Contents

Introduction

Under 40 per cent of 18–21-year-olds voted in the 2005 general election. Some politicians and journalists take this to mean that young people are getting less interested in politics. However, all other research – and my own teaching experience – suggests that young people feel strongly about core political issues like crime, education, the environment and international relations, and that many have a keen appetite for direct action. They may be disengaged from, or disillusioned with, mainstream party politics and politicians – the 'grey men in grey suits' – who are seen, at best, as boring and, at worst, as dishonest. But young people are far from apathetic about the issues that matter most to their lives.

This book was therefore written to provide students of UK government and politics with a source of information which is readable, topical and relevant not only to exam syllabuses but also to contemporary political events and issues. There is growing concern in the real political world about the oddities of the UK electoral system, the growing power of modern governments, the spin of modern party politics, the loss of civil liberties, the impact of the EU and the bending and breaking of the political rules. All of these issues, and more, are addressed in this book.

As an exam textbook, it also highlights concise definitions of key terms and concepts and gives up-to-date and succinct summaries of the core topics in British politics, as well as sample exam answers, source materials and stimulus questions, quizzes and other exercises, with answers.

The book is aimed mainly at students of AS UK Politics, but other students and teachers may find it useful as an introductory text for more advanced study, and even the general reader may find it of interest.

Acknowledgements

The publishers gratefully acknowledge the following for permission to reproduce copyright material. Whilst every effort has been made to trace the copyright holders, in cases where this has been unsuccessful or if have inadvertently been overlooked, the publishers will be pleased to make the necessary arrangements at the first opportunity.

- 'Old Spin, New Spin' by Stephen Gardner, Managing Editor of www.euro-correspondent.com copyright © Stephen Gardner. Reprinted with the kind permission of the author.
- 'Politics not parliament' by George Monbiot, The Guardian, 1st May 2001. Copyright © George Monbiot. Reprinted with the kind permission of the author.
- 'Scrap anti-terror detention law' from BBC News website 18th December 2003. Copyright © BBC. Reprinted with permission of BBC News.
- 'How to Vote: Mayor of London Ballot Paper', 'European Parliament Ballot Paper', and 'London Assembly Ballot Paper' all from The Metro, 9th June 2004. Reprinted with permission of Solo Syndication, London.
- list of major and minor parties that took part in the General Election 2005.
- 'All change: what the constitution means for the states of the union' The Times, 21st June 2004 copyright © NI Syndication. Reprinted with permission.
- 'It's The Sun wot won it' 1992 conservative victory, front page. Copyright © NI Syndications 1992. Reprinted with permission.
- 'Inquiry into opinion polls urged' from BBC News website 31st May 2004 copyright © BBC. Reprinted with permission of BBC News.
- 'Friends of the Earth Logo' copyright © Friends of the Earth. Reprinted with permission.
- 'New bypass for blackspot' from BBC website 29th October 2003. Copyright © BBC. Reprinted by permission of BBC News.

- 'What kind of May Day protester are you? Quiz' Guardian Unlimited 2004 copyright © Guardian Newspapers Ltd 2004. Reprinted with permission.
- 'The backlash against NGOs' by Michael Bond, extracted from April 2000 issue of Prospect Magazine www.prospect-magazine.co.uk. Reprinted with the kind permission of the author and Prospect Magazine.
- 'Compulsory National Identity Cards: What are the arguments?' from BBC website 28th June 2005. Copyright © BBC. Reprinted with permission.
- Graph 'small earthquake' The Economist, June 14th 2004 copyright © The Economist Newspaper Limited, London 14th June 2004. Reprinted with permission.
- Royal Borough funding of total expenditure 2004–5. Royal Borough of Kensington and Chelsea 2004/2005. Reprinted with permission.
- 'What a difference a mayor makes: new leadership for local communities' K Day, December 1999. From New Local Government Network. Reprinted with permission.
- 'Voter turnout in EU elections'. Reproduced with the kind permission of The European Parliament.
- 'Europe's Cinderella or Ugly Sister?' adapted from an article by Paul Reynolds, from BBC News website 3rd June 2004. Copyright © BBC. Reprinted with permission.

Photo credits:

(p.1) Winston Churchill: Illustrated London News V1 (NT)
(p.5) May Day disturbances: TNT/Alamy (A3PABB)
(p.7) Joseph Goebbels: Illustrated London News V2 (NT)
(p.11) UK police maintaining order: Corel 734 (NT)
(p.14) UK passport: Photodisc 44B (NT)
(p.17) US Constitution: Comstock/Alamy RF (AE4000) (NT)
(p.18) Lord Falconer, Law Lord: David Willis/Alamy (AM0C15)
(p.46) Tony Blair: David Mansell/Alamy (AG2356)
(p.46) Michael Howard: Jack Sullivan/Alamy (AXABBC) (NT)
(p.55) Robert Kilroy-Silk: Trevor Smith/Alamy (ATBB8C)
(p.61) Charles Kennedy MP: Philip Wolmuth/Alamy (A59B8F)
(p.67) George Galloway: iWitness/Alamy (AT0749)
(p.77) Miners conflict: Julia Martin/Photofusion/Alamy (AM294D)
(p.80) Greenpeace protest on Big Ben: Colin Edwards/Alamy (APDF95)
(p.84) Anti-war demonstration: Lisa Barber/Alamy (AM1C4D)
(p.94) House of Commons: Peter Adams/Digital Vision BP (NT)
(p.98) Tony Blair/PMQ: Empics/PA
(p.99) Tony Blair during a Commons select committee hearing: Empics/PA
(p.107) Queen Elizabeth II: Corel 654 (NT)
(p.110) Government Cabinet: Phil Noble/Empics/PA
(p.111) Tony Blair: Jack Sullivan/Alamy (A56D65) (NT)
(p.125) Release of the Birmingham Six: Sean Dempsey/Empics/PA
(p.126) Fox hunting: Corel 449 (NT)
(p.131) UK Judge: Photodisc 44B (NT)

Acknowledgements

(p.144) Local council meeting: Paul Doyle/Photofusion/Alamy (AFT847)

(p.148) Dame Shirley Porter: Tom Vickers/Empics/PA

(p.150) Ken Livingstone: Paul Doyle/Alamy (ARAA7A)

(p.164) European Parliament Building: Image Source/Alamy (ABE695) (NT)

(p.168) UKIP rosette: Jack Sullivan/Alamy (AX6C1E)

(p.169) Euro currency: Ingram ILG V1 CD1 (NT)

(p.175) European flag: Corel 461 (NT)

Every effort has been made to contact copyright holders and we apologise if any have been overlooked. Should copyright have been unwittingly infringed in this book, the owners should contact the publishers who will make the necessary arrangement at the first opportunity.

1

Political power and participation

■ What is politics?

key terms

power

The ability to do, or make others do, something based on the capacity to reward or punish

influence

Persuasive effect on others' ideas or actions

authority

Rightful, legitimate power based on consent

Winston Churchill

Politics is about the study and exercise of **power**. Power is the ability to make people do things by the ability to reward or by the threat or use of punishment, force or violence. Power may take various forms – economic, political, military, social or personal – and is a matter of degree. The epitome of power is the lawless gang which rampages through the streets generating fear and terror, or – at national level – the brutal military junta or rebel militia men who impose arbitrary violence and death, such as in Sierra Leone throughout the 1990s. However, power need not involve violence or even the threat of violence. If a strike by transport workers forces you to walk to school, that involves power because you have been made to do something unwillingly; whereas a persuasive publicity campaign by a pressure group, such as Comic Relief or Greenpeace, is simply **influence**.

Influence is persuasive effect upon others' ideas or actions; it may or may not be intended, organised or even consciously perceived, but it is based on respect or agreement (whether reasoned or unreasoned), and is therefore closer to **authority** than to power.

Authority is the ability to make people do things because they think the power holders have that right. Authority involves legitimate power based on consent, respect and support. It may derive from election, but also from tradition (for example, the House of Lords or the monarchy); from intense personal magnetism and character – known as 'charisma' (for example, Christ, Churchill, Gandhi or Hitler); or from the office rather than the character of the individual, that is, from due process, training, rules, laws and principles (for example, the police or civil service, doctors or teachers).

1

Question

Distinguish between 'power' and 'authority'.   *(5 marks)*

Authority is the basis of any democracy. Almost every country in the modern world, including the UK, claims to be a democracy. However, when countries as diverse as the USA and Cuba lay claim to the label, its meaning is obviously not clear-cut. In the UK, most people would point to the ballot box as proof of our democracy, but the concept goes much further than this.

■ What is democracy?

Democracy – from the Greek *demos kratos* – literally means 'people power', or self-government of the people, by the people, for the people. In its original form, it meant the right of all qualified citizens directly to decide upon matters of general concern. This form of government began in the ancient Greek city state of Athens in the fifth century BC, where all qualified citizens would gather regularly to vote directly on issues of concern. (Famously, however, only adult, free men were qualified citizens – women, slaves and non-Athenians were excluded.)

Any form of direct decision-making or direct action by the people which increases their own control over their own lives may therefore be 'democratic' in this literal sense of 'people power' – be it a vote on an issue at local, workplace or national level, a boycott, a strike, a riot or a revolution. 'People power' may thus be legal or illegal, peaceful or violent.

HANDS UP ALL THOSE WHO THINK WOMEN SHOULD GET THE VOTE.

key terms

franchise

The right to vote

direct democracy

'People power', or self-government of the people, by the people, for the people

referendum

A direct public vote on a political issue or policy; (plural referenda)

indirect/ representative democracy

The election by qualified citizens of candidates to political office to make decisions on behalf of the electorate

oligarchy

Political elitism, or rule by the few

This helps to explain why, until the nineteenth century, the very idea of 'people power' was often called 'mobocracy' or 'tyranny of the majority' and was feared by the ruling elites in countries like the UK, who asserted that the people – the 'mob' – were dangerous, unintelligent, fickle and incapable of making responsible political decisions. However, industrialisation and the factory system brought together an increasingly organised and educated workforce which used its collective economic power to demand a greater political voice; while at the same time the rising class of industrial owners and entrepreneurs, in competition for social dominance with the old landed aristocracy, was seeking a political power base. Industrial workers and employers, together with an emergent 'middle class', thus found some common cause in the extension of the **franchise** – that is, the right to vote. Hence the idea of 'democracy' has gradually become accepted – indeed, positively lauded – in most countries, though it is invariably practised in a limited form.

Scarcely any modern industrial society can claim to practise **direct democracy** in the way that the Ancient Greeks did. Switzerland perhaps comes closest, with its very frequent **referenda** – direct public votes on political issues and policies – in a very decentralised political system. However, throughout much of the twentieth century, Switzerland kept holding referenda on whether women should have the right to vote – and, since only the men had the right to vote in those referenda, women did not get the vote at all until 1971.

It is widely argued that most modern industrial states are too big and complex for such direct democracy to be possible. This is debatable: large states can be sub-divided into small political units, and modern technology could, in theory, enhance the capacity for direct political participation. Interactive TV and internet websites are now commonplace. This two-way media facility could easily be applied to the process of political decision-making, if the political will was there. Perhaps, however, political leaders are too reluctant to surrender their power, and/or most people are too apathetic to take it, for the possibility of more direct democracy to be considered seriously in countries like the UK.

The UK is not, therefore, a direct democracy. Like most other modern states, it claims to be an **indirect** or **representative democracy**. This involves the election by qualified citizens of representatives who govern over, and on behalf of, the people. Mere vote-casting is, obviously, a limited form of 'people power' and participation. It actually involves the voters giving away their political decision-making power to a few representatives who then make most of the key political decisions in society. All representative democracy therefore entails **oligarchy** or elitism: rule by the few. In the UK, representative democracy – the extension of the franchise – developed in the nineteenth and twentieth centuries under pressure from popular movements such as Chartism, the trades union movement and the suffragettes; and it was, in part, a conscious effort on the part of the political power-holders to forestall radical demands for more direct or extensive political democracy. In the words of the modern Conservative politician Lord Hailsham, 'If you don't give them reform, they will give you social revolution.'

analyse
this

Distinguish between two different types of democracy.

(5 marks)

Possible answers

1 **Good answer:**

In a direct democracy, political decisions on all major issues are made directly by all qualified citizens, as in the ancient Greek city-states. However, even there, women and slaves were not allowed to participate; and it is often argued that this system is not feasible in large, modern states. Therefore most societies today have a system of indirect or representative democracy, where representatives are elected to govern on behalf of the voters – that is, to reflect the voters' views, interests and/or social background. This may be a pluralist system – that is, multi-party (e.g. the UK) or single-party (e.g. the former USSR), but it is inevitably oligarchic or elitist.

2 **Weak answer:**

Direct democracy is where people do it themselves, whereas with indirect democracy other people do it for them, which isn't really democratic at all.

3 **Weak answer:**

In direct democracy, everyone votes for everything, like in Ancient Greece, though actually women and slaves didn't, so it wasn't really very democratic, and anyway it's not possible in big, complicated societies, whereas in Greece it was only in small cities, so it doesn't really happen now except in some African tribes, and referenda like on the EU in 1975 are a bit like direct democracy. Instead voters vote for representatives to represent them, i.e. indirect, usually in a party system like the UK's two-party system which is called pluralist, or the old Soviet Union's one-party system which isn't democratic anyway, but anyway only a few people are doing the ruling, which is oligarchy.

Say why each of the above examples is good or bad. If you were the examiner, how many marks (out of 5) would you give to each one? (For the answers, see page 176.)

Nevertheless, all modern states – whatever their type of economic or political system – have some valid claim to call themselves democratic if they contain elements of one or more of the following:

- **People-power**: for example, referenda, effective pressure groups, trades unions, etc.

- **Participation**: democratic participation may take many forms, from voting and standing for political office to meetings, marches, demonstrations, peaceful law-breaking and violent political opposition. Even riots have democratic claims, since they are 'people power' in the literal sense – although all states and governments will deny those democratic claims when such activities are directed against themselves.

talking point

Participation in any kind of political activity beyond voting is very much a minority phenomenon in the UK. Surveys indicate that only about 10 per cent participate in politics through pressure group membership. Under 5 per cent undertake various forms of direct action, and under 2 per cent are involved in a wide variety of political activities such as party campaigning and political protests. However, the more recent surveys do indicate that more people are becoming actively involved in public campaigns and protests.

Which of the following forms of political activity would you consider doing? Why or why not?

		Yes	No
a)	Voting for a political representative	☐	☐
b)	Signing a petition	☐	☐
c)	Completing an opinion poll	☐	☐
d)	Contacting your MP	☐	☐
e)	Attending a political meeting	☐	☐
f)	Joining a political party	☐	☐
g)	Joining a pressure group	☐	☐
h)	Producing a leaflet or poster	☐	☐
i)	Setting up a website	☐	☐
j)	Going on a demonstration	☐	☐
k)	Going on strike	☐	☐
l)	Peaceful law breaking (e.g. smoking a joint)	☐	☐
m)	Damaging property (e.g. painting protest graffiti)	☐	☐
n)	Injuring persons	☐	☐
o)	Rioting	☐	☐

May Day disturbances

- **Representation**: this can mean different things.

The strongest interpretation of the concept of 'representative' is that of a delegate: an elected power-holder who acts exactly as instructed by his or her voters, thus reflecting and implementing the voters' wishes on every issue. This does not apply to UK MPs – and it would be difficult for them, in practice, to consult all of their voters on every issue.

Alternatively, representation can mean the reflection of voters' interests, even if the decisions are not popular. (This form of representation is commonly claimed by politicians when they are, for example, increasing taxes or closing hospitals.) It may apply to UK MPs, but they are also closely tied to the aims and interests of their parties.

Finally, it can mean the reflection of voters' social backgrounds and typicality by the political representatives: for example, the percentage

key
terms

representation

A form of indirect democracy reflecting the views, interests and/or typical social background of the electorate

responsible (party) government

Executive accountable to Parliament and public (through party system, manifesto and mandate); or wise and sensible government in the best interests of the people

of female, ethnic minority, young or gay MPs in Parliament. MPs in the UK are now more representative of the wider public in this sense than ever before, but they are still quite atypical. For example, only 19 per cent of MPs currently are female, and only 15 out of 646 (under 2 per cent) are black or Asian compared with 8 per cent of the wider UK population.

● **Responsibility**: this concept can also mean different things. **Responsible government** means, primarily, government which is answerable and accountable – either directly to the voters or, as in the UK, to Parliament and thereby indirectly to the voters. A secondary interpretation is the idea of wise and sound government in the national interests of the voters.

● **Consent**: most modern states rest on the general agreement of the people that the governors have the right to govern and that the people will accept and live by the decisions of the governors (even if many people did not vote for them or do not agree with the decisions made).

The problem with defining democracy in terms of consent is that, especially in the modern age of mass media, consent can be created by political power-holders – through manipulation of information and of public opinion – to legitimise their rule. In Nazi Germany, for example, there was undoubtedly a substantial degree of mass, active

talking
point

In the UK, people cannot vote until they are 18. Some people argue that, at 16, young people in the UK can work, pay taxes, marry or join the army and, therefore, they should also be entitled to vote. Voting at 16 is already the official policy of the Liberal Democrats, the Scottish and Welsh Nationalists and the Green Party.

The right to vote (some examples)

State	Voting age
Japan	20
UK	18
Serbia	16 if employed, otherwise 18
Bosnia-Herzegovina	16 if employed, otherwise 18
Brazil	16; compulsory from 18
Sudan	17
Indonesia	17
North Korea	17
Nicaragua	16
Cuba	16
Iran	15

Western European politicians regard many of the countries listed above as 'undemocratic' because of the illiberal nature of their political regimes. Does the age at which people are entitled to vote make any difference to this evaluation, or not?

key
term

political socialisation

The instilling of political attitudes and values through agencies such as family, media, education, peer group, church, etc.

support for the regime; but there was also a well-developed and effective system of political indoctrination and propaganda in the schools and mass media, which made it difficult to distinguish real from manufactured political consent.

Most commentators would agree that the same point applies, to a greater or lesser degree, in every political system. People do not emerge from the womb as little flag-waving Nazis, communists, royalists or parliamentarians; they learn to accept and support the system in which they live through a process of **political socialisation**. Through the various agencies of family, school, work, peer group (friends and colleagues), media and religion, we each acquire the necessary attitudes and values to enable us to accept and adapt to the system in which we live, and to enable that system itself to survive. All individuals, in all states, are subject to this process of socialisation – sometimes by open indoctrination, often by more subtle, less honest and usually more effective methods.

The relationship between politicians, media and public opinion is, therefore, a complex one, like a dog chasing its tail – it is often hard to know which is leading and which is following. Anti-democratic philosophies would argue, anyway, that governments should not follow public opinion because it is uncertain, divided, manipulable, fickle, ignorant or selfish. The most cynical views would say that modern 'democracy', the world over, consists of the power-holders telling people what they want (socialisation) and then duly giving it to them (representation).

analyse
this

Old spin, new spin

Joseph Goebbels

Spin is essentially a technique of political communication invented for the twentieth century model of the mass media. Its roots can be traced back even before that – Napoleon had a Bureau of Public Opinion. But it was between the two World Wars that spin was really pioneered. Nazi propagandist-in-chief Joseph Goebbels harnessed the power of the emerging mass media, especially radio and cinema, to promote his venal creed.

His techniques were refined in post-war America, in particular from the 1952 presidential campaign onwards.

In the twenty-first century, however – as Blair has discovered to his cost – the traditional model of spin is increasingly out of date. The mass media, for which spin was invented, has been in decline for years. 'Old' spin has been made redundant by new technology.

Two examples from the Iraq War controversy illustrate how the internet spells the death of spin. Tony Blair's February 2003 'dodgy dossier' was largely plagiarised from an online article and was almost immediately exposed by a mouse-wielding academic and his trusty search engine. The Hutton Inquiry, meanwhile, has released an unprecedented selection of government documents direct to the public via the internet, an implicit recognition of the power of this new medium to rise above spin.

Potentially, these new developments can safeguard and even extend democracy by making government more transparent. At future elections, voters will be able to compare party manifestos online, votes will be cast online, and four years later voters will be able to search the archive to find out if the elected party kept its promises – and send an email direct to the Prime Minister if they didn't.

But there is also a dark side. A more direct relationship between government and citizens gives the government more power to control the information it puts out. Proliferation of the internet offers vast opportunities for monitoring online behaviour, for collecting vast amounts of data and for profiling and categorising anything and everything.

The new digital media landscape contains both opportunities and threats for democracy. In the future, government will need to be scrutinised as never before.

Source: by Stephen Gardner, from www.nthposition.com 2003

1 What is 'spin'?

2 Why has the 'new' Labour government been accused of 'spin'?

3 In what ways does the 'new digital media landscape' contain both 'opportunities and threats for democracy'?

Question

What are the main criticisms of democracy? *(20 marks)*

■ Liberal democracy

Representative democracies take many forms: one, two or multi-party systems, etc. The UK, like the USA and most European countries, claims to be a **liberal democracy**. This is a representative system embodying the concepts of diversity, freedom of choice and individual rights and freedoms (as opposed to collective equality or mass participation). It asserts the following principles:

- *Free and fair elections*: most adult citizens will have the right to vote in regular, competitive and secret ballots; diverse candidates and parties will be free to campaign in opposition to the government of the day; and the election results will be honestly counted, accepted and presented

- *Pluralism*: diverse centres of economic and political power; thus competitive private ownership in the economy and, especially, two or more parties in the political system, together with many pressure

analyse
this

Politics not parliament

When Tony Benn announced his intention to retire as an MP he said he was 'leaving parliament to go into politics'. He didn't need to explain what he meant. To the thousands of activists championing the issues which governments have neglected, Parliament has been peripheral to the life of the nation for years.

It's not hard to see why. The first and most obvious reason is that MPs are no longer permitted to represent their constituents. The lavish use of the parliamentary whip, the increased efficiency of the party machines, the fudged reform of the House of Lords, and the marginalisation of even the Cabinet as the government is run by unelected advisers, have all helped to sever the links between the people and their representatives.

As the government is gradually removed from effective, democratic supervision, unprecedented opportunities emerge for undemocratic lobbying. While petitions signed by one million electors are binned, [multi-national newspaper owner] Rupert Murdoch is admitted to Downing Street every time he knocks.

There is, both Tony Blair and Gordon Brown have assured us, 'no alternative' to neo-liberal globalisation. This leads to, although they would never express it this way, the gradual privatisation of everything, brokered by means of the Private Finance Initiative. It means the deregulation of business activities, resulting in even lower environmental, workplace and consumer standards.

So the electorate is left to wonder why, in a UK that has never been richer, public services are falling apart, the state pension is dwindling and schools are being privatised. Why, though no one wants them, we are being forced to accept genetically modified crops. Why the government that promised traffic reduction, rail renationalisation and integrated transport has instead relaunched the road building programme.

While the government insists that there is no alternative, those seeking to promote one are treated as dangerous outcasts. Non-violent campaigners have been reclassified as terrorists by the new Anti-terrorism Act, while the Investigatory Powers Act and the new Criminal Justice Act allow the security services to intercept emails and raid computers without a warrant. Yet, in the absence of an independent, investigative press, peaceful protest is now among the few means of raising the issues that will determine the future course of most people's lives. We are, as a result, entering a new age of activism.

These are, as a result, exciting times. While extra-parliamentary activism will make little difference to the outcome of the next election, the concerns it expresses will become harder to ignore. With or without the help of a marginalised parliament, Britain's politics at future elections will bear little resemblance to those of today.

Source: George Monbiot, *Guardian*, 1 May 2001

1 What is 'extra-parliamentary activism'?

2 Why, according to George Monbiot, are growing numbers of people resorting to such activism?

3 What may be the merits and the dangers of such activism?

groups. This should generate competition and hence freedom of choice and effective representation of many different views and interests

- **Political equality**: one person, one vote, one value – which implies a proportional system of voting, where the percentage of votes received by a party equates with the percentage of political seats (MPs) granted to them. It also implies equal opportunity to stand for political office and equal opportunity to be elected to office. There are, however, always restrictions on those qualified to stand for office. For example, in the UK, to stand as a Westminster MP, a person must be 21 or over (some, especially Liberal Democrats, think it should be 18) and must pay a deposit of £500. This last is intended to discourage 'frivolous' candidates, but it effectively excludes many serious contenders who do not have the financial backing of a large party

- **Constitutionalism**: government within clear and enforceable rules which set limits to political power

- **The rule of law**: a fair, just and impartial legal system which should include legal equality – the principle that everyone (including the government) is equally subject to the same laws and has equal access to the law – and an independent and impartial judiciary

- **Limited government**: checks and constraints by various other bodies, for example the courts and pressure groups, upon the power of government, to safeguard individual liberties

- **Open government**: non-secretive government, to ensure that government is honest and accountable to the people

- **Civil rights and liberties**: essential public freedoms, preferably enshrined in law.

Exam questions often ask: to what extent is the UK a liberal democracy? That is, how far do these principles apply within the UK political system? Later chapters will examine this question in detail.

Question

What is meant by 'pluralism'? *(5 marks)*

■ Political culture and citizenship in the UK

The United Kingdom is a **state**. A state is an independent entity with ultimate political power and authority – that is, **sovereignty** – over all of the individuals and groups within its territorial boundaries. It is made up of

key terms

state

The formal, abstract, sovereign political power over a given territory, usually comprising legislature, executive and judiciary and usually possessing a legal monopoly of coercive power

sovereignty

Ultimate legal and political power and authority

government

The executive, policy making branch of the state

society

The body of people within and under the power of the state

nation

A group of people who share a sense of common culture, based on common ties of, for example, language, religion, race, territory and/or history

political culture

The predominant set of political values held by the citizens of a particular state

UK police maintaining order

all the formal institutions of political power such as the Crown, legislature, executive, judiciary, army and sometimes the Church. It has a legal monopoly on the use of violence, but will often use consensus – agreement – as well as coercion – force – to keep order.

The **government** is the executive agent of the state; it enforces the rulings of the state and acts under its authority. In other words, it runs the country. Whereas the state is said to be a permanent, abstract entity (for example, the Crown), the actual people and the institutions of government come and go (for example, the monarch and Prime Minister).

Society is the body of people within and under the power of the state – both individuals and informal power bodies, such as pressure groups.

A **nation** is a group of people who share a sense of common culture, based on common ties of, for example, language, religion, race, territory and/or history. One state may embrace many nations. For example, the Scots, Irish, Welsh and English in the United Kingdom all have a separate and distinct sense of nationhood. Thus the UK – a sovereign state – contains at least four different nations. (Alternatively, one nation may be spread across many states: for example, the Jews were a nation without a sovereign state until the creation of Israel in 1948.)

Political culture in the UK

The term **political culture** encompasses the predominant values and attitudes of the people within a particular state, which are both a cause and a consequence of the formal political system of that state. A political culture may encourage participation (for example, small but strong democracies like Switzerland), passivity (as in authoritarian regimes like

Tsarist Russia), conflict (in countries with violent histories such as Ireland and Israel), compromise (for example, in very pluralist systems such as Sweden) – and so on.

The UK likes to call itself 'the mother of democracies'. It was the first country to industrialise and, until the twentieth century, it was the leading industrial power in the world. There is a fairly close correlation between industrialisation and the development of liberal democracy – with the significant exceptions of the fascist and communist regimes in the twentieth century. UK democracy can probably be said to originate from 1832, when the franchise – the right to vote – began to be extended to more and more people: from male property holders and then male householders to all adult men and, in 1918, to older women. In 1928, almost all men and women aged 21 were allowed to vote; this established the principle of 'universal adult suffrage' in the UK. The voting age was lowered to 18, under a Labour government, in 1969.

Number of persons having the right to vote in the UK

Date	Number per 100 adults
1800	3
1832	5
1867	13
1884	25
1918	75
1928	100

Throughout the nineteenth and twentieth centuries, the UK has had a comparatively stable democracy with relatively little use of domestic political violence – except for Ireland; no major political upheavals (such as the revolutions throughout Europe); relatively low levels of political extremism (neither fascism nor communism took strong hold in the UK); and with substantial respect for individual rights and liberties, an independent judiciary and the legitimacy of political opposition.

Traditional conservative philosophy, especially, would attribute this stability to the pragmatic flexibility of key institutions such as the Church, Crown and House of Lords which, by accepting gradual reductions in their own power, prevented major political conflicts and, at the same time, ensured their own survival and continuing political influence. Others would point to the relative social homogeneity – that is, social and cultural similarities – of the people in the UK. Class has been the dominant division in UK politics because other factors such as religion, language, nationality and race – which have torn many other states apart – have had quite limited impact.

From more critical perspectives, however, this view of UK political culture, as a stable and harmonious example to the modern world, is rather smug, self-satisfied and complacent. Change is afoot within the UK. Critics might argue the following points:

Turnout in UK general elections	
1918	58.9%
1922	71.3%
1924	70.8%
1927	76.6%
1931	76.3%
1935	71.2%
1945	72.7%
1950	84.0%
1951	82.5%
1955	76.7%
1959	78.8%
1964	77.1%
1966	75.8%
1970	72.0%
1974 (Feb)	78.7%
1974 (Oct)	72.8%
1979	76.0%
1983	72.7%
1987	75.3%
1992	77.7%
1997	71.5%
2001	59.0%
2005	61.0%

- There is a growing imbalance between the political institutions, with government becoming more centralised and powerful, and Parliament – the heart of UK democracy – losing ever more power and status. (See Chapter 2.)

- Growing nationalist sentiment in Scotland and Wales might not be 'bought off' with limited devolution; it might, conceivably, result in the actual break-up of the UK in the foreseeable future. (See Chaper 9.)

- As voters become more disillusioned with mainstream politics, party membership and voter turnouts are falling and the politics of direct action are increasing. There have been significant incidents of public disorder and violence – especially, but not only, during the 'radical right' Thatcherite phase of government in the 1980s, when economic deprivation (and perceived injustices such as the poll tax) prompted widespread inner-city rioting.

Since then, the growing politics of 'anti-capitalism' seek to challenge the whole economic and political system upon which political culture in the UK is based.

- There are growing curbs on civil liberties in the UK in the twenty-first century (largely justified by references to terrorism, illegal immigration and asylum) which, say critics, are quite fundamentally undermining the rights and freedoms all of UK citizens.

All of these issues and arguments will be examined more fully in later chapters.

Questions

True or false?

1 Authority requires election.

2 All representative democracy entails oligarchy.

3 Democracy simply means 'one man, one vote'.

4 Over 40 per cent of Westminster MPs are women.

5 England is not a state.

UK citizenship

What does it mean to be a UK citizen? Narrowly, **citizenship** is an individual's legal membership of, and recognition by, a state which grants mutual rights and obligations between state and citizen. Broadly, a

key term

citizenship

An individual's legal membership of, and recognition by, a state which grants mutual rights and obligations between state and citizen

UK passport

citizen is an individual with rights in relation to the state – as distinct, for example, from the concept of a 'subject' subservient to the state and the monarchy. Since the UK is a monarchy, it is debatable whether its members are citizens, or subjects, or both.

UK citizens are granted a passport which gives them the right to live and work in the country and the right to travel in and out of the country. Usually the right to work entails the obligation to pay taxes. Similarly, an individual who is on the voting register may be called up for compulsory jury service as a civic responsibility. The concept of citizenship, therefore, implies both rights and duties for both the individual and the state.

Legal citizenship is not granted to everyone who lives in the UK. Non-citizens – so-called 'aliens' – are not granted the same rights to live, work and vote within the state as are UK citizens. A succession of nationality and asylum laws since the 1960s has restricted rights of legal citizenship in the face of the UK's post-imperial heritage of immigration, unemployment and racialism. In this sense, the idea of 'citizenship' excludes many people as much as it includes others; and this exclusive use of the concept goes back centuries – as far back as ancient Athenian democracy where citizenship was granted only to some adult males and not to resident foreigners, women, slaves or children.

Even among those who are granted legal citizenship in the UK, there are still widespread economic and social inequalities, with many people remaining poor and disadvantaged. This has led the various political philosophies and parties to develop different interpretations of citizenship.

The post-war (1945) development of the welfare state embodied the modern liberal and socialist concept of 'social citizenship' and was intended to extend the social and economic rights of citizenship – such as a job, and access to free education, health and welfare services – to everyone. However, this liberal or social democratic version of citizenship, in practice, came to be seen, especially by conservatives, as requiring too much state involvement, bureaucracy and cost. Thatcherites spoke critically of the 'nanny state' fostering a 'dependency culture'; hence the alternative New Right conservative – Thatcherite – interpretation of citizenship which emerged in the 1980s.

According to the ideology of the New Right, the 'good citizen' is an individual who makes an active and responsible contribution to the

talking point

Some countries today, for example Belgium and Australia, regard voting not only as a right but as a legal and civic obligation. Voting is therefore compulsory in these countries, and people may be fined if they do not vote. Perhaps this is one reason why, in the 1999 European elections, turnout in Belgium was 89 per cent while in the UK it was just 23 per cent.

community: whether by joining their local Neighbourhood Watch scheme; by 'walking with purpose' (to quote Conservative leader Michael Howard's much-mocked description of voluntary street patrols); by picking up litter; looking after the young, the old and the sick through family or 'care in the community'; by becoming a school governor or by running a profitable business. This concept of the 'active citizen' is actually more about civil obligations than about civil rights, and it is at odds with the notion that the state has a duty to provide for the citizen in terms of welfare and protection against need or deprivation. This New Right approach, according to liberal and socialist critics, is very divisive with its often outspoken disapproval of the poor, passive, dependent and needy.

Yet another, more personal and emotional, concept of citizenship is rooted in a sense of cultural identity and belonging associated with feelings of nationalism and patriotism. Thus, some people may feel as if they belong to a country even if that country is not a sovereign state (for example, Scotland or Wales), or even if they are denied legal citizenship by the state which they claim as their own (for example, asylum seekers within the UK).

The concept of citizenship also has an increasingly international dimension. For some, Europe is a common home and cultural identity. Article 8 of the European Union Maastricht Treaty establishes 'citizenship of the European Union' for every legal citizen and worker of a member state.

Finally, a growing perception of, and concern about, looming environmental crisis on the world scale (for example, global warming) has given impetus to the rise of green politics with an emphasis on our common citizenship of Planet Earth, with universal, environmental rights and obligations which transcend geographical and political boundaries.

Questions

Quiz

Briefly answer the following questions.

1 Give examples to illustrate the difference between 'political power' and 'political influence'.

2 Where did democracy originate?

3 Name one European country which holds frequent referenda.

4 What percentage of the UK population is black or Asian?

5 What are WMDs?

6 How many parties are currently represented in the House of Commons?

7 In what year was universal adult suffrage established in the UK?

8 Give one example of a right, and one example of a duty, accruing from UK citizenship.

9 Name one country where voting is legally compulsory.

10 What, in political terms, is an 'alien'?

2

The UK constitution

The US constitution

■ What is a constitution?

If you have played or watched a good game of football or rugby recently, you will have understood and enjoyed it all the more because it was played according to certain rules which were (usually!) followed by the players and firmly enforced by the referee. If a state is to be run successfully, it also needs rules.

A **constitution** is the set of rules and principles by which a state is governed. If a constitution is outlined in a single, legal document it is described as **written** or **codified** – for example, the US constitution.

The UK constitution is described as **unwritten** or **uncodified**, because there is no single, legal document called 'The UK Constitution' which we can pick up and browse through. This is mainly because the UK has had no major political upheavals or revolutions in the last couple of centuries which might have required it to write out a clear statement of new rules. There are rules, but they have evolved gradually and piecemeal, over centuries; and they derive from many different sources – some are written and some are not, some have the force of law and some do not.

■ Sources and features of the UK constitution

Many – but not all – of the rules of the UK constitution are **laws**, that is, rules of state which are enforceable by the courts and judges. There are, in turn, several different types of law:

● **European Union law** (since the UK joined the EU in 1973): takes precedence over UK law; for example, the worldwide ban on the sale of UK beef which was imposed by the EU during the BSE ('mad cow') scare in the 1990s

17

Lord Falconer as Secretary of State for Constitutional Affairs – formerly Lord Chancellor – is head of the Law Lords

key terms

laws

Rules of state which are enforceable by the courts and judges

conventions

Unwritten customs which are traditionally regarded as binding, but which have no legal force

unconstitutional action

An action which breaks any part – that is, any rule – of the constitution

manifesto

Booklet of policy proposals issued by every party before each general election

- *Acts of Parliament (statute law)*: for example, the House of Lords (Amendment) Act 2003 which changed the composition of the House of Lords

- *common law*: ancient, unwritten law; for example, the powers of the Crown

- *case law (judge-made law)*: judicial interpretations of common and statute law, in new court cases, which then set a precedent for future cases. For example, in 2003, the Law Lords (the most senior judges in the UK) ordered the Home Secretary to hold a public inquiry into the murder, in a young offenders' institution, of Asian teenager Zahid Mubarek by his racist cellmate.

Other rules of the constitution are not laws, but may still be very important:

- *historical documents and constitutional writings*: for example, Magna Carta (1215), and Walter Bagehot's influential book *The English Constitution* (1867). These are not legally binding, but are very influential

- *conventions*: these are unwritten customs which are traditionally regarded as binding, but which have no legal force; for example, the practice that the Queen chooses, as Prime Minister, the leader of the majority party in the House of Commons. Some of the most important rules of the UK constitution are simply conventions, not laws.

An action is **unconstitutional** if it breaks any part – that is, any rule – of the constitution. This usually refers to government action. The government may break a law and be ruled illegal in the courts – *ultra vires* (this is Latin for 'beyond their legal powers'): for example, the Labour government's secret agreement to extend genetically modified (GM) crop research in 1999; and also the indefinite detention and illegal deportation of some asylum seekers. Alternatively, an unconstitutional action may break a convention rather than a law: for example, in 1998, Labour Prime Minister Tony Blair appointed his friend and Scottish media tycoon, Gus MacDonald, as a junior industry minister in his government, although MacDonald was neither an MP nor a peer. This breached the important convention that government ministers should be chosen from within Parliament to give them democratic legitimacy. Another example: the Labour government has, to date, refused to hold referenda (see below and Chapter 3) on electoral reform and on joining the European single currency, despite promises to the contrary in their **manifesto** (that is, their booklet of policy proposals issued before the general election). However, manifesto promises – like many of the important rules of the UK constitution – are not legally binding. It is therefore often hard to know what is 'unconstitutional'.

It is even possible that a rule of the constitution may, itself, break the 'spirit', if not the letter, of the constitution. Acts of Parliament are laws which, by definition, add to the rules of the constitution. However, a series of new laws on anti-terrorism, law and order and asylum seekers passed since 2000 are – though perfectly legal – very illiberal and potentially con-

key terms

rule of law

A principle which seeks to ensure 'just' law which is applicable to all; thus there should be legal equality, clear, consistent and impartial laws and an independent judiciary

parliamentary sovereignty

Parliament has supreme law-making power, and can make, amend or repeal any law without challenge from any other UK body or institution

straining of all UK citizens' civil liberties. Many critics, therefore, regard these laws as undermining the basic principles of UK liberal democracy.

Because the UK constitution derives from so many different sources and types of rules – which have developed, piecemeal, over so many centuries – the rules may, sometimes, be downright contradictory. Here are two examples:

- According to eminent (this usually means dead) constitutional commentators such as A.V. Dicey (1835–1922), the 'twin pillars' of the UK constitution are the **rule of law** – the principle that everyone is equal under the law – and **parliamentary sovereignty** – the principle that Parliament is above the law (see page 27). Sometimes eminent commentators were, apparently, a bit dense.

- A second example: in UK elections for the Westminster Parliament, voters choose one local MP to represent a single geographical area (a **constituency**) and voters are, therefore, said to have a one-to-one personal relationship with that MP. For this reason, if an MP defects

analyse this

Some key conventions of the UK constitution

➡ The tradition that the Queen chooses, as Prime Minister, the leader of the majority party in the House of Commons. It is law that the monarch appoints the Prime Minister; and, according to law, she could choose anyone (such as the leader of Her Majesty's Opposition, the Leader of the Liberal Democrats, or her gardener . . .) but the government is granted some democratic legitimacy if the head of government also heads the majority party in the elected House of Commons

➡ All of the powers of the Prime Minister – which, by law, largely still belong to the monarch; but which, by tradition, have passed to the PM – again, to give them democratic legitimacy

➡ The very existence, structure and powers of the Cabinet

➡ The doctrines of collective and individual ministerial responsibility (explained in Chapter 7), by which government ministers should resign if they cannot publicly defend their own government policies, or if they make mistakes

➡ The concept of parliamentary sovereignty (see below), which only exists because UK judges have always accepted that the will of the elected House of Commons should prevail over that of the non-elected judges.

This illustrates the fact that some of the most important and 'democratic' rules of the UK political system do not have the force of law, but are merely long-standing customs and practices – highlighting the potential danger that they can, quite easily, be bent or broken.

1 What are meant by 'conventions' of the constitution?

2 What may be the benefits of conventions over laws?

3 What may be the disadvantages or dangers of conventions?

key terms

constituency

a geographical area represented by an elected MP

mandate

The authority of the government, granted by the voters, to govern according to the promises in their manifesto

flexible constitution

A constitution which requires no special procedures for amendment, but can be changed by an ordinary Act of Parliament

rigid constitution

A constitution which requires a special legal process for change

from one political party to another between general elections, no new election is held – on the grounds that the electorate voted for the person and not for the party label. However, a conflicting principle of the UK constitution is the 'doctrine of the **mandate**'. This is the idea that the winning party at a general election has been granted the authority – a mandate – by the voters, to govern according to the promises in their manifesto. This theory rests on the assumption that the electorate are voting, not for the individual candidate, but for a party label and package of party proposals.

The UK constitution is thus, in many ways, uncertain, inconsistent and even unknowable. This is a problem for a political system which claims to be a liberal democracy operating within clear and enforceable rules.

The UK constitution is also **flexible**, i.e. it requires no special procedures for amendment, but can be changed by an ordinary Act of Parliament. This means that even a major change to the UK political system – such as the abolition of the monarchy – could be implemented by a one-vote majority in the House of Commons (in the same way as any minor change, such as a law on littering). Thus, there is no distinct body of constitutional law. A **rigid constitution**, by contrast, requires a special process for change: for example, the US constitution requires two-thirds of Senate and House of Representatives' votes, plus three-quarters of all of the state legislatures; and the Irish constitution requires a referendum (a direct vote on an issue by the electorate) for major change.

In theory – *de jure* – therefore, the UK constitution is unwritten, flexible and unitary. In practice – *de facto* – however, all of these features are changing.

The UK constitution is, in practice, becoming more written and legally codified, mainly because of the growing quantity and impact of EU laws and regulations, which take legal precedence over all other sources of the UK constitution; and also because of the large number of constitutional reforms introduced by law within the UK since 1997 – such as devolution, reform of the House of Lords and the introduction of a UK Bill of Rights. This trend will continue.

Again, in practice rather than theory, the UK constitution is gradually becoming more rigid as the principle becomes increasingly accepted and expected that referenda (direct votes by the people) should be held on issues of major political change such as electoral reform, devolution and joining the European single currency. Although such referenda in the UK are, in theory, invariably merely 'advisory' to maintain the semblance of parliamentary sovereignty (see page 27), no government could, in reality, ignore a referendum result.

Finally, the unitary nature of the UK is already challenged by the power of the EU over the UK Westminster Parliament; and it is likely to come under more challenge from below as the Scottish, Welsh and Northern Irish assemblies become more established and confident in their roles.

talking point

Source: BBC News website,
18 December 2003

Scrap anti-terror detention law

Terror laws allowing the indefinite detention of foreign nationals without trial should be revoked, an influential parliamentary committee says.

MPs and peers on the privy council review committee made the call in their review of the 2001 anti-terror bill.

The committee members acknowledged measures against terrorism would be needed for 'some time to come'.

The report said: 'Providing effective powers . . . while protecting individual rights can be difficult.'

The committee said Section 4 of the Anti-terrorism, Crime and Security Act 2001 – which allows indefinite detention without charge or trial – should be replaced with a measure that 'does not require the UK to derogate [opt out] from the right to liberty under the European Convention on Human Rights'.

'Other countries have not found it necessary to have any such derogation and we have found no obvious reason why the UK should be the exception.'

They added: 'While this power has not been used injudiciously or excessively it raises difficult issues of principle and it does not meet the full extent of the threat – for example it does not deal with British nationals.'

The 2001 Act also includes measures tackling weapons of mass destruction and terrorist finance and property.

Powers which allow public bodies such as the Inland Revenue to disclose information to help investigations and prosecutions are not limited to terrorism cases.

Amnesty criticism

Amnesty International, whose report Justice Perverted looked into the Act, claims the laws are creating a 'Guantanamo Bay in our own back yard'.

The human rights group says foreign nationals are being denied the presumption of innocence until proven guilty.

It says the UK has created a different justice system for foreigners, who are held indefinitely without charge, and is not meeting international standards.

In 2004 the Law Lords ruled that such **internment** was contrary to human rights law and all of the detainees were subsequently released.

key terms

internment

Indefinite detention of suspects without charge or trial (introduced in the UK in 2001)

Note that a constitution may be written but also flexible, for example New Zealand. Thus there is no necessary connection between these two concepts. The UK constitution is rare in being both unwritten and flexible.

The UK constitution is also **unitary**: that is, it has one sovereign legislature – namely, the Parliament at Westminster, which has ultimate legal authority over all other bodies within the UK. Although there are local government councils and there are now also local Parliaments throughout the UK, these bodies are still subordinate to the central, sovereign, Westminster Parliament; and their existence and powers are wholly determined by Westminster, which can limit the powers of the local bodies or, indeed, abolish them altogether at any time. The frequent suspension by Westminster of Stormont – the Northern Irish Parliament (because of political conflicts during the peace process) – is one example of Westminster's legal supremacy. (This does not mean that the law must be exactly the same throughout the whole of the UK; but differences – for example, between Scottish law and English law – are only those allowed, or ordered, by Westminster.)

This unitary system contrasts with a **federal constitution** such as that of the USA or Australia, where the local executive and/or legislative bodies have strong and autonomous powers within their own defined areas of responsibility. The centre has decision-making power over matters such as national security, defence and foreign affairs but it cannot impose on the powers of the local bodies – nor vice versa. The central and local power bodies are, in theory, equal and autonomous and there are mutual checks and balances between them. A federal system is, therefore, more decentralised.

unitary constitution

A constitution with one sovereign legislature which has ultimate law-making power and authority over all other bodies within the state

federal constitution

A constitution where the central and local powers are equal and autonomous, with mutual checks and balances against each other

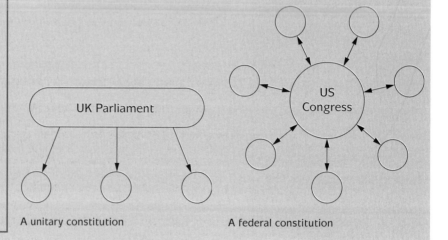

A unitary constitution

A federal constitution

Questions

1 What is an uncodified constitution? *(5 marks)*

2 What are the main sources of the UK constitution? *(15 marks)*

3 Why has the UK constitution been criticised? *(30 marks)*

This whole question should take 30 minutes in the exam. If you do the arithmetic precisely, you will see that you should spend the following amounts of time on each section:

a) 3 minutes maximum

b) 9 minutes maximum

c) 18 minutes maximum.

The best technique is not to make a few points at length but, rather, to make several points in a very precise and concise way, adding a real, topical example to illustrate each point.

Try it!

key terms

legislature

The branch of state responsible for the making of laws or 'legislation'

executive

The branch of state responsible for running the country through the execution and administration of laws and policies; often also called the 'government'

judiciary

The branch of state responsible for the interpretation and enforcement of the laws – that is, the judges

separation of powers

Non-overlapping personnel and powers of the legislature, executive and judiciary

■ The UK system of government

Back to our analogy of a football game: if it is to be understood and played successfully, it needs rules, it needs officials to implement those rules fairly and consistently – raising and spending money in the process – and it needs a referee or association to enforce the rules if they are broken.

Similarly, any state has three branches:

- a **legislature**, which makes the laws

- an **executive**, which implements the laws and policies

- a **judiciary**, which interprets and enforces the laws.

The UK executive, or government, decides and carries out the policies by which the country is run – whether that means raising taxes, imposing university tuition fees or going to war. However, all of these policies must be lawful. Therefore, every year, the government must submit its new policy proposals to the legislature to be legalised. If Parliament – the legislature – defeats a government bill, the government cannot implement that policy.

If the three branches of state – legislature, executive and judiciary – are completely united, the system may be a tyranny. Liberal democratic theory advocates the **separation of powers** – non-overlapping personnel and powers of the legislature, executive and judiciary – to ensure checks and balances between the different parts of the system and hence more freedom for the citizen. The United States has a substantial degree of separation between the legislature (Congress), the executive (President and Cabinet) and the US judiciary. The UK, however, does not practise extensive separation of powers.

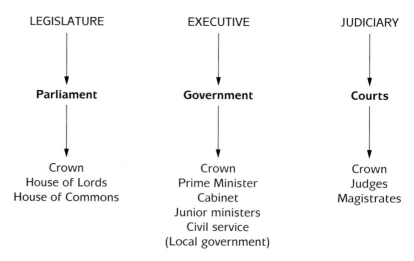

The UK system of government

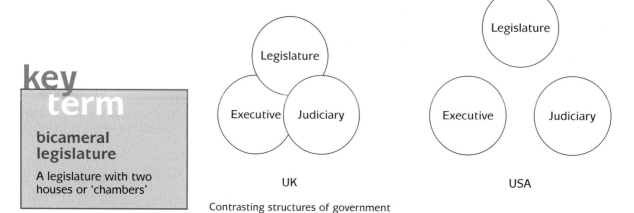

Contrasting structures of government

key term

bicameral legislature

A legislature with two houses or 'chambers'

In the UK, the legislature is called 'Parliament' and it has two houses or 'chambers' – the Commons and the Lords. Thus it is a **bicameral legislature**. The Lords is a wholly unelected House – a rarity in twenty-first century world politics.

In the USA, the legislature is called 'Congress' and it also has two chambers – the House of Representatives and the Senate – both elected.

In Russia, the legislature also has two chambers – the State Duma and the Federation Council – again, both elected.

States such as Denmark and Sri Lanka, by contrast, are 'unicameral' – that is, their Parliaments have only one (elected) chamber.

■ Parliamentary government

The main overlap in the UK system is between the legislature and the executive. The term **parliamentary government** refers to this overlap between Parliament and government: that is, the executive (government, i.e. PM and ministers) is chosen from within the legislature (MPs and peers) and is, in theory, subordinate to the legislature.

The main example of government's subordination to Parliament is an important convention of the constitution that, if a government is defeated in a 'vote of no confidence' by the House of Commons, it should resign. The last time that this happened was in 1979, when James Callaghan's Labour government was defeated by just one vote in the Commons (rumour has it that one MP refused to come out of the loo to vote!). However, it is important to note that this defeat was inflicted upon a **minority government** with under 50 per cent of the seats in the Commons.

Step 1

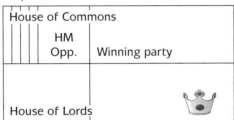

At each general election, the voters elect 659 MPs into the House of Commons, usually on the basis of a party label. Assuming that one party wins over 50% of the seats …

Step 2

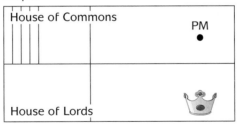

The Queen appoints, as Prime Minister, the leader of the majority party in the Commons.

Step 3

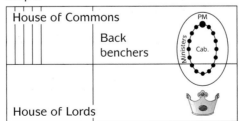

The PM then appoints his/her senior Cabinet ministers, and wider team of junior ministers, from within both the Commons and the Lords.

The formation of parliamentary government in the UK

key terms

representative government

a form of political decision-making by elected representatives who should reflect the views, interests and/or typical social background of the electorate

presidential system

A system where the executive is separately elected from the legislature and the two bodies are in theory equal, possessing checks and balances against each other

Government is also responsible, i.e. accountable, to Parliament through Question Time, debates and votes on government bills, parliamentary committees and financial scrutiny. Thus, through its link with Parliament – and especially with the elected House of Commons – the UK is said to have government which is both **representative** – reflective of the voters' views and interests – and **responsible** – that is, accountable and answerable for its actions, to Parliament and thus, indirectly, to the voters.

The United States and many other countries, by contrast, have a **presidential system**. This does not (confusingly) refer to the fact that they have a President and the UK does not. It means that the executive – the President – is directly elected by the voters, quite separately from Congress (the American legislature); the President is not allowed to be a member of Congress, and he is, in theory, equal (rather than subordinate) to the legislature, with mutual checks and balances between them.

analyse this

The UK constitution: reasons for controversy and change

➡ The long-term dominance of the Conservative party in post-1945 governments

➡ Perceived 'elective dictatorship' especially since 1997 (see below)

➡ Lack of checks and balances within the UK system, for example weaknesses of Parliament versus executive, Opposition versus government, Cabinet versus PM, local versus central government

➡ Improper use of the royal prerogative powers (by Prime Ministers and ministers)

➡ Ongoing secrecy of governments

➡ Perceived 'politicisation', for example of judiciary, civil service, police, Church and education

➡ Regional inequalities and imbalances

➡ Loss of civil liberties

➡ The uncertainty, flexibility and breakability of constitutional rules

➡ The impact of the European Union

1 What is a 'constitution'?

2 Why may it be dangerous to have one party in power for very long periods of time?

3 Can you think of any reasons why the basic freedoms of citizens might be limited?

■ Parliamentary sovereignty

Sovereignty is unrestricted power and authority. It applies to a body which can act or take decisions without hindrance from any institution above, below or within it. A body has internal sovereignty if it has the power to make decisions binding on all of its own citizens. A body has external sovereignty if it can control its own affairs without being blocked by outside bodies and states. And, to complicate matters, there are different kinds of sovereignty – for example, legal, political and economic sovereignty.

In federal states, internal sovereignty is divided between national and local powers; they are, therefore, based upon the paradoxical idea of shared sovereignty. However, the UK is a unitary state. Therefore, perhaps the main pillar of the UK constitution is, in theory, the legal sovereignty or supremacy of Parliament. This suggests that Parliament is the supreme law-making body in the UK, and that no institution in the country can override its laws. Thus no Parliament can bind its successors – that is, any future Parliament may amend or repeal any previous law passed by any previous Parliament. Also, Parliament is not bound by its own laws (statutes), but instead by a special body of law known as parliamentary privilege. (This exempts MPs from much ordinary law; for example, they cannot be sued for slander for words spoken in Parliament.)

However, Parliament's external sovereignty is now limited in practice by the European Union, whose laws have formal sovereignty over all member states – for example, fishing quotas, the world-wide beef ban and the 48-hour working week. This is the only formal override upon Westminster's legal supremacy. In theory, however, Parliament could legislate to withdraw from the EU at any time. Therefore, it remains technically sovereign – although, in practice, withdrawal from the EU seems unlikely.

There are also many other, informal, constraints on parliamentary sovereignty, both external and internal:

- membership of the EU, which means that large quantities of law now come from Europe, not from Westminster

- other international courts and laws, such as the European Court of Human Rights, which, in 1998, ruled against the UK government's ban on gays in the army

- big business, the City and other economic power bodies such as the international currency dealers, who, in 1992, forced the UK's fallout from the European exchange rate mechanism (ERM) which was paving the way for the euro

- pressure groups, for example, the huge extra subsidies given to the beef farmers in the 1990s to compensate them for lost sales due to the BSE scandal; and also the Countryside Alliance who persuaded the Labour government for years not to fulfil its manifesto promise to abolish fox hunting

- the media, for example, on clamping down on asylum seekers.

Parliament can pass **retrospective law**, that is, backdated law, which may have effect for days, months or years before it was even passed. At its most extreme, this means that Parliament could – in unlikely theory – pass a law which says 'As from now, it was illegal for you to have been walking down that particular road last week. Which you did. You are therefore nicked.' This breaches the principle (in an important theory called the 'rule of law', outlined later) that the law should be 'knowable' at the time that we are breaking it.

In June 1998, for example, retrospective law stopped tax exemptions for overseas earners (which prompted the Rolling Stones to cancel their UK tour). Also, after 11 September 2001, Parliament hastily imposed a retrospective increase in the criminal penalty for terrorist hoaxes from six months to seven years; and, in 2003, they watered down the 'double jeopardy rule' – the principle that you cannot be tried twice for the same crime – and this change has been backdated to apply to people who were tried and acquitted years ago.

" BUT THE COURT FOUND ME
NOT GUILTY LAST WEEK..."

key terms

retrospective law
Backdated law

political sovereignty
The ultimate electoral power and authority of the voters

elective dictatorship
Lord Hailsham's thesis of excessive executive (government) power, between elections, over Parliament and the public

Ultimately, Parliament is constrained by the **political sovereignty** of the electorate, who may occasionally simply refuse to obey the law of Parliament (for example, the mass refusal to pay the poll tax in 1989/90) – and who choose the MPs in the Commons and can therefore, in effect, sack Parliament.

Most importantly, Parliament tends to be dominated, from within itself, by a 'majority' government (that is, an executive whose party holds over 50 per cent of the seats in the Commons) which, with strong party discipline and backbench support, can usually ensure that its legislative proposals are passed by Parliament. No majority government has been forced to resign by a vote of no confidence in the House of Commons since the 1880s.

In his 1976 Dimbleby Lecture, Lord Hailsham therefore used the term **elective dictatorship** to suggest that a majority government, in control of a sovereign Parliament, with a flexible constitution, could effectively change the constitution at will. This argument gained renewed strength after the general election of 1997 when Labour won a massive 179 majority of seats over all of the other parties combined in the House of Commons (on a minority of the votes cast – see Chapter 3) and seemed, to many critics, virtually unstoppable. Thus, for example, within its first year in office, Labour had pushed through many unpopular policies which were not in its manifesto, such as cuts in lone parents' and disabled peoples' benefits, the introduction of students' tuition fees, increasing taxation of pension funds and completing the Millennium Dome.

The – rare – exceptions to this balance of power within Parliament are:

- a minority government, for example the Conservatives by April 1997

- a successful backbench revolt, for example MPs blocked a second VAT rise on domestic fuel in 1996

- defeat by the House of Lords, for example peers in 2003 blocked curbs on the right to jury trial.

Sharp readers will have noticed that most of these examples pre-date Labour's 1997 election win. The post-1997 Labour governments have never, yet, been defeated by a backbench revolt – given their large majority of seats in the Commons. They have been obstructed by the House of Lords but, usually, only temporarily because the elected House of Commons – arithmetically dominated by the government – has the ultimate legal power to overturn the unelected Lords' decisions.

Questions

1 Outline the main principles of the constitution. *(20 marks)*

2 Examine the weaknesses of having an unwritten constitution. *(20 marks)*

■ Recent reforms of the UK constitution

Constitutional change: a twelve-point plan (since 1997)

The following list includes only the proclaimed and 'progressive' changes enacted by the Labour governments since 1997:

- a Scottish Parliament with legislative and tax-varying powers

- a Welsh assembly with executive powers

- power-sharing institutions in Northern Ireland following the 1998 Good Friday Agreement

- an elected Mayor and Greater London Authority for London, and elected mayors in other towns and cities

- new electoral systems for the devolved assemblies, the European Parliament and local mayors

- greater use of referenda

- opting-in to the EU Social Chapter

- granting independence to the Bank of England

- the removal of all but 92 hereditary peers from the Lords

- the 1998 Human Rights Act, which incorporates the European Convention on Human Rights into UK law

- the Freedom of Information Act 2000, which requires the release of more official information by 2005

- the Political Parties, Elections and Referendums Act 2000, which regulates party funding and spending.

Each of these reforms will be explained and analysed in future chapters.

Other changes perceived by (often critical) observers, in practice since 1997 – such as the centralisation of the executive, the politicisation of the civil service, Prime Minister Blair's growing **presidentialism** and growing curbs on the civil liberties of UK citizens – may be equally real, but less legitimate, examples of changes to the UK constitution.

key terms

presidentialism

A style of government leadership (often attributed to Prime Minister Tony Blair) that is populist and personalised, aloof from Cabinet and dismissive of Parliament

Questions

1 What is meant by sovereignty?

2 What is meant by calling UK government 'parliamentary government'?

3 Define the word 'control' in the phrase 'parliamentary control of government'.

4 What is meant by 'the rule of law'?

Questions

True or false?

1 In the UK, the law is made by the judiciary.

2 A constitution is basically a set of rules.

3 In a state, the government is often referred to as 'the executive'.

4 In the UK, the government is the legally sovereign body.

5 Governments are required by law to fulfil their manifesto promises.

6 Parliament could pass a law abolishing the monarchy by the same procedure as it can pass any other bill.

7 In the UK, certain people can be imprisoned indefinitely without trial.

8 England has its own Parliament.

9 UK voters directly elect the Prime Minister.

10 If a constitution is written, it must also be rigid.

Questions

Quiz

Say what is wrong with each of the following statements, and why.

1 The legislature – Parliament – is elected by the people.

2 The two elements in parliamentary government are the House of Commons and the House of Lords.

3 In parliamentary government, the executive is elected from the majority party in the legislature.

4 In parliamentary government, the Cabinet and ministers are taken from the House of Commons.

5 The legislature is often, in theory, subordinate to the executive.

6 The UK constitution is unwritten, therefore flexible.

7   The UK constitution is flexible, therefore the UK has no constitutional laws.

8   A minority government has a minority of the votes but a majority of the seats.

9   A coalition government is where two or more parties have merged to form a single governing party.

10   A manifesto is what the government proposes to do, and the mandate is what they actually do when they get in.

3

Electoral systems and referenda

■ The right to vote

The right of all adults to vote for elected representatives in free, fair, secret and competitive elections is widely regarded as the defining feature of a liberal democracy, such as the UK claims to be. However, even this apparently basic criterion begs questions: for example, who is defined as 'adult'? At present, most people over the age of 18 can vote in the UK, but 16-year-olds may work, pay taxes, get married and join the army, yet cannot vote. The Liberal Democrats have long advocated giving the vote to 16-year-olds, and the Labour government began to consider this idea at the end of 2003. This was mainly because of falling turnouts in recent elections. In the 2001 general election, only 59 per cent of qualified voters actually voted – the lowest turnout since the 1920s. If voting numbers continue to decline, it could damage any future government's claim to democratic legitimacy.

Even 18–21-year-olds were only granted the right to vote in the UK as late as 1969. The gradual extension of the franchise (the right to vote), from a very few male property owners, dates from the 1832 Reform Act. Those still not allowed to vote are members of the House of Lords, non-UK citizens, under-18s, certified mental patients, prisoners under sentence and people disqualified for corrupt electoral practices (such as bribery).

For the Westminster Parliament, there are 646 single-member constituencies in the UK: England has 529, Scotland 59, Wales 40 and Northern Ireland 18 (roughly in proportion to their populations). These are geographical areas, each represented by one Member of Parliament (MP).

A **general election**, involving all UK constituencies, must be held when Parliament has run its full five-year term (under the Parliament Act 1911) or is dissolved earlier when the Prime Minister of the day calls for a general election.

key terms

general election

The election of all Westminster MPs to the House of Commons at intervals of no more than five years

33

key term

by-election

Election in a single constituency when an MP dies, loses the seat through disqualification or quits for other reasons

A **by-election** takes place in a single constituency when the MP dies, loses the seat through disqualification (for example, for corrupt electoral practice or by being granted a peerage – a seat in the House of Lords) or quits for other reasons. By-elections are inevitably used as pointers to the current popularity of the government and other parties but they are, by definition, singular events where factors come into play which do not feature in general elections. Very few seats are 'safe' in by-elections. The Conservatives did not win a single by-election between 1988 and 1997 – a factor which helped PM John Major to lose his slim majority entirely by the time of the 1997 general election. In 2003 the Liberal Democrats inflicted Labour's first by-election defeat for 15 years, in Brent East.

Question

Why is voting behaviour often so different in by-elections from general elections?

(15 marks)

key terms

proportional representation

Umbrella label for systems of election which produce seats in proportion to the parties' share of votes cast

simple majority

More votes or seats than any other single candidate or party; not necessarily 50 per cent

■ Electoral systems

Of the 61 per cent who voted in 2005, only 35 per cent voted for Labour – and yet the Labour Party won 55 per cent of the seats in the House of Commons. This is because of the particular electoral system used for UK general elections.

There are many different electoral systems used around the world, and even for different bodies within the UK. Some electoral systems are designed to produce just one winner (locally or nationally); all votes for losing candidates do not count – thus, they are 'wasted' votes. These are non-proportional systems. Other electoral systems are designed to produce seats in the legislature which are (more or less) in proportion to the votes cast for each party (locally or nationally). These systems are called **proportional representation** (PR).

Types of electoral system

Non-PR systems	*PR systems (mixed or full)*
First-past-the-post	Additional Member System (AMS)
Alternative Vote (AV)	Alternative Vote Plus (AV+)
Supplementary Vote (SV)	Single Transferable Vote (STV)
Second ballot	Party List System (a) Closed or (b) Open

key terms

absolute majority

Over 50 per cent of votes or seats

safe seat

A constituency where one particular party is virtually certain to win every time

Non-proportional representation

First-past-the-post

This is the system used for elections to the Westminster Parliament. It entails one vote per person in single-member constituencies – that is, one MP is elected to represent a single local area; and the one candidate with the most votes wins the constituency, with or without an **absolute majority** (over 50 per cent of the votes cast).

Advantages of first-past-the-post

- The first-past-the-post system is simple, quick and cheap.

- One person, one vote is a basic form of political equality.

- It is said to favour the two-party system as it usually produces a single-party, majority government and a second, strong Opposition party in the House of Commons; hence strong and stable government which is clearly accountable to the voters. However, this must be qualified: the system produced minority governments – with under 50 per cent of the seats in the Commons – in the 1970s; and a two-party system has both advantages and disadvantages – the latter including lack of choice and diversity (especially in **safe seats** which one particular party is virtually certain to win every time), unfair representation of minority parties and their voters, and a majority-seat government with a minority of votes cast. The rise of the Liberals – now Liberal Democrats – since the 1970s has undermined the two-party system; as have the marked regional differences in party support, for example in Scotland, and northern versus southern England – producing a clear north–south, Labour–Conservative political divide and, critics say, 'two Britains'.

- It is also sometimes said that the two-party system created by the first-past-the-post electoral system reflects a 'natural' political divide between conservatism and radicalism. However, the substantial third-party vote since the 1970s belies this argument, as do the substantial policy similarities between the two main parties since the 1997 election.

- Finally, it is said that contact between MP and constituents is closer than in large, multi-member constituencies. In principle there is, indeed, a one-to-one relationship; but, in practice, MPs need not even live in their constituencies and contact with voters is often negligible, especially in safe seats (though these are now declining as voters become more volatile). Do you know the name of your MP?

Disadvantages of first-past-the-post

- Since any vote for a losing candidate is 'wasted', i.e. not directly represented at all in the Commons, all votes do not carry equal weight; i.e. the system does not grant one person, one vote, one value, and political equality is denied. Voters may therefore be discouraged from voting for minority parties, or from voting at all.

% of votes won by each candidate

Candidate		%	
Smith (Labour)	☒	40%	This candidate wins the seat
Brown (Conservative)	☐	30%	All of the votes for these losing candidates are 'wasted'
Clark (Liberal Democrat)	☐	20%	
Green (Green)	☐	10%	

A first-past-the-post ballot paper

- Because many or most MPs have fewer than 50 per cent of the votes cast in their constituencies, no government since the 1930s has had an absolute majority (over 50 per cent) of votes cast, though most have had an absolute majority of seats in the Commons. This usually produces a powerful government which the majority of people voted against – arguably an 'elective dictatorship' (to use Lord Hailsham's phrase) of an unrepresentative kind. Opinion polls suggest that around 60 per cent of voters now favour a system of PR.

- Until the 1997, 2001 and 2005 general elections when the Conservatives were under-represented in the Commons, the two main parties had both been consistently over-represented, while the Liberal Democrats especially – because of the geographical dispersal of their votes – have been consistently under-represented.

- Occasionally, a government may have more seats but fewer votes than the 'losing' party, for example the Conservatives in 1951 and

The party with the most *seats* becomes the government ...

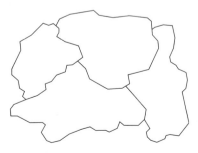

although another party may have more *votes*.

key
terms

independent candidate

A candidate who is not a member of any political party

consensus politics

A period when the two main parties share very similar policies

adversary politics

A period when the two main parties are polarised, advocating very different policies

Labour in February 1974 (because of unequal constituency sizes and winning margins).

● **Independent candidates** (with no party attachment) have very little chance of success. This may exclude quality and diversity from the system.

● Finally, in the period of economic boom from the 1950s to mid-1970s, the two-party system was based on **consensus politics**, when the two main parties shared very similar, centrist policies in support of the mixed economy, welfare state, full employment and nuclear defence. This was praised by some for producing moderation and stability, but was criticised by others for its lack of innovation and choice. Conversely, the recessions of the 1980s were said to have produced **adversary politics** with more right-wing Conservative governments and a more influential left-wing in the Labour Party. The opposite pros and cons were advanced – more diversity and choice, but also more risk of a 'pendulum swing', i.e. sharp policy reversals between different governing parties.

However, after four successive election defeats, the Labour Party in the 1990s shifted increasingly to the right in pursuit of disaffected Conservative voters. The post-1997 period has witnessed a new kind of political consensus based upon a more right-wing agenda of low taxation and inflation, privatisation of services and authoritarian law and order policies.

The 2005 general election result

	% votes cast	No. of seats	% seats
Labour	35	356	55
Conservative	32	197	31
Liberal Democrat	22	62	10
Other	10	30	5
Turnout 61%	100	100	100

Notes and novelties

● Unprecedented third term for Labour.

● Overall Labour majority: 66 seats (down from 179 in 1997, and 167 in 2001).

● Lowest vote (35%) for any winning party since the 1920s, before universal suffrage.

● Only 39% of 18–24 year olds voted.

● Record 127 female MPs – 19%; 1% more than 2001.

● Record 15 Asian and black MPs – three more than 2001.

● First ever black convervative MP, in Windsor. They have two in total.

- The Liberal Democrat tally of seats was highest by a third party since 1923.

- Two independent MPs: Richard Taylor and Peter Law.

- One seat (safe Conservative) not filled because election postponed due to the death of one of the candidates.

- 170 'parties' stood candidates.

Other non-proportional voting systems

Alternatives to first-past-the-post are many and varied; they need not involve proportional representation.

The following three non-PR systems, unlike first-past-the-post, all produce a single winner with over 50 per cent of the votes cast. They may, therefore, have more claim to democratic legitimacy than first-past-the-post.

The alternative vote

Voters list candidates in order of preference; the last candidate(s) are struck out and their votes are redistributed according to the second choices marked on their ballot papers until one candidate has an absolute majority (over 50 per cent) of the votes (for example, Australia).

The supplementary vote

This is preference voting, similar to the alternative vote, but with the voter allowed only two preferences. All candidates except the first and second are eliminated; the losers' second preferences are redistributed and the candidate with over 50 per cent of first and second preferences combined is the winner. This is the system used to elect the London Mayor.

HOW TO VOTE

MAYOR OF LONDON BALLOT PAPER

■ This paper will be in pink and has its own barcode for security. It will have the names of all ten of the candidates, and you should mark one as your first choice and one as your second choice.

■ If you choose the same candidate as your first and second choice, then your first choice will be counted, and your second choice disregarded.

■ If you just make a first choice, your paper will still be counted. But if you make a second choice and not a first one, then your paper will not be counted.

Source: *The Metro*, 9 June 2004

The second ballot

Voters put one cross against one candidate; if no candidate gets 50 per cent, the last candidate(s) are struck out and new ballots are held until one candidate has over 50 per cent (for example, France). This is the method which Conservative MPs used in 2001 to produce a shortlist of two possible party leaders, who then went to a vote by the whole Conservative Party membership.

Proportional representation

This label covers a wide variety of electoral systems where seats are won more or less in proportion to votes cast. PR, in one form or another, is used throughout Europe, has long been advocated by the Liberal Democrats and support for it has grown in the UK since the 1970s: partly because the first-past-the-post system failed in the 1970s to produce majority governments, and partly because the increasing third-party vote since the mid-1970s has highlighted the distortions of first-past-the-post. The 1997 Labour government manifesto promised a referendum on the issue, but they have never yet held one.

Advantages of PR

All forms of PR are said by supporters to share the same basic advantages: they are more representative of voters' wishes as expressed at the ballot box; fewer votes are 'wasted', therefore greater participation may be encouraged; minority parties are more fairly represented; there are less likely to be safe seats with low turn-outs and poor quality MPs; voters may have more choice and therefore candidates may be of better quality; the two-party system (which may have both pros and cons) is usually eliminated and the end result is more pluralist; and the possibility of single-party 'elective dictatorship' is greatly diminished.

It is sometimes argued against PR that it generally demands more knowledge and activity of the voters (for example, to rank candidates in order of preference), and hence may discourage participation. Conversely, however, voters may welcome the opportunity to be better informed and to exercise greater choice, and turnout may actually increase.

Above all, if there are more than two main parties competing, a proportional allocation of seats to votes will tend to produce a **hung parliament** where no party has over 50 per cent of the seats. The consequences – and pros or cons – of a hung parliament are not clear-cut. For one thing, a hung parliament in post-war Britain is rare; and, given the nature of the UK constitution, when it happens the 'rules' are uncertain, for example, who may be chosen as Prime Minister, which parties should form a government, when and whether a fresh election should be called, etc.

A hung parliament need not result in **coalition government** (i.e. two or more parties in executive office). More often in the UK the result has been a single-party, minority government with under 50 per cent of the seats in the Commons. For example, from February 1974, Labour under Harold Wilson hung on for eight months as a minority government, boosting its

key terms

hung parliament

A parliament where no one party has over 50 per cent of the seats

coalition government

Two or more parties in executive office

own popularity with pension increases and rent freezes before calling a new election in October 1974 and winning a small overall majority.

The Liberal Democrats argue in favour of coalitions. They prefer to call a hung parliament a 'balanced parliament'; they favour centrist coalitions, arguing that these would curb elective dictatorship, encourage moderation and continuity, promote greater stability of national direction and policy and therefore be more efficient than the present, potential 'swing of the pendulum'. Certainly a hung parliament usually ensures better attendance in the Commons and harder working MPs, while coalition governments can draw on a wider pool of talent, and may be quite stable. Equally, one-party government may be 'unstable' if it adopts sudden policy changes, for example John Major's forced withdrawal from the ERM in 1992.

Disadvantages of PR

The case against these arguments, and against PR, is that no one votes for a coalition; there is no clear authority, or mandate, for compromise politics. Coalition government may also give disproportionate power to small parties, and may therefore be as unrepresentative, in its own way, as the first-past-the-post system.

talking point

The Liberal Democrats came fourth in the Scottish parliamentary elections (behind Labour, the Scottish Nationalists and the Conservatives) in both the 1999 and 2003 elections but, nevertheless, they have been in a coalition government with Labour in Scotland since 1999. This is sometimes cited as an example of 'proportional representation producing disproportional power'.

Nor is there any inherent virtue in centrism which, from a critical or radical standpoint, may be seen as stagnation. If the Blair 'project' and Liberal Democrats' goal of a permanent, centrist consensus or coalition was to be achieved, it could amount to a new form of elective dictatorship and a retreat from pluralism.

It is now necessary to examine the main types of PR individually, because each has its own particular characteristics, merits and demerits. Beware of generalising in exam answers.

The single transferable vote (STV)

STV is based on multi-member constituencies. Voters list candidates in order of preference. Any candidate obtaining the necessary quota – not necessarily a majority – of first preference votes is elected. (The quota is a formula designed simply to ensure that there are not more winners than there are seats available within each constituency.) Any winners' surplus votes are redistributed among the other candidates in proportion to the second preferences on the winning candidates' ballot papers and so on until all seats are filled. If too few candidates achieve the quota by that process, the last candidate(s) are dropped and their votes are redistributed in proportion to the second preferences on their ballot papers. This system is used in Ireland and also for the Northern Irish Assembly; and it has long been advocated by the Liberal Democrats.

The party list system

This is the most common, and purest, form of PR. The elector votes for a particular party list of candidates, and seats are allocated to each party in exact proportion to votes received. The party seats are then allocated to specific candidates (for example, Switzerland, Israel).

There are two varieties of the party list system:

● *Bound/closed list*: the elector simply votes for a party label and then the party chooses the candidates to fill the seats. This system was employed in Iraq's first 'free' election (after the overthrow of Saddam Hussein) in 2005. The obvious criticism of this system is that the voter has no say in who are the actual MPs, who are likely to be loyal party placemen.

Shortly after they came to power in 1997, the Labour government introduced the closed party list system for elections to the EU Parliament, generating loud protest from some left-wing Labour MPs who feared that they would be frozen out by the process. The House of Lords rejected the closed list system for EU elections a record six times, but the government in the Commons pushed it through nevertheless. By 1999, some independent-minded and popular MEPs, for example Labour's Christine Oddy (Coventry and North Warwickshire), were pushed so far down the party lists as to be effectively deselected by the leadership, with the voters having no say in the process.

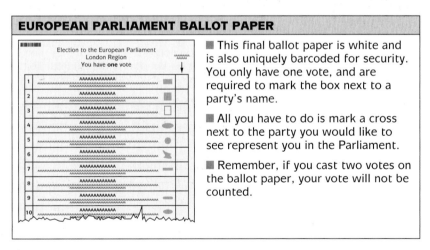

EUROPEAN PARLIAMENT BALLOT PAPER

■ This final ballot paper is white and is also uniquely barcoded for security. You only have one vote, and are required to mark the box next to a party's name.

■ All you have to do is mark a cross next to the party you would like to see represent you in the Parliament.

■ Remember, if you cast two votes on the ballot paper, your vote will not be counted.

Source: *The Metro*, 9 June 2004

● *Free/open list*: the elector may have several preference votes, and may vote for many candidates within one party list or even across different party lists. Each party wins seats in proportion to their total votes received, and those seats are then given to the candidates with the most personal votes within each party list. This may be quite complicated, but it allows the voter much more choice, together with very close proportionality.

Mixed proportional systems

Some electoral processes combine two systems – one PR and one not – in one procedure, in an attempt to get the best of both worlds. In these arrangements, each voter has two votes, and two different kinds of MP are produced – one with a local, single-member constituency and one who is a regional or national representative. Two such systems are described here.

Additional Member System (AMS)

This combines first-past-the-post and PR. The ballot paper has two parts and the elector has two votes. One vote is cast for a candidate to win a seat in a single-member, first-past-the-post constituency. The second vote is cast for a party label, and a number of set-aside or 'top-up' seats in the legislature are filled by non-constituency candidates – additional members – chosen through the closed party list system (see above) in exact proportion to the votes cast for each party on the second part of the ballot paper. This retains single-member constituencies but also provides top-up proportionality for parties which would otherwise be under-represented by first-past-the-post alone. The Scottish Parliament, Welsh Assembly and London Assembly are elected by AMS on a ratio of about 60 per cent first-past-the-post seats to 40 per cent 'top-up' PR seats.

LONDON ASSEMBLY BALLOT PAPER

■ The London Assembly ballot paper is yellow and orange and also has a unique barcode for security. For the Assembly, you have two votes: one for an Assembly member for your constituency and one for a London-wide candidate.

■ If you vote for a constituency member and not a London-wide candidate or vice versa, your vote will still be counted.

■ You cannot vote for two members from the constituency category or the London-wide list, as your vote will not be counted.

Source: *The Metro*, 9 June 2004

Alternative Vote Plus (AV+)

This is a novel combination of electoral systems, devised and recommended by the Jenkins Commission in 1998 for future Westminster parliamentary elections. It combines the Alternative Vote for 80 per cent of the (single-member constituency) seats at Westminster, with 20 per cent of (non-constituency) top-up PR seats to be chosen by a closed party list system. This only contains a very limited element of PR because Tony Blair's aides urged Roy Jenkins to water down his original ideas; and the idea was, anyway, never adopted in the UK. This system is not actually used anywhere.

analyse
this

2005 estimated results using diverse electoral systems (number of seats out of 646)						
	F-p-t-p	*AV*	*AV+*	*STV*	*AMS*	*Party List*
Labour	356	426	355	336	297	226
Conservative	197	110	174	142	200	206
Lib. Dems.	62	84	84	129	109	142
SNP/Plaid Cymru	10	10	15	23	19	45
Others	20	16	18	16	21	27

1 Calculate the percentages (out of 646 seats) represented by each of the figures above.

2 Compare these with the percentage of votes won by each party in 2005.

3 Which electoral system is (a) least and (b) most representative of votes cast?

talking
point

Electoral deposits are the sums of money required from each candidate who stands in an election. They are intended to deter frivolous candidates. The deposit is returned to candidates who win over 5 per cent of the votes cast.

- Westminster deposit: £500 per candidate

- EU Parliament deposit: £5,000 per candidate

- London mayoral election deposit: £10,000 per candidate

Political equality, not.

Questions

Quiz

Briefly answer the following questions.

1 Which system seems to give the most power to the parties in choosing MPs?

2 Which system seems to produce the closest proportion of seats to votes?

3 Which system does not have single-member constituencies? List three advantages and three disadvantages of multi-member constituencies.

4 Which system(s) produce one winning candidate with more than 50 per cent of the votes cast?

5 Which system(s) produce two types of MPs, one with a local constituency and one without? Suggest two advantages and two disadvantages of this arrangement.

6 Which system requires the electorate to turn out to vote more than once? Give one advantage and one disadvantage of such a system.

7 Which system(s) allow for cross-voting between parties and/or candidates? Give two possible advantages and two disadvantages of cross-voting.

8 Which system(s) are likely to give more accurate representation to minority parties? Give two advantages and two disadvantages of such systems.

9 Suggest one reason why STV is not purely proportional.

10 List four reforms to the present first-past-the-post system (other than the various other electoral systems discussed above) which may make it more 'democratic'.

key terms

electoral deposit

The sums of money required from each candidate who stands in an election

class or partisan dealignment

The breakdown, since the 1970s, of long-term patterns of consistent voting for a political party which were based mainly on social class

■ Some factors influencing voting behaviour

Social class and occupation

These have long been the most important influences on voting in the UK. Historically, the wealthier upper and middle classes were more likely to vote Conservative and the working class were more likely to vote Labour; while centrist parties such as the Liberal Democrats have suffered from their lack of class identity. However, there have always been exceptions. Lower-income Conservative voters used to be classified by sociologists either as 'deferential' voters (regarding the Conservatives as superior governors) or as 'secular' or 'instrumental' voters (seeking personal advantages such as tax cuts).

This analysis is now regarded as too simplistic. Since the 1970s, voters have become more volatile and quicker to change sides, and the old class allegiances are weakening – a process known as **class or partisan dealignment**. There are several suggested reasons for this process.

- The traditional manual working class has markedly declined in size with structural changes in the economy and rising unemployment in the 1980s. Trade union membership has also fallen for the same reasons and, with it, some of the traditional working-class values of equality, collectivism, solidarity and 'old' Labour support. Rising living standards for those in work, together with increasing home and company share ownership, geographical mobility (often due to the break-up of traditional working-class communities, for example after coal pit closures), population shifts to the south, privatised and non-unionised work have also weakened traditional working-class values and voting patterns.

● Many workers looked to the Conservatives in the 1980s for promised tax cuts and council house sales. Other key policy issues, such as defence, law and order and local government, also caused problems for Labour at that time.

● As the Conservative and Labour parties were seen to be polarising throughout the 1980s, growing support for the centre parties increased the distortions of the first-past-the-post electoral system.

● In the 1997 election, as 'new' Labour adopted almost wholesale the Conservatives' tax and spend policies, they won over many middle-class voters for the first time.

Other important factors cut across class divisions.

Regional variations

Labour is stronger in inner-city areas, and in Scotland and Wales where the Conservatives won no seats at all in 1997. The Conservatives are stronger in rural areas and in southern England. These patterns are linked to both class and local culture. The Liberal Democrats have pockets of support in Wales, south-west England and the Scottish Isles and borders.

Sex, age and race

Historically, women tend to vote Conservative more than Labour. More young people in 2005 voted Labour: 52 per cent of first-time voters as opposed to 20 per cent for the Conservatives and 24 per cent for the Liberal Democrats. However, voting turnout is lowest among young people. Surveys of ethnic minorities consistently show around 70 per cent support for Labour, 25 per cent for the Conservatives and 5 per cent for the Liberal Democrats.

Religion

Roman Catholics and non-conformists tend to be less Conservative than are Anglicans; but this influence is declining and, again, may be linked to class. The invasion of Iraq has undermined support for Labour among Muslim voters.

Mass media

TV and newspapers both create and reflect public opinion and can highlight particular political issues (such as education, unemployment), party images and personalities as a basis for voting. For several decades, the national press in the UK was largely Conservative (hence the *Sun*'s

The media both create and reflect public opinion

notorious front-page headline after the 1992 Conservative victory, 'It's the Sun wot won it').

Uniquely, however, Blair courted and won over the Rupert Murdoch stable – the *Sun*, *The Times*, *The Sunday Times* and the *News of the World* as well as Sky TV and other international broadcasting media – before the 1997 election. Whether they helped to swing the result or simply anticipated the inevitable is a matter of conjecture.

Personal experience

Family, friends and work associates can help to shape a person's political opinions; parental influence is particularly strong (and is, of course, linked again to social class).

Party image and party policy

Tony Blair

Because of the first-past-the-post and parliamentary systems – when we vote for a single, local MP we are indirectly voting for a national government – electors tend to vote for a party label more than for an individual candidate. Some voters look closely at the parties' past records and present policies; many vote on the basis of a broad party image (united or divided, pro-spending or cutting, pro- or anti-welfare, helping the poor or the wealthy, etc.), although this may not always correspond to the parties' actual policies when in power. For example, much is made of the economic 'feel good' factor; but, paradoxically, the economy was in serious decline when the Conservatives won again in 1992 and was recovering well when they lost in 1997.

Party leaders

Growing emphasis has been put upon the image and popularity of the party leaders – especially since the 1997 election when the main parties' policies have been quite similar. In 1992, the 'Kinnock factor' clearly put off a significant number of voters who felt that he lacked stature and gravitas; he was also the object of a sustained campaign of character assassination by the *Sun* newspaper. Conversely, in 1997 Tony Blair was perceived to be leading an increasingly moderate and disciplined party in contrast to the feuding Conservatives; and he was careful not to repeat Neil Kinnock's over-exuberance and premature triumphalism. In 2001, William Hague was widely perceived as a rather weak leader heading a party which was still divided, old and out of touch. Michael Howard was seen as more experienced and competent than recent Conservative leaders, but his unpopular record as a Cabinet minister in the Conservative governments of the 1980s and 1990s told against him in 2005.

Abstentions

Michael Howard

Qualified voters may choose not to vote for many reasons: lack of information about, or interest in, the election (especially in local council elections, by-elections and European elections; and also in safe seats where campaigning may be minimal and the outcome is a foregone conclusion); dislike of all available parties or candidates, or lack of effective choice (again, especially in safe seats); difficulty in getting to the polling station (though the local parties may provide transport for some voters). In sum, the main reasons are apathy, disillusionment, protest or practical difficulties. The young, the poor, ethnic minorities and the unemployed are the most likely to abstain – or not to register at all – which tends to hit the Labour vote hardest. (In London in 2005, for example, 24 per cent of black people were non-registered compared with 6 per cent of white people.)

This is an increasingly important issue, given the low turnouts for all recent elections. Some new methods of vote-casting are being tried in various parts of the country to see if they encourage higher voter turnout, including all-postal ballots in some regions.

Summary of election turnouts 1997–2005 (%)

General election May 1997	71
Northern Ireland Assembly May 1998	70
Scottish Parliament May 1999	57
Welsh Assembly May 1999	46
Local government elections May 1999	29
European Parliament June 1999	23
General election June 2001	59
London Mayor and Assembly 2004	37
General election May 2005	61

analyse
this

General election results 1970–2005

Date	Party	Votes (millions)	% Votes	Seats	% Seats
1970	Cons*	13.145	46.4	330	52.4
	Lab	12.179	42.9	287	45.6
	Lib	2.118	7.5	6	1.0
	Others	903	2.2	7	1.1
1974	Cons	11.869	37.9	297	46.8
(Feb)	Lab*	11.639	37.1	301	47.4
	Lib	6.063	19.3	14	2.2
	Others	1.762	5.6	23	3.6
1974	Con	10.465	35.8	277	43.6
(Oct)	Lab*	11.457	39.2	319	50.2

AS Government and Politics

	Lib	5.347	18.3	13	2.1
	Others	1.920	6.6	26	4.2
1979	Cons*	13.698	43.9	339	53.4
	Lab	11.510	36.9	268	42.2
	Lib	4.314	13.8	11	1.7
	Others	1.700	5.5	17	2.7
1983	Cons*	13.103	42.4	397	61.0
	Lab	8.462	27.6	209	32.2
	Lib/SDP	7.776	25.3	23	3.6
	Others	1.420	4.6	21	3.2
1987	Cons*	13.760	42.3	376	59.4
	Lab	10.030	30.8	229	36.1
	Lib/SDP	7.341	22.6	22	3.5
	Others	1.398	4.3	23	3.5
1992	Cons*	14.092	42.0	336	51.6
	Lab	11.560	35.4	271	41.6
	LibDem	5.999	17.9	20	3.1
	Others	1.998	5.6	24	3.7
1997	Lab*	13.517	44.4	419	63.6
	Cons	9.593	31.5	165	25.0
	LibDem	5.243	17.2	46	7.0
	Others	2.513	8.5	29	4.4
2001	Lab*	10.725	40.6	413	62.7
	Cons	8.357	31.6	166	25.2
	LibDem	4.814	18.3	52	7.9
	Others	2.471	9.1	28	4.2
2005	Lab*	9.556	35.2	356	55.1
	Cons	8.772	32.3	198	30.6
	LibDem	5.982	22.0	62	9.6
	Others	2.821	10.5	30	4.6

* Governing party

1 Check the percentages of votes and seats gained by the Labour and Conservative Parties in February 1974. Which party became the governing party and why?

2 Check the percentages of votes and seats gained by the Labour and Liberal/SDP Parties in 1983. How would you explain the discrepancies?

3 Compare the number of votes cast, and seats won, for the Liberal Democrats in 1997 and 2001. How did they manage to win fewer votes, and yet more seats, in 2001?

48

Questions

True or false?

1 Democracy has existed in the UK ever since Saxon times.

2 The Reform Act 1832 gave the vote to all men over the age of 21.

3 General elections must normally be held at least every five years.

4 The Prime Minister decides when a general election is to be held.

5 A by-election is held to elect local councillors.

6 Judges and police officers are legally disqualified from voting.

7 In a general election, the winning party is the one with the most votes.

8 A 'coalition' is a government composed of people from more than one party.

9 Only 22 per cent of the qualified electorate in the UK voted for Labour in the 2005 general election.

10 The influence of social class upon voting behaviour in the UK is declining.

■ Referenda

A referendum is a direct vote by the electorate on a policy issue offered by the government, usually in the form of a question requiring a 'yes' or 'no' answer. Switzerland – a very small and decentralised country with only 5 million voters – is the world record holder in the number of referenda which it holds, accounting for an estimated half of the referendum ballots worldwide.

Referenda provide an element of direct democracy in a representative system (even though, in the UK, they are invariably only 'advisory' to maintain the semblance of parliamentary sovereignty). They can be educative, increasing public awareness and understanding of an issue because all sides are likely to bombard the voters with information and arguments. They help to legitimise the resulting policy decision and to promote consensus behind it within both the government and the public.

On the other hand, referenda may oversimplify a complex issue by reducing voter choice to a simple 'yes' or 'no'.

Referenda may also reduce voter choice by merging two or more issues in one question – for example, in the referendum on an elected London council and mayor in 1998. Voters may also be subjected to very one-sided campaigns – for example, in the 1975 European and 1998 Scottish referenda – or to misleading propaganda rather than informative facts. Even the wording of a referendum question may be perceived as 'leading' or biased. The proposed wording of the euro referendum is 'Should the United Kingdom adopt the euro as its currency?' The Conservatives have complained that the question 'makes no mention of the fact that the pound will be replaced if people vote yes'. The vote may be so close as to call into doubt the legitimacy of the policy; for example the referendum on Welsh devolution was won by under 1 per cent. Cynics may go so far as to suggest that UK governments will only offer referenda when it suits them and when they are sure they are going to win – hence the timing of the Northern Ireland referendum and delaying of the referendum on the euro.

In summary, referenda may be used simply to legitimise what governments intend to do anyway, whilst at the same time allowing governments to evade responsibility and blame the voters for any unpopular consequences. They are also, of course, quite time-consuming and costly.

Given the UK's flexible constitution, there are no legal rules at all about when and how referenda should be held. In 1998, the Neill Committee on Public Standards recommended that there should be equal state funding for both sides in referenda campaigns, and that the government of the day should remain neutral. The government promptly rejected both ideas.

Questions

1 Outline two differences between a referendum and an election.　*(5 marks)*

2 Describe the circumstances of three referenda held in the UK.　*(15 marks)*

3 What are the disadvantages of referenda?　*(30 marks)*

4

Political parties and MPs

■ Political parties

A **party** system implies political decision-making and representation on the basis of formal, organised groups of (more or less) like-minded people who stand candidates for election on a common policy programme. A party system may contain only one party – which would widely be seen as a dictatorship – or two, or many. A party system, of any type, has merits and demerits as compared with, for example, representation and political decision-making by independent individuals. The issues involved include representative and responsible government, pluralism and elective dictatorship.

Advantages of a party system

● Parties provide the basis for the choice of a Prime Minister and the formation of a legitimate and unified government.

● Parties provide the basis for a coherent and comprehensive body of policies for government.

● Parties organise and crystallise public opinion into coherent blocks.

● Parties educate public opinion through their activities inside and outside of Parliament, and through the media (though they may also try to manipulate and mislead public opinion for party advantage).

● Parties provide effective organisation, financing and campaigning for candidates.

● According to the 'doctrine of the mandate', an elected government is authorised, or even obliged, to implement the policy proposals contained in its party manifesto; the party system is therefore essential for representative government.

● The convention of collective responsibility, whereby government is accountable to Parliament and hence to the electorate, assumes an

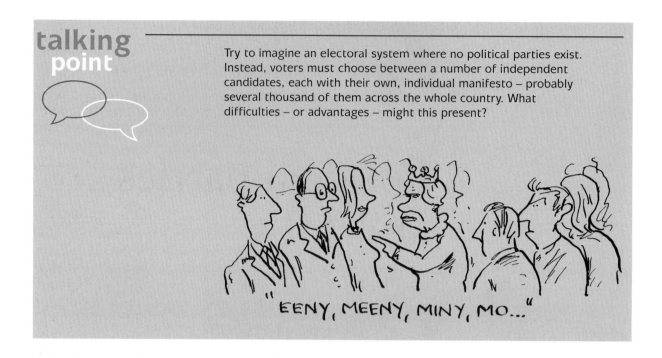

talking point

Try to imagine an electoral system where no political parties exist. Instead, voters must choose between a number of independent candidates, each with their own, individual manifesto – probably several thousand of them across the whole country. What difficulties – or advantages – might this present?

" EENY, MEENY, MINY, MO..."

executive united around a common body of policy. The party system is therefore essential for responsible government.

● The party system provides stability and consistency of government.

Disadvantages of a party system

● A single-party, majority government based on strong party discipline may amount to elective dictatorship.

● Parties may encourage partisan conflict for its own sake, undermining effective government.

● Voters have no choice between the policies of any one party.

● Voters have no say in the parties' candidates (though 'open primaries' could be introduced, as in the USA).

● The party system discourages close, personal contact between MPs and voters.

● The party system undermines MPs' independence and individualism.

● The national or local party machines may have excessive power – for example, over MPs – at the expense of the voters.

● The party system may permanently exclude some minority views, or may neglect important issues which cut across orthodox party lines (for example, moral issues such as abortion or capital punishment).

● The party system excludes able independents.

■ The UK party system

The major and minor parties taking part in the 2005 general election

Conservative **C**; Labour **Lab**; Labour and Co-operative **Lab Co-op**; Liberal Democrat **LD**; Plaid Cymru **PC**; Scottish National Party **SNP**; Green **Green**; Ulster Unionist Party **UUP**; Democratic Unionist Party **DUP**; Social Democratic and Labour Party **SDLP**; Sinn Fein **SF**; Alliance **Alliance**; Workers' Party **WP**; Alliance for Change **AFC**; Alliance for Green Socialism **Green Soc**; Alternative Party **AP**; Anti-Corruption Forum **Anti-Corrupt**; Asian League **AL**; Blair Must Go Party **BMG**; British National Party **BNP**; British Public Party **BPP**; Build Duddon and Morecambe Bridges **Bridges**; Burnley First Independent **Burnley**; Campaigning for Real Democracy **CRD**; Chairman of Sunrise Radio **Sunrise**; Christian Democrat **Ch D**; Christian Peoples Alliance **CPA**; Church of the Militant Elvis Party **Elvis**; Civilisation Party **CP**; Clause 28 Children's Protection Christian Democrats **Clause 28**; Communist Party **Comm**; Communist Party of Britain **Comm Brit**; Community **Community**; Community Action Party **CAP**; Community Group **CG**; Countryside Party **Country**; Croydon Pensions Alliance **Croydon**; Death Dungeons & Taxes Party **DDTP**; Defend The Welfare State Against Blairism **Def Welfare**; Demanding Honesty in Politics and Whitehall **Honesty**; Democratic Labour Party **Dem Lab**; Democratic Socialist Alliance – People Before Profit **Dem Soc All**; Direct Customer Service Party **Customer**; English Democratic Party **EDP**; English Democrats – Putting England First **England**; English Democrats Party **Eng Dem**; English Independence Party **Eng Ind**; English Parliamentary Party **EEP**; Extinction Club **Ext Club**; Fancy Dress Party **FDP**; Fathers-4-Justice **Fathers**; Fit Party For Integrity And Trust **Fit**; Forward Wales Party **FWP**; Free Party **Free**; Free Scotland Party **Free Scot**; Freedom Party **FP**; Get Britain Back Party **GBB**; Green **Green**; Grey Party **Grey**; Imperial Party **IP**; Independent **Ind**; Independent J **Ind J**; Independent – Vote for Yourself Party **Ind Vote**; Independent B **Ind B**; Independent Batchelor **Ind Batch**; Independent Bell **Ind Bell**; Independent Booth **Ind Booth**; Independent Br **Ind Br**; Independent Braid **Ind Braid**; Independent Cam **Ind Cam**; Independent Community Candidate Empowering Change **Community**; Independent Green **Ind Green**; Independent Haines **Ind Haines**; Independent Hill **Ind Hill**; Independent Hinkles **Ind Hinkles**; Independent Hunt **Ind Hunt**; Independent John **Ind John**; Independent K **Ind K**; Independent Keys **Ind Keys**; Independent Kidderminster Hospital and Health Concern **KHHC**; Independent KI **Ind KI**; Independent Labour **Ind Lab**; Independent M **Ind M**; Independent Masters **Ind Masters**; Independent McBride **Ind McBride**; Independent N **Ind N**; Independent Nazir **Ind Nazir**; Independent P **Ind P**; Independent Pev **Ind Pev**; Independent Pr **Ind Pr**; Independent Prachar **Ind Prachar**; Independent R **Ind R**; Independent Sh **Ind Sh**; Independent Sib **Ind Sib**; Independent Stone **Ind Stone**; Independent T **Ind T**; Independent United Unionist **Ind UU**; Independent W **Ind West**; Independent Walsh **Ind Walsh**; Independent Working Class Association **IWCA**; Independent X **Ind X**; "Iraq War, Not In My Name" **Iraq**; Islam Zinda Baad Platform **IZB**; Isle of Wight Party **IOW**; Jam

Wrestling Party **Wrestling**; John Lillburne Democratic Party **JLDP**; Justice Party **JP**; Kidderminster Hospital and Health Concern **KHHC**; Left Alliance **Left All**; Legalise Cannabis Alliance **LCA**; Liberal **Lib**; Liberated Party **LP**; Local Community Party **Local**; Lower Excise Duty Party **Low Excise**; Marxist Party **Marxist**; Max Power Party **Power**; Mebyon Kernow **Meb Ker**; Monster Raving Loony Party **Loony**; Motorcycle News Party **MNP**; Muslim Party **Muslim**; National Front **NF**; New Britain Party **NBP**; New England Party **NEP**; New Millennium Bean **Bean**; Newcastle Academy with Christian Values Party **NACVP**; No description **ND**; No description Bardwaj **ND Bardwaj**; Northern Ireland Unionist **NI Unionist**; Northern Progress For You **Northern**; Open-Forum **Forum**; Operation Christian Vote **OCV**; Pacifist for Peace, Justice, Cooperation, Environment **Pacifist**; Pathfinders **PF**; Peace Party, non-violence, justice, environment **PPN-V**; Peace and Progress Party **Progress**; Pensioner Coalition **Pensioner**; Pensioners Party Scotland **PPS**; People's Choice **Choice**; People's Justice Party **PJP**; Personality And Rational Thinking? Yes! Party **PRTYP**; Pride in Paisley Party **Paisley**; Pro Euro Conservative Party **Pro Euro C**; ProLife Alliance **ProLife**; Progress Democratic Party Members Decide Policy **Prog Dem**; Progressive Democratic Party **PDP**; Progressive Unionist Party **PUP**; Protest Vote Party **Protest**; Public Services Not War **PSNW**; Publican Party – Free to Smoke (Pubs) **Publican**; Qari **Qari**; Rainbow Dream Ticket Party **Dream**; Rate Payer **RP**; Reform 2000 **Reform**; Reform UK **Ref UK**; Removal of Tetra masts in Cornwall **Masts**; Residents Association **RA**; Residents and Motorists of Great Britain **Res Motor**; Respect the Unity Coalition **Respect**; Rock & Roll Loony Party **R & R Loony**; SOS! Voters against Overdevelopment of Northampton **SOS**; Save The National Health **SNH**; Save the Bristol North Baths Party **Baths**; Scottish Freedom Referendum Party **Scot Ref**; Scottish Independence Party **Scot Ind**; Scottish Labour **Scot Lab**; Scottish Senior Citizens Party **Scot Senior**; Scottish Socialist Party **SSP**; Scottish Unionist **Scot U**; Seeks A Worldwide Online Participatory Directory Online; Senior Citizens Party **Senior**; Silent Majority Party **Silent**; Socialist **Socialist**; Socialist Alliance **Soc All**; Socialist Alternative Party **Soc Alt**; Socialist Environmental Alliance **Soc EA**; Socialist Labour Party **Soc Lab**; Socialist Party **Soc**; Socialist Unity Network **Soc Unity**; St Albans Party **St Albans**; Stuckist **Stuck**; Tatton Group Independent **Tatton**; The Common Good **Common Good**; The Millennium Council **MC**; The Peace Party – non-violence, justice, environment **TPP**; The People's Choice Making Politicians Work **Work**; The Resolutionist Party **The RP**; The Speaker **Speaker**; Their Party **TP**; Third Way **Third**; Tigers eye the party for kids **TEPK**; Truth Party **Truth**; UK Community Issues Party **UKC**; UK Independence Party **UKIP**; UK Pathfinders UK **Path**; UK Pensioners Party **UKPP**; United Kingdom Unionist **UKU**; Unrepresented People's Party **Unrep**; Veritas **Veritas**; Virtue Currency Cognitive Appraisal Party **Currency**; Vote for yourself rainbow dream ticket **Vote Dream**; WWW.XAT.ORG **WWW.XAT.ORG**; Wessex Regionalist **Wessex Reg**; Women for Life on Earth **WFLOE**; Women's Coalition **Women's Co**; Workers' Revolutionary Party **WRP**; World Revolutionary Party **World Rev**; Xtraordinary People Party **XPP**; Your Party (Banbury) **YPB**; familiesfirst.uk.net **FFUK**; telepathicpartnership.com **telepath**.

talking
point

There are currently ten parties in the House of Commons (including the Scottish and Welsh nationalists and the Northern Irish parties) and 170 'parties' stood candidates in the 2005 general election! Many of them, of course, were very small groups indeed, often more like pressure groups pursuing a single cause and standing candidates merely for publicity. Some of them, as you can probably guess from their labels, were rather frivolous – but even these served a valuable function in a pluralist democracy by providing a channel for political participation and protest.

Robert Kilroy-Silk, UKIP

There are several possible ways of describing the party system in the UK – and all of them have some validity, depending upon which part of the political system, and which time period, is under scrutiny.

- A **multi-party system** is one where many parties exist and there is a fairly even balance of power between them. Clearly, as shown above, many parties exist in the UK and even within Parliament. There are also clear regional differences in the parties' strengths: for example, in Scotland and Wales, the Scottish and Welsh nationalist parties are the formal 'Opposition' (i.e. the second largest parties). In local government, too, the small parties, such as the Greens and the BNP, do better than at national level. Finally, because of its unique history, there is a completely different party system in Northern Ireland, based upon nationalist and unionist parties. The main UK parties, such as the Labour and Conservative parties, usually do not even stand candidates in Northern Ireland.

- A **two-and-a-half party system** is one where two parties dominate but a third party plays a significant role. The Liberal Democrats won 22 per cent of the votes cast in the 2005 general election; they have been in a coalition government with Labour in Scotland since 1999; and, in the 2004 local elections, the Liberal Democrats pushed Labour into third place.

- A **two-party system** is one where, although many parties exist, only two dominate the legislature and have any real prospect of winning government power. The first-past-the-post system of election transforms – or deforms – a multi-party system in the country into a two-party system in Westminster. Only the Labour and Conservative parties have formed (single-party) governments since 1945; almost 90 per cent of Westminster MPs are Labour or Conservative; the constitution recognises only Her Majesty's Government and

AS Government and Politics

key term

Her Majesty's Opposition

The second largest party in the legislature and an official part of the constitution

Her Majesty's Opposition; and Westminster parliamentary procedures such as pairing and Opposition Days – even the two-sided layout of the Commons' chamber – assume and reinforce the two-party system.

- A **dominant party system** is one where one particular party is in executive power for significantly longer periods of time than any other party (whether with a small or large majority). The Conservatives, by 1997, had been in power for the previous 18 years, for two-thirds of the post-war era and, indeed, for over two-thirds of the twentieth century. Perhaps 'new' Labour may be heading the same way in the twenty-first century? It is rather too soon to tell.

The main disadvantages of a dominant party system are:

- The governing party becomes complacent, arrogant and even corrupt.

- Government becomes stagnant and runs out of useful ideas.

- Alternatively, government casts around for new ideas for their own sake, which may generate policy instability.

- The Opposition lacks information and experience over the long term, especially in a system as secretive as the UK's.

- Institutions such as the civil service, police and judiciary may become 'politicised'.

- Large sections of the electorate are long excluded from representation by government and may become apathetic or angry; they may turn to direct action, etc. Even supporters of the governing party may get fed up and develop the 'time for a change' sentiment so evident in the 1997 general election.

- 'Elective dictatorship' is the phrase used by Lord Hailsham to describe periods of time in the UK when the governing party has such a large majority in the Commons that they can overwhelmingly dominate it and push through almost any decision they want. Within its first year in office in 1997, Labour had pushed through many unpopular policies which were not in its manifesto, such as lone parents' benefit cuts, disabled people's benefit cuts, students' tuition fees, a five-year public sector pay squeeze and increasing taxation of pension funds.

Question

Distinguish between two types of party system. *(5 marks)*

key terms

New Right conservatives

Economic Conservatives – Thatcherites – who emphasise private property, the free market, individual enterprise and self-help, reducing inflation, public spending and taxation

Eurosceptics

People doubtful about, or quite hostile to, the UK's involvement in the EU and further European integration

traditional political conservatives

Older school of Conservatives who emphasise social stability and consensus, traditional institutions (for example, monarchy, Church and Lords), the nuclear family and public duty

■ Principles, policies and organisation of the major parties

The Conservative Party

This is the oldest of the three main parties. Under Margaret Thatcher in the 1980s, it was led by economic conservatives – the **New Right** – who emphasised private property, the free market, individual enterprise and self-help, reducing inflation, public spending and taxation (at the expense of employment, if necessary). This ideology was inherited from eighteenth-century 'classical' liberals. Paradoxically, within New Right conservatism, the stress on 'rolling back the frontiers of state' in the economy was combined with a very illiberal agenda of growing political centralisation and authoritarianism, for example in law and order, anti-immigration, and strict social and moral policies reflecting 'Victorian values'. The New Right tend also to be strongly **Eurosceptic** – that is, hostile to the European Union to a greater or lesser degree. They came to the fore in the late 1970s as a reaction against: the consensus politics of the post-war period; the 'excessive' state intervention in the economy – for example, the many nationalised industries and the welfare dependency of the 'nanny state'; the influence of the trade unions in 1970s' politics, perceived by the New Right conservatives as excessive; and the 'permissive society' of lax moral values since the 1960s.

There is also, however, still an older school of more **traditional political conservatives** in the party (for example, Lord Howe) who emphasise social stability and consensus, traditional institutions (for example, monarchy, Church and Lords), the nuclear family and public duty. These 'wets' (a derogatory label coined by Mrs Thatcher) combine traditional Toryism with a Keynesian (liberal) approach to economic

" WHAT THIS COUNTRY WANTS IS LESS TAX AND MORE LAW AND ORDER . " (Margaret Thatcher)

policy, favouring some state intervention, a mixed economy, public spending, welfare and pro-European policies – for example, Michael Heseltine and Kenneth Clarke. Successive leaders – John Major, William Hague, Iain Duncan Smith and Michael Howard – have leant more towards the Thatcherite wing of the party, which has caused continuous internal party conflict, especially over Europe.

All Conservatives advocate private property, hierarchy, strong defence and law and order. In November 2003, Michael Howard became leader of the Conservatives (unopposed, therefore no party election) after his predecessor, Iain Duncan Smith, was defeated in a vote of no confidence by his own MPs. Howard vowed to lead 'from the centre' and promised his MPs a free vote on the Labour government's proposed gay partnerships bill. However, in his 2004 frontbench reshuffle, he sacked key 'modernisers' and replaced them with right-wing Eurosceptics such as John Redwood. By the 2005 general election, the party was promising a largely Thatcherite agenda, including tax cuts, curbs on immigration and asylum and 40,000 extra police.

The Labour Party

Labour, founded in 1900, historically was similarly divided between a more centrist, **social democratic** leadership which favoured 'freedom, fairness and fraternity' in a mixed, mainly private enterprise, economy combined with some state control and planning, welfare and multilateral nuclear disarmament within international bodies such as NATO and the EU; and the more radical left-wing **democratic socialists** (for example, Tony Benn), who sought extensive collective ownership, workers' democracy, welfare, social equality, greater political participation and political reform (for example, abolition of the House of Lords), unilateral nuclear disarmament and withdrawal from NATO and the EU.

In 1995, Labour abandoned Clause Four of its founding constitution (about common ownership), the most sacred totem of 'old' Labour values. This was the most symbolic moment of the shift from 'old' to **'new' Labour**, pioneered by Neil Kinnock and then John Smith before Tony Blair took over as leader.

> 'To secure for the workers by hand or by brain the full fruits of their industry, and the most equitable distribution thereof that may be possible, upon the basis of the common ownership of the means of production, distribution and exchange and the best obtainable system of popular administration and control of each industry or service'
>
> Clause Four of the Labour Party constitution (1918), which was emblazoned on all Labour Party membership cards until 1995

The key phrase in Clause Four is 'common ownership': that is, collective or state (as opposed to private-for-profit) ownership of businesses and industries – a central principle of socialism.

key terms

social democrats

Moderate 'old' Labour advocates of a mixed economy and moderate welfare

democratic socialists

Radical left-wing 'old' Labour advocates of extensive collective ownership, workers' democracy, welfare and equality of outcome

'new' Labour

A term used by Tony Blair for the first time at the 1994 Labour Party conference to describe the modernised, more right-wing Labour Party, repositioned to attract more middle-class voters

However, as then Trade Secretary Stephen Byers said in 1999, 'new' Labour is about 'wealth creation, not wealth distribution'. Blair's 'Third Way', as he calls it, is more right-wing than either of the old Labour schools of thought: although it has elements of social democracy within it, it has chosen largely to continue Conservative New Right economic, taxation and law and order policies, combined with the 'wet' Conservatives' pro-European stance and a liberal programme of constitutional reforms. Senior Conservative Lord Onslow said of the 'new' Labour government in its early days, 'They're buggering up the constitution and ruining fox hunting. Otherwise, it's a perfectly sound Tory government.'

Or, as left-winger Tony Benn said in 2003, 'One of the reasons why the Conservative party is in such a mess is because there is a much better Conservative party in office'.

This is not wholly fair: there are 'old' Labour, social democratic, aspects to the Labour government's policies, such as the minimum wage; and there are liberal constitutional reforms such as the Human Rights Act; as well as Conservative policies on freezing income tax, privatising parts of the public services and pursuing increasingly illiberal law and order policies. 'New' Labour is not ideologically coherent.

Examples of 'old' Labour policies enacted by the post-1997 Labour governments

- Amsterdam Treaty: opted into the EU Social Chapter, for example the minimum wage – although it was set at a low £3.60, and lower for under-21s – and was therefore criticised by the trade unions. It has since been raised to over £5 per hour

- Employment Relations Act 1999: enhanced workers' rights of trade union recognition and parental leave

- Record increases in spending on education and health

- Goals to eradicate child and pensioner poverty.

- Railtrack forced into administration 2001 – 'de-privatisation'

- Brown's 2002 budget added 1 penny in the pound onto National Insurance to help fund the NHS

Examples of 'new' Labour policies enacted by the post-1997 Labour governments

- 1997 cuts in lone parents' benefits and 1998 cuts in disabled peoples' benefits

- 1999 welfare-to-work reform policies: similar to the US Workfare system with compulsory interviews and job offers

- Privatisation of air traffic control, the Tote, the London tube, etc.

- Private Finance Initiatives (PFIs) in the NHS

- Top-up university tuition fees

- Crime and Disorder Act 1998: introduced the UK's first child jail for 12–14-year-olds, curfews for under-10s, electronic tagging of 10-year-olds, etc.

- Draconian 2001 anti-terrorism laws

- £300 million of taxpayers' money to compensate Railtrack shareholders in 2002

- Radical constitutional reforms: devolution, local government, Lords, Bill of Rights, Freedom of Information Act, etc.

Labour's broken promises since 1997

✗ Guaranteed nursery places for all four-year-olds

✗ A new University for Industry

✗ An end to waiting for cancer surgery

✗ A ban on tobacco advertising

✗ A complete ban on handguns

✗ A review of ministerial accountability to remove abuses

✗ A referendum on the voting system for the House of Commons

✗ An independent National Statistical Service

✗ A referendum on a single European currency

✗ The protection and promotion of human rights as a central part of foreign policy

✗ Swift and fair decisions on asylum seekers

✗ No top-up university tuition fees

The Liberal Democrats

This party emerged out of the break-up of the SDP/Liberal Alliance after the 1987 election and the merger of most of its members under the leadership of Paddy Ashdown. They are much the same, philosophically, as the old Liberal Party. They favour a largely private enterprise economy but with positive state intervention to promote positive individual freedom through, for example, the provision of welfare, and legislation to promote freedoms such as access to official information and the prevention of discrimination. They were, historically, the party most enthusiastic about civil liberties and issues of constitutional reform – notably a written constitution and Bill of Rights, proportional representation, devolution or federalism and a democratically reformed second chamber. 'New' Labour has stolen many of their ideas (in limited form). However, the Liberal Democrats' ideas on constitutional reform go further than Labour's, to include proportional representation for Westminster and local authorities, an elected second chamber, elected regional assemblies for England and a Supreme Court able to veto legislation and to resolve disputes within a federal UK with a codified consti-

Liberal Democrat leader
Charles Kennedy

tution. Of the three main parties, only the Liberal Democrats are fully committed to the development of a federal Europe.

By 2005, the Liberal Democrats seemed to the left of Labour on several issues: for example, a 50 per cent tax rate on incomes over £100,000, separation of the Church and monarchy, legalisation of cannabis for medical use and further devolution and Lords reforms. They did historically well in the 2005 election, winning 62 seats, partly due to skilful **tactical voting** by Labour and Conservative supporters whose favourite parties had no prospect of winning in their constituencies. In 2003, the Liberal Democrats inflicted Labour's first by-election defeat for 15 years, in Brent East. They are now the most distinctively different of the three main parties, with their tax-raising agenda, opposition to the invasion of Iraq and to compulsory national identity cards.

The smaller parties

The Scottish and Welsh nationalists are now the official opposition in the Scottish and Welsh assemblies but did poorly in the 2003 elections, at the expense of the more left-wing Greens and Scottish Socialist Party. The Greens celebrated their thirtieth anniversary in 2003, and now have a record 62 local councillors (but no MPs at Westminster).

The right-wing, anti-European UK Independence Party (UKIP) won 12 seats in the EU Parliament in June 2004 and, a few months later, pushed the Conservatives into fourth place in a by-election in Hartlepool. However, such small parties cannot do well under first-past-the-post.

Finally, the racist British National Party, by 2004, had 18 local councillors.

key terms

tactical voting

Ignoring your favourite candidate or party and, instead, voting for the candidate or party most likely to defeat your least favoured candidate or party

Question

What factors helped to explain the massive swings from the Conservatives to Labour since 1997? *(30 marks)*

Organisation and financing of the major parties

The structure of the major parties used to reflect their different philosophies and principles. For example, traditional conservative ideology stressed political hierarchy, 'natural governors' and loyalty to leadership; the Conservative leader was therefore responsible for policy-making, party headquarters and internal appointments (for example, the chairman and Shadow Cabinet). The conference was not a policy-making body, but a political rally intended to demonstrate unity and loyalty to the leader. The Labour Party's philosophy, by contrast, demanded greater internal party democracy: the Shadow Cabinet was elected by the Labour MPs; conference was a policy-making forum; and the Labour leader had much less formal power – until Tony Blair.

The positions are now almost reversed. As the Conservative Party became more internally democratic, Tony Blair centralised the Labour Party. The Labour leadership has simply ignored recent conference defeats on, for example, foundation hospitals in the NHS. There has also been a big decline in Labour membership since 1997, from 405,000 to 180,000 – the lowest for over 70 years.

The Conservative Party is financed largely by private firms and individuals, whereas the Labour Party was previously always financed largely by trade unions. However, this, too, has changed, with Labour looking increasingly to private donations – even setting up a 'Thousand Club' for wealthy individual donors like Bernie Ecclestone of Formula One. In 2002 Labour received a large, and much-criticised, donation from *Daily Express*/porn publisher Richmond Desmond. By 2005, trade union funding of Labour had declined from 90 per cent to under 30 per cent.

There were several scandals about party funding in the 1990s: for example, the Conservatives took money from what their critics called 'foreign crooks' such as fugitive businessman Asil Nadir; and Labour had its Ecclestone affair, where the 1997 Labour government received a £1 million donation from Formula One boss Bernie Ecclestone – which coincided with an exemption for motor racing from a ban on tobacco sponsorship. The Labour government asked the Committee on Public Standards to establish clear rules about party funding. In 1998 the following rules were proposed:

- foreign donations banned

- blind trusts abolished

- all national donations of £5,000+ and local donations of £1,000+ to be made public

- anonymous donations of £50 or more banned (but *how*?!)

- £20 million ceiling on each party's national election campaign spending

- tax relief on donations up to £500

- increased state funding for opposition parties

- shareholders to approve company donations and sponsorship

- equal state funding for both sides in referenda campaigns, and government should remain neutral

- an Electoral Commission to oversee the rules with the power to impose heavy fines.

The government almost immediately rejected the idea that it should remain neutral in forthcoming referenda such as on the single European currency, but legislated on the rest of the proposals in 1999. The government was also obliged to return Bernie Ecclestone's £1 million donation.

Questions

Quiz

1 List five functions of a political party.

2 Distinguish between a dominant party system and an elective dictatorship.

3 Which of the three main parties is the most pro-European?

4 When was the Labour Party founded?

5 What was Clause Four?

key terms

backbenchers

MPs in the House of Commons who are not, in addition, members of the government, the shadow government or major spokespersons for their party

constituents

Residents of a local area represented by an MP

■ MPs

Backbenchers are MPs in the House of Commons who are not, in addition, members of the government or of the shadow government – i.e. they are not members of Cabinet, junior government ministers or Opposition shadow ministers. The role of backbenchers – of any party in the Commons – is to legislate, to scrutinise the executive and to represent their voters as elected representatives. This may involve them in: debates and votes on bills in the House – and, occasionally, in backbench revolts; introducing their own private members' bills; asking questions of the PM and ministers at Question Time; undertaking parliamentary committee work; and representing their **constituents** (local voters) both inside and outside of the House – for example, by holding regular 'surgeries' in their constituencies where they can meet their local voters and hear their political complaints.

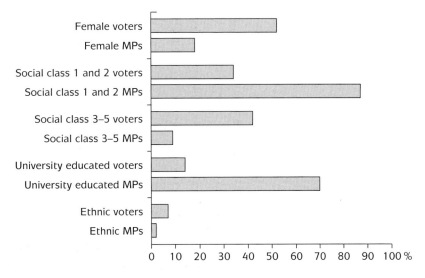

MPs' representation (2005)

Question

How socially representative are MPs?   *(15 marks)*

analyse
this

UK MPs must be UK subjects, over 21 years of age. Those disqualified from membership of the Commons include those disqualified from voting, plus: undischarged bankrupts, clergy of the established churches, judges, civil servants and other Crown officials, heads of nationalised industries and directors of the Bank of England, and those convicted of corrupt practices at elections.

Shared political ideology and natural party loyalty – together with ambition for higher public office and quite ruthless party discipline – usually combine to ensure that most back-benchers toe the party line and vote in support of their leadership. This usually means that the majority of MPs in the Commons support the actions and policies of the government of the day.

1   Why, do you think, are the categories of people listed above barred from being MPs in the House of Commons?

2   Why do most MPs, most of the time, 'toe the party line'?

3   What principled political arguments might there be (a) in defence of, and (b) against 'quite ruthless party discipline'?

Some AS questions ask about the diverse roles and conflicting loyalties of MPs; the key concepts of 'representation' and 'responsibility' should be addressed in exam answers. Who – or what – should MPs 'represent'? How feasible or valuable are different theories of representation? To whom should MPs be accountable or 'responsible'?

The diverse roles of an MP

Legislator

MPs are elected as law-makers to a national legislative assembly. They debate and vote on parliamentary bills in the House and in standing committees. They are constrained by party discipline from speaking or voting against the party line on a two- or three-line whip (see below), on pain of suspension from the party. However, backbenchers may assert themselves by rebelling collectively against a bill. This usually happens when MPs see the bill as contrary to the basic principles of their party. Backbenchers may also introduce their own legislation in the form of private members' bills. However, there is usually little time set aside for private members' bills and in procedural terms they are easily defeated, especially if the government of the day does not support them. Therefore few are passed (though good publicity may be won for the issue involved): on average, over 50 are introduced in each parliamentary session but only around half a dozen are passed.

Controller of executive

According to the theory of parliamentary government, MPs – regardless of party – are supposed to scrutinise, check and publicise the activities of the government, through, for example, debates, votes on government bills, Question Time, parliamentary committees and control of government finance as well as via the media, etc. Some MPs have made their mark in this role: for example, radical Labour MPs such as Dennis Skinner are a constant thorn in the flesh of the Labour government.

MPs are, however, constrained in this role by:

● the power of a majority government to push through bills: for example in 2004, top-up university tuition fees were forced through despite a 72-strong revolt by Labour MPs

● lack of time available to backbenchers in the Commons

● lack of information granted to Parliament by government in the UK's highly secretive system: for example, in 2002, about GM crop contamination

● lack of office, research and secretarial facilities available to MPs (though a new building, Portcullis House, goes some way towards remedying this)

● MPs' own personal ambitions for promotion to the rank of minister – see the next point!

Trainee minister

All ministers should, by convention, be selected from either the Commons or the Lords. (In the USA, by contrast, the executive may be drawn from the ranks of big business, the army, lawyers, academics, state governors, etc. as well as Congress.) Parliamentary work – in debate, in committee, and in the constituency – may provide some useful training for future executive office. However, since ambitious MPs may hesitate to offend their party leaders, MPs who see themselves as 'trainee ministers' may do little to control or criticise their own governing party. The parliamentary system thus creates 'role conflict' for many backbenchers.

Representative

MPs are also, of course, elected to express the views or interests of their voters, individually or severally.

The term **party whip** was invented by Conservative MP Edmund Burke in the eighteenth century. He likened the disciplining of MPs on voting to the process of 'whipping in the hounds' during a fox hunt. Party whips are senior MPs in the Commons or peers in the Lords who have been selected by the leadership of their party to act as a channel of communication – i.e. information, guidance and party discipline – between the leadership and the party members in each House. The Chief Whip is the most important whip in each party – an MP of substantial power and authority.

party whips

Senior MPs in the Commons, or peers in the Lords, who have been selected by the leadership of their party to act as a channel of communication and party discipline between the leadership and the party members in each House

An example of a Conservative whip

WEDNESDAY, 30th OCTOBER
3. **Enterprise Bill:** Consideration of Lords Amendments.

Important divisions will take place and your attendance at 3.30pm and until the business is concluded is essential

---

THURSDAY, 31st OCTOBER

Tabling:	To be announced
House meets at **11.30am** for:	**Trade and Industry Questions**
	Minister for Women Questions
At about **12.30pm:**	**Business Questions**

Main Business
Debate on **Defence in the UK** on a Motion for the Adjournment.

Your attendance is requested.

Friday, 1st November
The House will not be sitting.

24.10.02

The provisional business for the following week will include:

Monday, 4th November
Adoption and Children Bill: Consideration of Lords Amendments.

There will be a 3-Line Whip from 3.30pm and until the business is concluded.

Tuesday, 5th November
Nationality, Immigration and Asylum Bill: Consideration of Lords Amendments.
There will be a 3-Line Whip from 3.30pm and until the business is concluded.

Wednesday, 6th November
Animal Health Bill: Consideration of Lords Amendments.

Consideration of any Lords Messages which may be received.

There will be a 3-Line Whip from 3.30pm and until the business is concluded.

talking point

The whips of each party issue an agenda of the week's business – a piece of paper also called the 'whip' – to their members. They indicate how important each item is by underlining it once, twice or three times. If an item is underlined three times – a 'three-line Whip' – this shows that the party expects their MPs to be present and to vote as instructed.

It is a serious matter for MPs to defy a three-line Whip and therefore it happens quite rarely. When it does occur, it can lead to the Whip being 'withdrawn' from an MP. Withdrawal of the Whip means expulsion from the party, although this may be temporary. For example, Labour's George Galloway was expelled from the party in 2003, for the way in which he expressed opposition to the invasion of Iraq.

George Galloway

However, MPs cannot be sacked from Parliament by their parties, because liberal democratic theory suggests that only the voters should have the power to elect or reject an MP.

The diverse loyalties and responsibilities of an MP

MPs have wide-ranging, and sometimes conflicting, loyalties. To whom MPs are – or should be – loyal or accountable is a matter of debate; the answer depends on political ideology, party structure and personal inclination. The demands on an MP's loyalty include the following.

The parliamentary party

Prime Minister Disraeli said in the nineteenth century, 'Damn your principles! Stick to your party.' The 'doctrine of the mandate' suggests that electors vote for a package of party policies as outlined in a manifesto, and therefore that MPs are most effectively representing the voters' wishes if they toe the party line. But what if the party breaks its manifesto promises?

Party conference

Whereas the annual Conservative conference is not a policy-making body but simply a jamboree – a political rally intended to demonstrate unity and loyalty to the leader – the Labour conference is, or at least was, a policy-making body. However, Labour conference members tend to vote for 'old' Labour policies. For this reason, the conference has been increasingly sidelined by the 'new' Labour leadership as a policy-making forum – for example, recent conference defeats on privatisation in the NHS were simply ignored by the Labour leadership.

Constituency party

The local party selects the MP and provides the electoral campaign back-up; rank-and-file activists may also have a good understanding of constituency needs. The local party can also deselect the MP – that is, they may decide not to choose that person as their party candidate at the next election. For example, Jane Griffiths, Labour MP for Reading East, in 2004 became the first MP to be deselected by her constituency party in ten years (despite – or perhaps because of – being a Blair loyalist). This usually terminates an MP's political career. Many MPs, therefore, pay special heed to the local party, even where this may jeopardise their standing with the national leadership.

Constituents

Total subservience to the party would negate the role of constituency MPs. Local voters' views and interests may conflict with national party policy or with the 'national interest' (if there is such a thing). However, it may also be difficult for MPs to serve diverse local interests: for example, farmers versus farm-workers; and it is hard for an MP to gauge the views of constituents as a whole.

Interest groups

Many MPs have special personal interests (for example, deaf Labour MP Jack Ashley campaigned on behalf of disabled people). They are often sponsored or lobbied by pressure groups and private companies to act on their behalf. About one-third of Labour MPs are sponsored by trade unions (Dennis Skinner, for example, is sponsored by the National Union of Mineworkers); here, the trade union pays some of the candidate's campaign costs in return for a voice in Parliament where possible.

talking point

Did you know that you can fax your MP, via the internet, simply by going to the website below and typing in your post code?

www.faxyourmp.com

Many other MPs, especially Conservatives, are paid personal fees (ranging from £1,000 to £20,000 per year) as consultants or directors by pressure groups, by private individuals and by companies seeking to promote their own interests. This generated the 'cash for questions' scandal of the 1990s, where Conservative ministers such as Neil Hamilton and Jonathan Aitken tabled parliamentary questions in return for money from outside interests, notably from Harrods' owner Mohamed Al Fayed. Then Prime Minister John Major set up a Commission on Standards in Public Life (or commission on 'sleaze' as it was popularly described by the media) under senior judge Lord Nolan, and later Lord Neill. In 1996 the following rules were agreed:

- MPs must register all outside interests with a Parliamentary Commissioner for Standards (currently Sir Philip Mawer).

- MPs must disclose sources and amounts of outside earnings.

- MPs are forbidden from tabling questions on behalf of outside paying interests and must declare such interests when speaking in debates.

- A new Commons Committee on Standards and Privileges has been established to enforce the new rules.

Many MPs also receive fees for media and other public appearances.

National interest

Conservative politician Edmund Burke argued, in 1774, that an MP was a member of 'a deliberate assembly of one nation with one interest, that of the whole', and that MPs should pursue the 'general good' according to their personal judgement. The concept of a 'national interest' is central to the philosophy of traditional political conservatism, but is denied by liberals (who perceive diverse individual interests) and by socialists (who perceive conflicting class interests). However, all governments bring the concept into play when it suits their policy objectives.

Conscience

This is the second feature of Burke's theory of the role of an MP: 'Your representative owes you not his industry only, but his judgement; and he betrays instead of serving you, if he sacrifices it to your opinion.' Private conscience for MPs is given expression, particularly, in free votes in the Commons (for example, on moral issues such as capital punishment, abortion and homosexuality laws), in private members' bills and in back-bench revolts. It may obviously conflict with party, constituency and other interests outlined above.

Questions

1 How has the role of MPs changed in recent years?   *(20 marks)*

2 Is this change undermining the representative nature of Parliament?   *(20 marks)*

Questions

True or false?

1 There are ten parties in the House of Commons.

2 The Labour and Conservative parties do not stand candidates in Northern Ireland.

3 There are no independent MPs in the House of Commons.

4 Being an MP is a part-time job.

5 The principle of the mandate ensures that the government's election promises will be carried out.

5

Public opinion and pressure groups

■ Public opinion

In a democracy, it is usually assumed that government should be responsive to **public opinion**; but this is a very difficult concept to define or measure. It is best defined as the majority view on a given issue at a given time; but if opinion is divided several ways, there may be no 'majority' view; or the view of a vocal or powerful minority may dominate.

It is often assumed that the party system and the government of the day best represent public opinion. However, given that the 2005 Labour government had the support of only 22 per cent of the registered voters (that is, 35 per cent of the votes cast on a turnout of just 61 per cent), other factors come into play. Public opinion may be expressed or assessed through: elections for other bodies such as local councils or the European Parliament; through referenda (for example, on remaining in the EU and on devolution within the UK); through television or radio chat shows, letters to the press or to MPs; through the internet (increasingly); through opinion polls; or through pressure group activity or direct action by individuals or groups.

Public opinion polls – surveys and questionnaires of representative samples of voters by professional pollsters – are paid a lot of attention by politicians and the media, and they can be quite reliable and informative indicators of people's views on key issues.

However, they may, sometimes, question an unrepresentative sample of people; they may offer limited options as answers; or they may shape the very responses they are trying to measure, simply by posing questions about an issue which some people may never before have considered. Political parties often carry out their own polls; and they may publish misleading results in an effort to boost their own vote. It is sometimes suggested that even professional opinion polls should be banned in the days before an election, because they may influence the result of the election itself: for example, if one party seems very strong – or, indeed, very weak – its supporters may not bother to vote at all.

talking point

Source:
www.news.bbc.co.uk,
May 2004

Inquiry into opinion polls urged

The government is being urged to hold a full inquiry into opinion polls and to introduce new laws to control them if necessary.

Thirty-eight MPs have signed a Commons motion querying the 'integrity, honesty and professionalism' of the industry. The MPs say there is a lack of regulation and transparency in the methodology used. They say polling techniques may be designed to get the results favoured by those who commission the polls.

The group of MPs is led by Barry Sheerman, Labour chairman of the Commons Education Committee. He told Radio 4's Today programme he was concerned some pollsters lacked experience. 'A number of the large players in the opinion polling business say that people can just set up to be opinion pollsters without any background at all and that is quite worrying.' Mr Sheerman said many small players offer cheap online polls but will not reveal their methodologies. 'So, you can't assess how accurate and reliable those polls are, and some of the polls may be polls producing the results that the people who pay for the polls want,' he said.

60% OF PEOPLE DISLIKE OPINION POLLS.

In voting and other forms of political activity, a distorted impression of public opinion may be conveyed, for example, by tactical voting, abstentions, and unequal degrees of political activism by different sections of the public (for example, the middle classes tend to be more politically active and vocal than the working class); or, simply, by selective media reporting of such activities.

Though public opinion is difficult to define or measure, it may influence Parliament or government: for example, the so-called 'greening' of the Conservative and Labour governments from the late 1980s onwards, when they paid increasing attention to environmental issues, in response to growing public concern and pressure group activity.

However, it may be argued that politicians should not follow every whim of public opinion because it may be ill-informed, selfish, fickle, emotional or irrational. One example of this may be Parliament's consistent rejection of capital punishment since the 1960s – despite opinion polls suggesting that almost 60 per cent of UK voters favour it.

analyse
this

Opinion polls seek to determine the views of the general public by putting questions to relatively small groups of people – perhaps only one or two thousand in total. There are several ways in which such a group might be selected, but two main ways are the use of a random sample or a quota sample. In the UK, for example, a random sample might consist of every thousandth name on the register of electors in various constituencies. A quota sample, on the other hand, seeks out specific groups of people whose composition is decided in advance – for example, specific numbers of males and females, working class and middle class, various age and gender groups, and so on. By this method, questions are directed at a group of people who are perceived to be, on the whole, a cross-section of the public.

Opinion polls have potential flaws: for example, if one section of the public disproportionately refuses to answer questions, or simply lies, this may skew the results; if polls are conducted via the internet or even by telephone, poorer voters may be excluded; and if the answers on offer are too limited, the results will, again, be distorted.

The belief that polling during election campaigns may actually influence voting behaviour has prompted some countries, such as France, to ban the publication of poll results in the run-up to the actual election.

1 If you were conducting a political survey, would you opt for a random or a quota sample – and why?

2 Should the publication of opinion poll results be banned in the run-up to a general election? Why/not?

3 Try to devise a short political survey and then put it to your fellow students. What insights and problems about polling have you gleaned from this exercise?

talking
point

Should the government simply do everything that majority public opinion appears to support? Why/not? Bear in mind that this question is central to diverse interpretations of such key concepts as 'democracy' and 'representation'.

■ Pressure groups

Pressure groups are organisations which seek to promote a cause or to protect a particular section of society, often by influencing government, Parliament or the public. Unlike parties, they do not stand candidates for election, and their aims and membership are often narrower; but they do often have close links with political parties. Pressure groups are usually centred upon promoting a single issue or upon representing a single group. Their aim is not to form the government but to influence it.

Two main types of pressure group are:

- **promotional or cause groups**, which seek to promote a specific cause, for example Countryside Alliance (rural issues), Shelter (housing), Friends of the Earth (environment)

- **protective or sectional or interest groups**, which seek to protect the interests of their own members as a particular section of society, for example **trades unions** and professional associations such as the NUM (National Union of Mineworkers), the Law Society (solicitors), the CBI (Confederation of British Industry), etc.

Question

Which of the above two types of pressure group may tend to have more power, and why?   *(5 marks)*

According to the writer Wyn Grant, pressure groups may, alternatively, be subdivided into **insider** and **outsider groups** depending on the closeness of their relationships with government, civil servants and other key policy-makers. UK farmers are often cited as an example of an insider group with close contacts with ministers and civil servants and with significant influence upon policy-making – for example, upon the government's decision to approve genetically modified (GM) maize production in 2004, despite strong public disapproval. It is more common for sectional than promotional groups to be insiders. Outsider groups, by contrast, have aims which are totally different from those of the government – for example, in the 1980s, the Campaign for Nuclear Disarmament (CND) had no influence upon the Conservative governments of the day despite its huge membership (over one million) and marches. Outsider groups may also use methods which are deemed unacceptable by the government; one example is the Irish Republican Army (IRA), which uses violent tactics.

Some outsider groups aim for insider status, either through a change in government or through a growth in their own influence or power. Other outsider groups aim to stay that way because they are ideologically opposed to the political system and to any governing party.

Friends of the Earth

A third way of categorising pressure groups is to subdivide them into permanent versus temporary groups. Temporary groups have limited and short-term goals and will disband if these are achieved – or, indeed, if they fail and the result cannot be reversed. The most common examples are groups seeking to prevent some building work in their local area such as an airport runway, a motorway or an asylum centre. (Their outlook is often described as the 'nimby syndrome' – the attitude of 'not in my back yard'.) Sometimes a particular event may lead to the formation of a pressure group: for example, the Snowdrop group which campaigned for the banning of handguns following the 1996 killings at Dunblane, and which was dissolved when its aim was largely achieved.

talking point

Source:
www.news.bbc.co.uk,
29 October 2003

New bypass for blackspot

Campaigners have won their battle for a bypass on one of south Cumbria's busiest roads.

The roads minister David Jamieson has agreed that the villages of High and Low Newton, on the A590, need a bypass. The plans will now form part of the government's transport programme which has seven years to run.

But Friends of the Lake District said it was 'utterly appalled' by the decision. The environmental group said the government was relegating the Lake District's landscape to the dustbin.

Notice that, in this example, there are two different pressure groups involved, with wholly conflicting views and aims. How would you summarise their diverse aims?

key terms

insider groups

Pressure groups which are regularly consulted by the ministers and civil servants who make policy decisions in the groups' special areas of interest and influence

outsider groups

Pressure groups which are not consulted by the policy-makers because they have aims and/or methods which conflict with those of the government of the day

Trades unions

A trade union is a protective organisation of workers which aims to protect its members' pay and working conditions. There are several types:

- industrial unions, for example the National Union of Mineworkers (NUM)

- white-collar unions, for example the National Association of Local Government Officers (NALGO)

- general unions, for example the Transport and General Workers' Union (TGWU).

Generally, the more skilled and specialised are its members, the more 'powerful' is the union.

In the 1960s and 1970s, during the period of consensus politics, trades unions were closely involved with governments – both Labour and Conservative – in shaping economic and industrial policy. Examples of trades union influence or power during this period included the Social Contract of 1973–8, when the unions agreed to pay restraints in return

key terms

corporatism

Tripartite (three-way) involvement and consultation of workers' and employers' groups with the government in economic policy-making

for promises of social benefits from the government; and also the involvement of the trades unions in government-created bodies such as the Advisory, Conciliation and Arbitration Service (ACAS) which often mediated in disputes with employers.

This **corporatist** approach of three-way co-operation between employers, trades unions and government in economic planning and decision-making was rejected by the Thatcher governments of the 1980s.

Legal curbs on trades unions since 1980

Successive laws passed during the Thatcher era have: prohibited sympathy and secondary action and mass picketing; required secret ballots of union members before industrial action, and for maintaining a political fund (i.e. union contributions to the Labour Party); allowed fines and 'sequestration', i.e. freezing and seizure of union funds by the courts; required unions balloting on industrial action in separate workplaces to win a majority vote in every workplace; and prohibited unions from disciplining strike-breakers even if a clear majority of members have voted for strike action. Employers are still allowed to sack strikers even after a ballot in favour of strike action.

The 'new' Labour governments have reversed none of these constraints, and trade union membership has fallen markedly since the 1980s.

The defeat of the miners in 1985, after a year-long strike over pit closures, was seen by the government and trades unions alike as a watershed in the decline of trades unions' power and rights. (In the years since then, for example, the UK coal industry has declined from 170 pits employing 180,000 miners, to just nine pits and under 5,000 miners).

Another turning point was Rupert Murdoch's 1986 'Wapping revolution', when he moved the production of his newspapers, such as *The Times* and *News of the World*, from Fleet Street to Wapping to be printed by new computer technology, thus eliminating the old crafts of the printers and excluding the unions – 5,500 workers were sacked overnight and there were mass union pickets and demonstrations at Wapping. These were illegal under the 1980 and 1982 Employment Acts, therefore the trade union involved had all of its funds sequestrated (confiscated). One 19-year-old picket was killed by a company lorry; although the jury

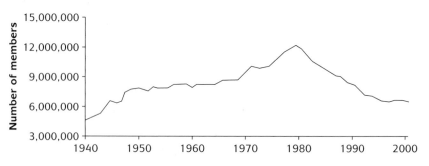

Trades union membership 1940–2002

Source: Trades Union Congress (TUC)

Police line during the miners' strike, Yorkshire 1984

returned a verdict of unlawful killing, there was no prosecution. Eighteen police officers were prosecuted for excessive violence on the picket lines, but all of the charges were dropped after long delays in bringing the cases to court.

The most powerful 'trades unions' now are the professional associations such as the Bar (barristers), Law Society (solicitors) and British Medical Association (doctors), which have a legal monopoly on their own professional services, regulate entry to their own professions, and often have the dual functions of protecting and disciplining their own members. Concern is sometimes expressed about these last aspects of their role and the possible conflicts of interest which may arise from it.

Although the 'new' Labour governments since 1997 have chosen not to reverse the 1980s' anti-union legislation, they have introduced the minimum wage and legislated for trades union recognition in large workplaces if most of the workers want it.

Case for the protection of individuals by trades unions

- The weakness of individual workers versus employers.

- The historical role of unions in advancing working people's conditions of work, health, safety, pay, living standards and pensions. They also provide services for their members such as legal aid in tribunal cases and retirement homes for sick miners.

- The representative nature of unions: unlike most promotional groups, members elect their leaders, who are usually 'delegates' rather than mere 'representatives' (i.e. union leaders are very closely bound by the direct instructions of their members); and together they represent a larger population sector than any other pressure groups (currently 8 million workers).

- Direct action by trades unions, for example strikes, may be seen as mass, direct 'people-power'.

- Visible union or workers' power, for example strikes, is a negative, uncertain and often counter-productive weapon of last resort, involving loss of pay and job security; it may thus be an indication of relative weakness, i.e. lack of alternative rights, powers and channels of influence for workers.

- Media coverage of unions and industrial action is often biased and hostile. For example, 95 per cent of all strikes are 'wildcat' or unofficial, but are portrayed as if 'bully-boy' union leaders are calling out unwilling members; employers' figures on the 'costs' of strikes are usually presented uncritically, omitting company 'savings' in wages, raw materials, fuel, etc.

- Thus public hostility to unions and industrial action is greater, the less direct experience people have of them (and people therefore tend to say 'the unions are too powerful', but also that 'my union is not strong enough on my behalf').

- Though workers' negative or disruptive power may be seen as significant and quite inconvenient by those members of the public affected by it, their power may be negligible if measured in terms of results – such as company closures, unemployment, redundancies, growing income inequalities, and continuing imbalances of decision-making power in the workplace between workers and employers.

- Contrary to popular myth, the UK was always well down the international league table on strike figures, even in the 1960s and 1970s when trades union power was perceived to be at its height.

Questions

What is meant by each of the following terms (all of which are related to the issue of trades unions)?   *(15 marks)*

a) Block vote

b) Closed shop

c) Corporatism

d) Functional representation

e) Sequestration

■ Pressure group methods

Pressure groups seek pressure points, not only at Whitehall and Westminster but beyond. Their methods include:

- **Direct links with government and civil service**: the most powerful (so-called 'insider') groups – such as the National Farmers' Union (NFU) – often have direct links with government ministers and civil servants, in a relationship of mutual need, for example for information, expertise and influence. Such groups rarely need to resort to public lobbying, street demonstrations, etc.; the most powerful and influential groups are therefore often, paradoxically, the least visible. A few groups – such as the farmers – have the statutory right to be consulted on relevant legislation and policy initiatives. Examples of the farming lobby's influence include: the forced resignation of junior health minister Edwina Currie, followed by new government subsidies to egg producers, after her (statistically accurate) remark in 1988 that 'most egg production' in this country was contaminated by salmonella; and the huge extra subsidies given to the beef farmers in the 1990s to compensate them for lost sales due to the BSE ('mad cow disease') scandal.

- Many pressure groups **work through Parliament, parties and MPs** by:

  - financing political parties: the Labour Party, historically, has been funded largely by trades unions, while the Conservative Party has been funded mainly by business and industry. However, since 1997, Labour has won increasing business support and finance and has been deliberately distancing itself more from the unions

  - **lobbying** (influencing) MPs in Parliament, through letters, leaflets, petitions, free gifts, dinners, trips and parties, and personal 'consultancy fees' for MPs. Since the 'cash for questions' scandal of the 1990s, MPs are bound by much stricter rules about financial links with pressure groups and other external interests

  - **sponsoring MPs**: many trades unions pay some part of a local Labour candidate's election campaign costs in return for support by a Labour MP – for example veteran MP Dennis Skinner (who used to be a coal miner) is sponsored by the National Union of Mineworkers

  - drafting and promoting private members' bills: for example, Liberal MP David Steel's 1967 (legalising) Abortion Act was largely drafted by the Abortion Law Reform Association, and later restraining bills (by Conservative MPs such as Ann Widdecombe) were backed by anti-abortion groups such as the Society for the Protection of the Unborn Child (SPUC)

  - seeking to influence government legislation: for example, the Lord's Day Observance Society successfully mobilised Conservative MPs into opposing Sunday shopping in 1986. Sunday

key terms

lobbying

Influencing politicians and policy-makers

sponsored MPs

MPs (usually Labour) whose campaign costs are aided by trades unions or other pressure groups

shopping in the UK was only introduced in the 1990s, because the EU insisted upon it

– hiring professional lobbyists (private public relations companies such as Hill and Knowlton) to promote a cause among MPs, for which clients may pay around £30,000 per year. There are now over 60 such organisations in the UK.

● Many UK pressure groups are increasingly **focusing their attention on the EU** rather than on domestic decision-making institutions – a reliable indicator of the shifting balance of power and influence towards Europe. For example, the Committee of Professional Agricultural Organisations (COPA) – comprising most of the national farmers' organisations, including the UK's NFU – is now based in Brussels.

● **Mobilisation of public opinion**: often a last resort for the least powerful but most visible cause groups is to seek to influence government indirectly through the voters: e.g. the Child Poverty Action Group, Shelter and Greenpeace. Methods used include conducting or publicising opinion polls, petitions, pickets, leaflets and letters, media adverts, demonstrations and staged public events, such as Greenpeace dumping 4 tons of genetically modified soya beans outside the gates of Downing Street in 1999 in protest over Prime Minister Blair's backing for GM foods. Concern is sometimes expressed where pressure groups' publicity tactics are emotive, obstructive, illegal or violent.

● **Illegal methods**: pressure groups may use **civil disobedience** – non-violent but unlawful action as a form of political protest – to gain publicity for their cause: for example, CND (anti-nuclear) protesters trespassing and cutting the perimeter wire at nuclear bases, refusing to pay taxes towards nuclear weapons and staging mass

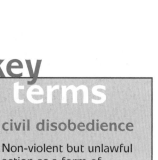

key terms

civil disobedience

Non-violent but unlawful action as a form of political protest

Anti-war civil disobedience by Greenpeace protesters scaling Big Ben, 2004

street 'die-ins' (obstruction); and Fathers4Justice protesters scaling Buckingham Palace, and handcuffing themselves to government ministers. These are examples of non-violent action. Sometimes, however, pressure groups even resort to the threat or use of violence: for example, the Animal Liberation Front planting bombs at animal experimentation centres and at shops which sell fur products. Such groups would argue that it is fair to counter violence with violence; and such methods may also win more publicity and political response than legal, peaceful methods. This raises questions about the role and responsibility of the media in their coverage of public participation and protest.

talking point

Source: Guardian Unlimited
© Guardian Newspapers
Limited 2004

What kind of May Day protester are you?

Anti-capitalism is a broad church. Are you a pacifist fluffy, pro-violence spiky or undercover investment banker?

You are exhausted after a long day of demonstrating. What do you do?

1 Head to the nearest Starbucks for a café latte

2 Hang out with friends at a local pub, exchanging tales of how you shouted abuse at literally dozens of policemen

3 Take off your white overalls, fire up your laptop and upload those protest pics onto a May Day protest website

4 Phone your solicitor from a police cell

What is your key May Day accessory?

1 A Louis Vuitton bag for storing your make-up/hair gel

2 A mobile phone so you can phone dad if you get in trouble

3 A large foam battering ram

4 A brick

Which of these phrases are you most likely to say?

1 I am never going to reach the protests unless this M25 traffic eases up!

2 What time do you think the protest is going to finish, only I've got a dentist's appointment at 4.30?

3 Can anyone think of a comedy acronym for our anti-capitalism collective?

4 This is going to be bigger than Seattle!

You are walking down Oxford Street when a group of Balaclava-clad people start smashing windows. What do you do?

1 Call the police – that's daddy's firm they are breaking into

2 Watch from a safe distance

3 Beg them to stop – it is meant to be a party, not a riot

4 Join in

You count which of the following among your ideological influences?

1 Posh Spice, Naomi Campbell, Bill Gates

2 Pre-mayoral Ken Livingstone, Chumbawamba, Happy Mondays

3 Ya Basta!, Zapatistas, and the hippy movement

4 Eta, Urban Alliance, Anarchist Federation

What will be your greatest thrill on May Day?

1 Looting a darling pair of sunglasses from Harrods

2 Getting home safely

3 Getting arrested for lying down in front of rush-hour traffic

4 Getting arrested for smashing up McDonald's

You miss a day off work to attend the May Day protests. What do you tell your boss?

1 I've been on a management training course

2 I've had 24-hour flu

3 I've been fighting capitalist forces in London

4 Nothing – being an anarchist is a full-time occupation

KEY TO ANSWERS

1 Undercover capitalist

Your motto: 'I hope they smash up Gap – I need some new jeans.'

You are about as committed to the anti-capitalist cause as George W. Bush is to the Kyoto protocol. You enjoy the thrill of dicing with the police, but you do not want to do anything that might jeopardise your graduate traineeship in merchant banking. You once belonged to the Young Conservatives but now it is cooler to be a May Day protester. Go home now, before mummy and daddy see you on TV and get worried.

2 Fair weather protester

Your motto: 'It's started raining – let's go to Burger King instead.'

You want to fight capitalism but can't quite bring yourself to go the whole hog. After all, those Nike trainers were gorgeous and a snip at only £80. You prefer to stay on the edge of the action and tend to flee at the first sign of trouble. Getting arrested is your biggest fear – after all, a criminal record could ruin your chances of getting onto that media studies course.

3 Fluffy

Your motto: 'White Overall Movement Building Liberation Through Effective Struggle forever!'

You love sticking two fingers up at authority, and you plump for fun, non-violent tactics such as street parties and fire-breathing to make your point. You are likely to belong to Reclaim the Streets or the Mayday Collective, have not visited a hairdresser in the last five years and sport at least one penny whistle. You will probably end May Day at a friend's squat, regaling your mates with tales of guerrilla gardening.

4 Spiky

Your motto: 'Anarchy in the UK!'

Brick in hand, balaclava on head, on May Day you'll sally forth to do battle with the evil capitalist forces of the world. You are likely to belong to the Anarchist Federation or the Urban Alliance, and be versed in the best ways to avoid police batons and smash windows. You will probably end up in court for your law-breaking activities, but what does that matter to a hard-core anarchist like you?

■ Pressure groups and parties

Differences between pressure groups and parties

Strictly speaking, there are clear differences between pressure groups and parties. Above all, pressure groups do not stand candidates for election – they merely seek to influence those in political office. Also, the aims and membership of pressure groups are usually narrower than those of parties. For example, most promotional pressure groups support a single cause such as the banning of fox hunting; whereas even small parties outside of Parliament, such as the British National Party (BNP), have a wide-ranging manifesto covering all major areas of political policy. Similarly, most protective groups seek to represent only one section of society – such as the National Union of Teachers (NUT), which seeks only to defend the interests of teachers; whereas even small parties seek much wider membership, support and representation. Political parties seek to bring together many interests and opinions into one single political group embracing a comprehensive ideology and capable of governing the country, whereas pressure groups can represent specialist interests and single issues – often in much more diverse, radical and popular ways.

Similarities between pressure groups and parties

As discussed in Chapter 4, many so-called 'parties' at general elections are really pressure groups who put up candidates simply for publicity –

An anti-war demonstration

not necessarily because they have any realistic hope of winning seats. The Stop the War Coalition group, for example, transformed itself into the Respect Party for the June 2004 elections by broadening its policy platform and putting up candidates. In 2005 it won one Westminster seat. The pressure group Fathers4Justice put up a candidate for the 2004 Hartlepool by-election; he won just 139 votes, but also considerable publicity.

Also, many small, extra-parliamentary parties (that is, parties outside of Parliament) – such as the Green Party – look and act much like promotional pressure groups such as Greenpeace. Indeed, some small parties – such as the United Kingdom Independence Party (UKIP) which really only seeks withdrawal from the European Union – are, in effect, single issue pressure groups. Equally, many large pressure groups – such as the CBI (Confederation of British Industry – the umbrella body for many private companies) and the TUC (Trades Union Congress – the umbrella body for most of the trades unions) – may have more real power, and closer links with Parliament through the main parties, than small parties such as the Natural Law Party. Labour was, of course, founded by the trades unions, is still to some extent financed by them and has strong organisational links with them. The differences between parties and pressure groups are therefore often blurred.

Question

To what extent have pressure groups become more important in recent years?   *(30 marks)*

■ Pressure groups and democracy

Arguments that pressure groups enhance democratic government

● Pressure groups enhance pluralism, that is, competing centres of power, choice and representation; almost all shades of opinion are represented. This is especially true where 'pro' and 'anti' groups co-exist – for example EXIT (in favour of euthanasia – mercy killing) versus EXIST (against euthanasia).

● Pressure groups 'fill the gaps' in the party system, for example by promoting causes which cut across party lines, especially on local or 'moral' issues such as abortion and capital punishment. This is especially true where there are only two large parties who may be quite close together on the political spectrum.

- Pressure groups provide channels of collective influence and power for the public where individual action (including voting) may be relatively weak or ineffectual.

- Pressure groups provide channels of direct participation for the public, going beyond mere indirect representation through Parliament.

- Pressure groups provide channels of communication between the government and the voters.

- Pressure groups seek to represent deprived or inarticulate sections of society (for example, Help the Aged, and the Child Poverty Action Group).

- Protective groups, especially, are usually internally democratic, in that their members elect their leaders.

- Trades unions, especially, are representative of large numbers of people (currently eight million in the UK); and their tactics of direct action – for example, strikes – may be seen as mass, direct democracy or 'people-power'.

- Pressure groups provide information, education and expertise for the public, Parliament and government (for example, environmental groups); therefore they are often consulted by MPs and the executive; and they may help to enhance open government by exposing significant events, information and issues.

- Pressure groups channel new issues and concerns onto the political agenda – for example, the environmentalist and women's movements.

- Pressure groups provide a check on parliamentary sovereignty and elective dictatorship, especially where the electoral system is unrepresentative and parliamentary opposition is weak; hence they provide additional checks and balances in the UK's liberal democracy.

- Pressure groups may promote continuity and stability of policy between successive governments.

- Pressure groups may enhance political stability by providing a safety valve for more radical political grievances and demands.

- Pressure groups may provide public services, for example legal aid and advice.

Arguments that pressure groups undermine democratic government

- Pressure groups may by-pass or usurp the elected representatives in Parliament and government; MPs may be reduced to 'lobby-fodder'. (Conservative Home Secretary Douglas Hurd, in 1986, likened them to sea-serpents, strangling ministers in their coils and distorting the constitutional relationship between government and electorate.)

- Their lobbying tactics may amount to near bribery and corruption of MPs.

> Some international pressure groups, such as Greenpeace control huge funds and have substantial influence in diverting investment and promoting campaigns which cut across national boundaries and government controls. 'When 122 countries agreed to stop using and selling land mines in 1997, the success was attributed not to the work of tireless government officials, but to the 1,000 or so non-governmental organisations (NGOs) in 60 countries which had lobbied ministers on the issue for years. At the signing ceremony in Ottawa, Jody Williams, the campaign's coordinator, remarked that NGOs had come into their own on the international stage. 'Together,' she said, 'we are a superpower.'
>
> Source: Michael Bond,
> 'The backlash against NGOs',
> *Prospect*, April 2000

- Pressure groups may be small, sectional or unrepresentative but very influential or powerful, at the expense of majority or 'national' views or interests.

- Insider pressure groups may have an excessively close and secretive relationship with the executive, excluding other views and interests – perhaps those of the majority.

- The collective power of pressure groups may undermine individual rights and interests, contrary to 'liberal democratic' principles.

- Promotional groups, especially, may be internally undemocratic – often with no election of leaders by members, leadership out of touch with their membership, etc.; or they may claim to speak on behalf of others, but without any consultation or mandate to do so.

- Pressure groups with constitutional aims may be internally dominated by people who seek to subvert liberal democracy itself: for example, the Anti-Poll Tax Federation and the Stop the War Coalition contained many anarchists.

- Pressure groups' methods may be illegal and/or coercive. In 2004, for example, the pressure group Fathers4Justice lobbed bags of purple flour from the public gallery of the Commons at the Prime Minister during Question Time; they drew attention to their cause, but received very negative publicity and encouraged the security services to turn Parliament into a fortress. (But note that many pressure groups would defend such tactics in theory and in practice – see Chapter 8.)

- Pressure group activities give powerless people a false sense of hope that they can have an impact and make a difference. It suits the ruling class or power elite that people channel their energies into narrow causes which do not question, challenge or threaten the fundamentals of the economic and political power systems.

Questions

Quiz

1   Suggest three possible criticisms of opinion polls.

2   Give two differences between promotional and protective pressure groups.

3   Which academic author devised the categorisation of pressure groups into 'insider' and 'outsider' groups?

4   Define 'insider' groups.

5   How many UK workers currently belong to trades unions?

6   List ten methods used by pressure groups.

7   What percentage of UK voters are members of any political party?

8   What is the main difference between parties and pressure groups?

9   What are 'extra-parliamentary parties'?

10 Give one example of a small party which looks and acts much like a single-issue pressure group.

Question

Why are some pressure groups more successful than others?   *(30 marks)*

6

Parliament

key terms

bill

Draft law going through Parliament

statute

Act of Parliament – a law passed by Commons, Lords and Crown

■ History and functions of Parliament

The UK Parliament at Westminster was created in the thirteenth century. It is now bicameral: that is, it has two 'chambers', or houses – the House of Commons and the House of Lords. It is headed by the monarch, and every new parliamentary **bill** (draft law) has to go through all three parts of Parliament before it can become a **statute** law, that is, an Act of Parliament.

Parliament is said to be the sovereign body in the UK political system – that is, it has legal supremacy.

Functions of Parliament

- Making the law
- Controlling the executive
- Representing the people

Subsidiary functions

- Debate and deliberation
- Controlling government finance
- Channel of communication between government and electorate

The above list of the roles of Parliament could provide a useful framework for longer and more analytical AS questions such as 'What problems does Parliament encounter in performing its various functions?' Such broad questions on the roles of Parliament also cover the electoral

talking point

There is a very strong convention that no modern monarch will refuse 'royal assent' to a bill, because it would be undemocratic for a non-elected monarch to challenge the will of the elected House of Commons. The last time a monarch refused royal assent for a bill was in 1707, when Queen Anne tried to block the Scottish Militia Bill.

system, the party system, the theory and practice of 'parliamentary government', the roles of MPs and peers and the impact of the EU and devolution – all of which, critics say, combine to limit Parliament's effectiveness in carrying out its functions today. Such exam answers should be very broad-ranging, concise and topical.

■ The House of Lords

Composition of the House of Lords

The House of Lords is a wholly unelected chamber. Until the 1950s, it was made up entirely of **hereditary peers** whose right to sit and vote in the chamber derived purely from a title inherited within the family. In 1958, **life peers** were established: members appointed by the Prime Minister of the day, for their lifetime only, whose titles are not hereditary. Nevertheless, for most of the twentieth century, hereditary peers still made up two-thirds of the Lords – almost 800 of a potentially huge chamber of 1,200 peers. (However, many of them rarely attended.)

Also entitled to sit and vote in the Lords are the 24 senior bishops of the Church of England (including the Archbishops) and the 27 most senior judges in the country, known as **Law Lords**. At their head is the Lord Chancellor, currently Lord Falconer. He has a constitutionally unique position: he is simultaneously the Speaker of the House of Lords, a Cabinet minister with departmental responsibilities and the head of the judiciary in England and Wales. Thus the office of Lord Chancellor has legislative, executive and judicial roles. This is a major breach of the principle of separation of powers, and the Labour government plans to abolish the office of Lord Chancellor and to separate out the three roles. They have already abolished the title 'Lord Chancellor'; Lord Falconer is now called the Constitutional Affairs Secretary.

Most peers are members of the main parties. However, there are around 200 **cross-benchers** – independent peers without any party affiliation (so called because of the chamber's seating arrangements), who include the Law Lords and bishops. These provide a relatively independent element which is absent from the Commons.

As long ago as 1909, Lloyd George criticised the hereditary peers in the following terms:

> They do not even need a medical certificate. They need not be sound in either body or mind. They only require a certificate of birth – just to prove that they were the first of the litter. You would not choose a spaniel on those principles.

The 1997 Labour government came to power with a manifesto commitment to abolish all of the hereditary peers, saying 'This will be the first stage in a process of reform to make the House of Lords more democratic and representative.' Most of the hereditary peers were abolished (i.e. excluded from the chamber, rather than losing their titles) in 1999. Lord Cranborne, then leader of the Conservatives in the Lords, did a secret deal with the Labour government to keep 92 hereditary peers in

key terms

hereditary peers

Lords whose right to sit and vote in the chamber derives purely from a title inherited within the family

life peers

Members of the Lords appointed by the Prime Minister of the day, for their lifetime only, whose titles are not hereditary

Law Lords

The most senior judges in the UK

cross-benchers

Independent peers without any party affiliation

return for the smooth passage of government legislation. (Much to the government's irritation, however, the Lords have been more obstructive ever since, asserting a new degree of legitimacy since reform.)

There was traditionally a large majority of Conservative peers in the Lords but this is no longer the case since most of the hereditary peers were excluded. There is no fixed limit to the number of peers in the Lords as there is for MPs in the Commons.

Also in 1999, Blair voluntarily gave up his prerogative power to veto the names of Conservative and Liberal Democrat nominees; and he announced a new appointments commission to nominate cross-bench peers; but the Prime Minister currently retains control of the numbers of new peers from each party, which is clearly the most significant power. Meanwhile, within his first three years in office, Blair had created more new life peers (over 200) than Margaret Thatcher did in her entire 11 years as Prime Minister.

It was widely expected that 'second stage' reform of the Lords would include a substantial elected element. In 2003, MPs were given seven free votes on options ranging from 0–100 per cent elected members of the second chamber; this successfully confused them so much that they voted against *all* of the options, leaving the UK with a wholly unelected second chamber – an option explicitly favoured by Prime Minister Blair.

The government has been accused by its critics of seeking simply to create a chamber which Blair could pack with his own appointees – 'Tony's cronies' – such as his former flatmate Charlie, now Lord Falconer of Thoroton. As one critic has said:

What of the pledge in the 1997 Labour manifesto to 'make the House of Lords more democratic'? Well, we now know exactly what the Prime Minister means by democracy. One flatmate, one vote.

Conservative leader Michael Howard's speech in response to the 2003 Queen's Speech

Analysis of House of Lords composition, 2005, by party strength

Party	Life peers	Hereditary peers	Bishops	Total
Labour	210	4		214
Conservative	160	50		210
Liberal Democrat	69	5		74
Cross-bench	148	33		181
Arch/bishops			24	24
Other*	7			7
TOTAL	594	92	24	710

Note: Excludes 12 peers on leave of absence.

* These are: L. Archer of Weston-super-Mare, Non-affiliated; L. Beaumont of Whitley, Green Party; L. Fitt, Independent Socialist; L. Grenfell, Non-affiliated; L. McAlpine of West Green, Independent Conservative; L. Stoddart of Swindon, Independent Labour; B. Young of Old Scone, Non-affiliated.

key term

money bills

Government bills concerned mainly with the raising or spending of public money

Powers of the House of Lords

As a wholly non-elected chamber, the Lords' powers are much more limited than those of the Commons. The Lords can play a useful role in amending and revising legislation, but they cannot touch **money bills**, i.e. bills which are largely about the raising and spending of government money. They have the power to delay other bills for a maximum of one year, after which the Commons can invoke the Parliament Act 1949 and simply override the Lords. The only kind of bill which the Lords can block entirely is any bill seeking to extend the life of Parliament beyond its five-year maximum legal term – in effect, that means any bill which seeks to postpone or cancel a general election. The Lords have never, yet, had to use this power.

If amendments by the Lords are not accepted by the Commons, usually the Lords will back down – but not always. They have repeatedly blocked curbs on the right to jury trial. By the end of 2004, the Lords had inflicted over 80 significant defeats on the government since reform of the Lords; but the government was determined to overturn all of them – further examples of elective dictatorship. For example, the government has invoked the rarely-used Parliament Act to override the Lords and push through the introduction of closed lists for EU elections, the lowering of the gay age of consent to 16 and the ban on fox hunting.

Question

Distinguish between the roles and powers of the House of Commons and the House of Lords.

(15 marks)

Defence of the Lords

One possible argument in defence of an unelected chamber is that its members gain knowledge and experience over their many years of service, and that they add stability and continuity to the law-making process. Since they have total job security (short of outright abolition), they are less beholden to their party and to the government than are MPs, and so peers may be more independent-minded and less vulnerable to party pressure.

People who have distinguished themselves in wider public life, such as in industry, the trades unions, education, science, the arts and local government, are often brought into the House of Lords. 'Expertise' is also, therefore, often cited as a merit of the Lords; examples include former Prime Ministers such as Thatcher and Callaghan; former Foreign Secretaries such as Hurd and Carrington; Law Lords such as Nolan and Neill; businessmen such as the banker Lord Williams of Elvel; and media people such as Lord Melvyn Bragg. Lord Hives was an expert on beekeeping, and contributed usefully to the Bees Act 1980! Following a

Lord Hives – beekeeping expert

positive report by the prestigious Lords' Science and Technology Committee, medical trials for cannabis use began late in 1999. (Of course, the Commons also contains experts in many diverse fields, i.e. election does not preclude expertise – though it may render it less permanent.)

However, it is hard to defend a wholly non-elected legislative chamber in a twenty-first century liberal democracy. The main problem about further reform is the lack of consensus amongst the main parties and politicians.

analyse this

Past proposals for reform of the Lords include:

➡ complete abolition of the House of Lords (in the radical 'old' Labour manifesto of 1983)

➡ 'functional representation' based upon pressure and interest groups, rather than upon a party system

➡ indirect election of representatives from regional bodies (in the Liberal/SDP Alliance manifesto of 1987)

➡ a directly elected second chamber based on proportional representation (suggested by Lord Hailsham in his 1976 lecture 'Elective Dictatorship').

AS Level exam questions often ask what reforms of the Lords you would recommend, and why.

Consider the following points:

➡ The first issue to consider is, what roles and powers should the second chamber have – that is, how strong should it be as a check upon the first chamber? For example, should its delaying power be extended? Should it be allowed to amend government money bills? If you want a substantially stronger and more effective second chamber than the present House of Lords, then it should be democratised to ensure that its powers are legitimate.

➡ How many members should there be in the second chamber?

➡ Should they all be elected or should some be appointed?

➡ Who should appoint the appointed members?

➡ By what system should the elected members be elected?

➡ What term of office should the elected members have?

➡ Should the upper chamber be elected on different constituencies from the Commons?

➡ Should the term of office coincide with that of the Commons or, like the US system, overlap?

➡ Should any such changes require a referendum?

The Labour government's plans for further reform of the Lords

In the 2003 Queen's Speech, the Labour government announced that it would legislate on the following changes:

- abolishing the office of Lord Chancellor
- creating a 'supreme court' of senior judges separate from the House of Lords
- creating an independent judicial appointments commission
- abolishing the remaining 92 hereditary peers

In 2004, the Lords voted to send the Constitutional Reform Bill – containing the first three of the changes listed above – to a special select committee of the Lords for further scrutiny because there had been very little consultation on the proposed changes. The government was furious, accusing the Lords of being obstructive; but reluctantly agreed to the process of committee scrutiny. When the bill was returned to the Lords, it was defeated, throwing the government's plans into confusion.

The government dropped a separate bill seeking to abolish the remaining 92 hereditary peers, in the face of its possible defeat in Parliament.

These events demonstrate that the power of the Lords, though limited, should not be under-estimated.

Labour's 2005 election manifesto pledges that 'In our next term we will complete the reform of the Lords so that it is a modern and effective revising chamber'. They propose to remove the remaining 92 hereditary peers and to consider an elected element – *but* also to reduce the delaying power of the second chamber to a maximum of 60 days.

■ The House of Commons

This section attempts to describe and assess the role of the House of Commons, under the headings of Parliament's three main functions already listed at the beginning of this chapter:

- making the law
- controlling the executive
- representing the people.

Making the law

Parliamentary sovereignty

The Westminster Parliament is the supreme – ultimate – law-making body within the UK. It can pass, amend or repeal any law without challenge from any other UK institution. Parliament cannot be ruled illegal, nor can it be bound by any laws of any previous Parliament. Thus no Parliament can bind its successors. All other rules of the constitution (for

Westminster

example, conventions) can be overridden by Parliament, which can also take back, by law, any power given away to any other bodies – for example, the European Union or devolved assemblies. Also, Parliament is not always bound by its own laws (statutes), but instead by a special body of law known as **parliamentary privilege**. (This exempts MPs from some ordinary law; for example, they cannot be sued for slander for words spoken in Parliament.) The Westminster Parliament is subject only to the political sovereignty of the people at a general election (as long as Parliament chooses not to ban elections).

There are two broad types of parliamentary bill:

- **public bills** – concern the general public interest:

  – government bills

  – money bills (a special type of government bill, which cannot be amended by the Lords)

  – **private members' bills** (introduced by backbench MPs – usually public bills)

- **private bills** – concern specific individual or group interests (for example, the Ipswich Market Bill 2004, extending the market's area): these breach the rule of law and the principle of legal equality; they are therefore subject to special procedures and scrutiny.

The stages of parliamentary legislation are usually quite lengthy and complicated:

1. *Preparation and consultation*: Government bills are drafted by lawyers and civil servants, and may be preceded by a consultation paper (**Green Paper**) and/or a draft proposal (**White Paper**) – so called simply because of the colour of paper upon which they are printed.

standing committees

Commons' committees of backbench MPs from all parties in the Commons, which scrutinise proposed legislation

2   *First reading*: a purely formal reading of the bill's title to alert the MPs, groups and interests concerned (a necessary process before the invention of printing, and it has lived on by tradition).

3   *Second reading*: this is the really important stage of the bill, when it is outlined by the relevant minister and debated in detail and voted upon in the Commons' chamber.

4   *Committee stage*: the bill goes to a **standing committee** of Commons' backbench MPs (proportionally reflecting the parties' strength in the Commons) who scrutinise and amend the details of the bill, clause by clause. The whips have substantial control of the committees' membership; thus, on average, only 5 per cent of committee amendments have not been previously agreed with the government and, of these, only 1 per cent succeed.

5   *Report stage*: the amended bill is reported back to the whole House of Commons.

6   *Third reading*: only minor amendments to grammar and wording can be made at this stage, and the whole bill is then passed or rejected by the Commons.

7   The bill now goes through similar stages in the Lords.

talking point

When a bill has been passed by the Commons, it goes to 'another place' – the Commons' quaint name for the House of Lords because, traditionally, the two Houses cannot name each other!

8   Then it is returned to the Commons, where Lords' amendments are debated and either accepted or rejected. A controversial bill may go back and forth between the two Houses several times, until one backs down.

9   *Royal assent*: nowadays a formality.

Although the parliamentary law-making process is usually slow and cumbersome, occasionally it may move very fast: for example, draconian new anti-terrorism laws were passed through Parliament in a single day in 1998, despite a significant backbench revolt.

Challenges to Parliament's law-making role

A major challenge to Parliament's law-making function has come from the UK's membership of the European Union, whose legislation takes precedence over the laws of member states. The assent of Parliament is not required. This effectively negates parliamentary sovereignty; although, technically, Parliament could legislate to withdraw from the EU at any time, in practice this is unlikely. The more policy areas that are transferred to the decision-making of the EU – for example, by the Single

key
terms

devolution

The delegating of some legislative or executive powers from central to regional bodies

delegated legislation

Laws made by bodies other than Parliament – for example, ministers or local authorities – by powers passed to them by Parliament

European Act 1986 and the Maastricht Treaty 1992 – the less law-making power rests with Westminster.

Devolution – the delegating of some legislative or executive powers from central to regional bodies, and especially the creation of a fairly powerful Scottish Parliament – has also lightened the load of Westminster considerably and may ultimately threaten its national sovereignty.

Delegated legislation is also known as indirect or secondary legislation, because it allows ministers, local authorities and others to make detailed regulations under powers delegated by Parliament in a parent Act. It can thus turn ministers into law-makers, breaching the principle of separation of powers. The National Health Service (Complaints) Regulations 2004 is one example among thousands each year.

Controlling the executive

This is the most controversial issue of all. In parliamentary government, the executive (government) is chosen from within the legislature (Parliament) and is, in theory, subordinate and accountable – responsible – to the legislature. Parliament is therefore supposed to examine, debate, criticise and check the activities of the government, to publicise executive actions, to convey public opinion to the government, and to authorise the raising and spending of money by government – through, for example, debates, votes on government bills, Question Time and committees. The ultimate form of control is a vote of no confidence in the government by the House of Commons, which would oblige the government to resign.

Her Majesty's Opposition (HMO) – the second largest party in the Commons – is a formal part of the constitution: the leader and whips are paid a special salary and HMO is given special time and opportunities in Commons' procedures which are unavailable to other parties. The Leader of the Opposition is traditionally consulted on bipartisan matters (for example, the invasion of Iraq), and is given a chauffeur-driven car. Twenty Opposition Days are set aside in the Commons' yearly timetable for debate and criticism of government, with the topics chosen by the Opposition. Nevertheless, the Opposition is clearly weak against a majority government.

Occasionally the Commons does persuade the government to back down on an issue – for example, the taxing of disabled people's benefits in 1998 – but invariably this is under pressure from the government's own back-benchers. The Opposition alone cannot 'control' a majority executive; its main function now is to present itself to the electorate as 'the alternative government'.

Frustration is demonstrated by low attendance of MPs. Another outlet for MPs' frustration is rowdiness in the chamber. Lively debate may be seen as a legitimate tradition of the House. For some commentators, however, MPs' 'bad' behaviour is a symptom of the crisis of legitimacy developing in an unrepresentative, adversarial, executive-dominated House of Commons where the parliamentary process is slowly breaking down.

Control of finance

Scrutiny and control of government finance should be the Commons' most significant check, but 'estimates' of how much money is required by each government department are only given three days per year of parliamentary time, and no Budget item has been defeated since 1910.

£400 billion per year of public money is checked by the Commons Public Accounts Committee (PAC) and National Audit Office (NAO) to ensure that it has been lawfully spent. However, the Public Accounts Committee has itself said that the Commons' control of government finance – 'Parliament's key constitutional function' – is 'largely a formality', because the estimates and accounts provided by Whitehall are both too vague about key financial categories and objectives, and too complex on minor details. The PAC can only criticise after the event, to little effect; for example, its criticism in 1998 of the under-priced privatisation of the Atomic Energy Authority as 'a staggering waste of public money'. The budgets of the security and intelligence services – an estimated £1,000 million per year – are not subject to parliamentary scrutiny at all. The PAC also often accuses apathetic MPs of simply ignoring their many critical reports about government waste and mismanagement.

Another outlet for MPs' frustration is rowdiness in the chamber

Question Time

Question Time – the noisiest and most publicised part of the Commons' day – epitomises government's accountability to Parliament; but many query the usefulness of the whole exercise, and it has been described as 'ritualised combat' and 'a punch and judy show'. In 1997 Blair reduced PM's Question Time (PMQT) to once instead of twice a week, without consulting Parliament at all. (Moreover, Blair himself has only voted in 5 per cent of Commons' divisions since 1997 – a record low. His rare attendance in the House reduces his personal contact with MPs and his ability to sense the mood of his own backbenchers.)

Tony Blair during Prime Minister's Question Time

Other ministers answer questions only about once a month under a rota system. Confident ministers, well briefed by their officials and advisers, can usually deal easily with oral questions by giving combative or evasive answers. Sycophantic questions planted by the whips and asked by docile backbenchers make the process even easier for ministers. As former MP Tony Benn said in 2001, 'Question Time now has so many planted questions, it might as well be called gardeners' question time.'

Nevertheless, a genuine rottweiler – especially from the minister's own party – highlights Question Time as a pure form of ministerial accountability, under the media spotlight, which can occasionally make or break ministerial careers.

Select committees

Departmental select committees, comprising backbench MPs from all of the parties, scrutinise each government department's policies, activities and spending. They generally conduct inquiries on specific departmental issues and publish reports, to which the government must respond. They have been called the single most important weapon of increased parliamentary influence in the twentieth century.

They do attract growing media attention (for example, the Foreign Affairs committee's 1998 investigation of the arms to Sierra Leone affair); absenteeism is low; they are quite independent-minded (for example, in 2000 the Transport Committee was highly critical of the government's plan to privatise air traffic control); and they have been able to extract valuable information from government (for example, in 1999, the Commons Agriculture Committee strongly rebuked the Agriculture

key term

departmental select committees

Commons' committees of backbench MPs from all of the parties, which scrutinise each government department's policies, activities and spending

A Commons select committee hearing

Secretary for hyping £1 million worth of new aid up to '£500 million'). The government has sometimes acted on their recommendations: for example, in 2004 the government took up the Home Affairs Committee's suggestion of more use of electronic tagging and other community sentences to reduce prison over-crowding. In 2002, PM Blair agreed that he would henceforth appear twice-yearly before a special Liaison Committee made up of all of the chairpeople of the select committees. In 2001, the attempted removal by the whips of two feisty Labour select committee chairpeople (Gwyneth Dunwoody on Transport and Donald Anderson on Foreign Affairs) was defeated by the Commons – the only real Labour government defeat by the Commons yet.

However, the select committees lack the time, resources, staff, expertise, power and, perhaps above all, the will, to be more than an irritant to the government. Often the government simply ignores the criticisms and recommendations of the committees: for example, in 2000 a joint report of four major committees criticised arms sales to Zimbabwe, but it was ignored by the government. Also in 2000, Blair refused to attend – and refused to allow his chief of staff/spin doctor Jonathan Powell to attend – the Public Administration Committee to justify the increase in special political advisers in Downing Street. The government has explicitly rejected suggestions from the Liaison Committee in 2002 for strengthening the committees' powers.

Moreover, the balance of party power on the committees reflects that of the Commons as a whole, so backbenchers of the governing party are usually in a majority on the committees – and most government backbenchers, of course, want to be frontbenchers and therefore may be unwilling to be too critical. Finally, the committees' membership is still heavily influenced by the whips.

In sum, most commentators agree that the select committees have done little to shift the real balance of power between executive and legislature, though they do have influence and provide information, detailed scrutiny and public criticism of government. Reformers say that they need bigger budgets, stronger powers, and more capacity to conduct research, initiate debates and interrogate ministers and civil servants more rigorously. Such solutions lie largely in the committees' own hands.

The Ombudsman

This is a parliamentary bureaucrat whose job it is to investigate public complaints about government maladministration – but who (again) lacks power and resources. The current **Ombudsman** – Ann Abraham – recently threatened to resign because the government is still too secretive and has also banned her investigations of ministerial conflicts of interest: for example, Blair's private gifts from foreign leaders.

In summary: some commentators argue that the task of Parliament is simply to scrutinise and sustain the government rather than 'control' it. However, most say that Parliament should control the government but usually cannot, for the following reasons:

Factors which contribute towards elective dictatorship

These include:

- majority governments
- party discipline
- government control of parliamentary time
- government secrecy and obfuscation, especially on finance
- government control of civil service personnel and information
- the growth of delegated legislation
- the lack of power of parliamentary committees and the Ombudsman
- lack of resources and facilities for MPs
- the weakness of the non-elected House of Lords
- the growing influence on government of extra-parliamentary bodies such as the EU, business, pressure groups and media.

For all of these reasons – but, above all, because of the power of a majority government in control of a sovereign Parliament with a flexible constitution – Lord Hailsham's phrase 'elective dictatorship' is often used to describe the UK system of government. (See Chapter 2.)

Representing the people

The extent to which Parliament represents the UK people depends, first, upon what is meant by the concept of a 'representative'. The pros and cons of Westminster's first-past-the-post electoral system are obviously central to this issue. So is the question of elective dictatorship when the government can use its majority to dominate the Commons.

---

key term

Ombudsman

A parliamentary bureaucrat whose job is to investigate public complaints about government maladministration

---

analyse
this

A political 'representative' may reflect:

➡ the *views and wishes* of the voters

➡ the *interests* of the voters as the representative sees them

➡ the *social background* and *typicality* of the voters.

1 Study the composition and proceedings of the present House of Commons over one week, through newspaper and television coverage and the internet.

2 For each of the above interpretations of the word, find one specific example where MPs are representative of the voters and one example where they are not.

3 Suggest ways in which MPs could be made more representative of their voters.

A further point to consider here is, again, the issue of devolution. In the 1997 election the Conservatives won no Westminster seats at all in Scotland or Wales, and some nationalists therefore argued that Westminster and Whitehall had no authority to control Scottish or Welsh affairs. The 1997 Labour government re-established the Northern Irish assembly in 1998 and new Scottish and Welsh assemblies were set up in 1999. These are widely seen as representing the regions better than Westminster does, not least because they are elected on at least partial proportional representation.

Parliamentary privilege is the exemption of MPs from some ordinary laws under the special laws and customs of Parliament. It is therefore a special category of constitutional law, which breaches the rule of law and principle of legal equality. It was originally a defence against the power of the Crown, and is now justified on the grounds that MPs can better represent the people if, for example, they have complete freedom of speech. Thus they are immune from slander or libel actions for words spoken in Parliament. This may be used to expose wrongdoing – for example, Labour MP Stuart Bell used parliamentary privilege to expose the scandal of 'cash for questions' in the 1990s.

However, this freedom may be abused by MPs: in 1999, Unionist MP Ian Paisley named and accused a man of being an IRA killer although the police said that the man was an innocent farmer.

Despite this 'absolute' freedom of speech, Sinn Fein MP Gerry Adams was permanently barred from the Commons by the Speaker after his election in 1997, because he refused – as a republican – to take an oath of allegiance to the Crown.

Other privileges – for example, freedom from arrest – may now seem anachronistic or excessive. The right of Parliament to control its own proceedings is, perhaps, quite reasonable, but its right to try and to punish outsiders for 'contempt of Parliament' is controversial.

Televising of the Commons (and its committees) since 1988 has enhanced open government and freedom of the media; and many MPs believe that TV – with its statutory duty of impartiality – presents a more balanced and fair view of party politics than does much of the conservative UK press. However, some MPs argue that it encourages bad behaviour by MPs and the public in the House, while others fear that selective broadcasting may trivialise, sensationalise or distort proceedings and undermine the authority of the Commons. Minority parties are under-represented in televised proceedings as they are in the Commons itself.

talking point

Should parliamentary privilege be abolished?

Question

What are the limits on the sovereignty of Parliament?   *(15 marks)*

Reform of the House of Commons

Since 1997, the Labour government has made a few small and piecemeal reforms of the Commons (apart from devolution, which was a major constitutional change):

● Changes to the Commons' timetable, so that its proceedings start and finish earlier in the day. This was done to reduce the number of late-night and all-night sittings and to make the place more 'family friendly', especially for its women members.

● A new building – Portcullis House, next door to Westminster – has given MPs added office space.

● PM Tony Blair cut PMQT from twice to once per week.

● PM Tony Blair has taken questions from the Commons' Liaison Committee (of select committee chairpeople) twice a year since 2002.

analyse
this

Consider the possible further ideas for reform of the Commons listed (in no particular order) below.

➡ Ombudsman: broader role (for example, over police); more staff; more power over Whitehall; more publicity

➡ Fixed-term elections

➡ Full-time MPs

➡ Abolition of external fees and payments for MPs

➡ Push-button or proxy voting for MPs in the House

➡ Reform of electoral system (Specify, and consider consequences.)

➡ More freedom of information for MPs and committees

➡ More free votes in the House

➡ Fewer MPs – for example, 400 – for a more efficient and professional House

➡ Restore PMQT to twice a week

➡ Regional Parliaments (devolution) for England

➡ More power (to scrutinise people and papers) and more publicity for select committees

➡ Abolition of all/obsolete parliamentary privileges

➡ Abolition of the 'guillotine', i.e. the time limit on committee stage of bills

➡ Less control by whips of committee appointments

➡ A well-paid and high status parliamentary career ladder which could provide an alternative to executive promotion for backbenchers

➡ More opportunities and (legal) assistance for private members' bills

➡ Reduction/abolition of notice for oral questions

➡ Better parliamentary scrutiny of delegated legislation

➡ Separation of powers – the executive elected separately from Parliament

1 Decide which of the above reforms you would and would not advocate in an exam answer on the subject, and why. As you do so, consider whether one reform may require, generate or preclude another – i.e. ensure that your choices are consistent and compatible.

2 Consider any possible problems arising from your chosen reforms; how would you counter or overcome them?

3 Can you add any more good ideas for reform to this list?

Questions

Quiz

Briefly answer the following questions.

1   When did a monarch last refuse assent to a bill?

2   What is a White Paper?

3   Who is responsible for drafting government bills?

4   List the stages of legislation for public bills.

5   What is a joint committee?

6   What is Hansard?

7   Once elected by the Commons, does the Speaker cease to be an MP?

8   List three functions of the Speaker.

9   Who is the present Speaker of the Commons?

10   What are Standing Orders?

11   What is a 'simple closure'?

12   What are 'the usual channels'?

13   List three functions of the whips.

14   What is 'pairing'?

15   What is meant by 'withdrawing the whip' from an MP?

16   Why might an MP seek a written rather than oral answer at Question Time?

17   What is the function of the Ombudsman?

18   What is the Consolidated Fund?

19   When was a government last defeated in the Commons on a vote of no confidence?

20   What is (a) the PLP and (b) the 1922 Committee?

Sample AS answer

Distinguish between the legal and the actual powers of Parliament.   (15 marks)

'Power' is the ability to do, or make others do, something regardless of their consent, based on the capacity to coerce, i.e. to reward or punish. Parliament's power is supposed to be based on authority – from elections for the House of Commons and tradition for the House of Lords.

In theory – *de jure* – the UK Parliament has legal sovereignty, i.e. it can make, amend or repeal any law and no domestic institution can override its laws. Thus it cannot be ruled illegal or unconstitutional; it can pass retrospective (backdated) law to legalise illegality – for example, sperm donors – and no Parliament can bind its successors – i.e. a future Parliament may amend or repeal any previous statute. Also, Parliament is not bound by its own statutes, but instead by a special body of law known as parliamentary privilege which exempts MPs from much ordinary law: for instance, they cannot be sued for slander for words spoken in Parliament. For example, Labour MP Stuart Bell used parliamentary privilege to expose the Conservative 'cash for questions' scandal in the 1990s.

Also in theory, according to the UK system of parliamentary government, Parliament should have the power to scrutinise and hold to account the executive, through debates, votes, Question Time, select committees, the Ombudsman, etc. This holds particularly true when the executive does not have a majority in the Commons, for example John Major's government before the 1997 election.

Parliament is also given the authority and power to represent the people through the first-past-the-post system of election for the Commons – for example, blocking the 1996 second VAT rise on domestic fuel. Though the Lords are not elected and therefore have limited power – one-year delay, for example War Crimes Act 1991 – they derive authority from such factors as tradition and expertise (at least in the eyes of traditional Tories), for example blocking the abolition of the office of Lord Chancellor in 2004.

However, the actual – *de facto* – powers of Parliament are limited, first by a majority government within Parliament, for example Labour (66 majority in 2005). The executive can effectively dominate Parliament due to party loyalty and discipline, control of the timetable, official secrecy, and the weaknesses of the select committees, Ombudsman and Lords – i.e. elective dictatorship (Hailsham).

The European Union can, since 1973, override Parliament – for example, on fishing quotas and the worldwide beef ban. This also means that both the European and UK courts can override Parliament's law where it conflicts with EU law – for example, on the 48-hour working week. Other international bodies such as the IMF and NATO also have influence.

Other constraints on the actual power of Parliament are: pressure groups – for example, the fox-hunting supporters (Countryside Alliance); the media – for example on asylum seekers; the City and other economic power bodies – for example, the UK's fallout from the ERM in 1992; and ultimately the 'political sovereignty' of the electorate, who choose the MPs in the Commons and who may, occasionally, simply refuse to obey the law of Parliament – for example, the poll tax.

7

Executive

■ What is the executive?

The executive consists of:

- the **Crown**

- the political policy-makers: Prime Minister, **Cabinet** – that is, the 20 or so most senior ministers – and other, junior ministers (around 100 altogether)

- the administrators: the **civil servants** – a hierarchy of non-elected, permanent, impartial and professional 'bureaucrats' (around 500,000 altogether) who administer the policies and machinery of government.

The work of the government is divided into around 20 policy departments – defence, foreign affairs, employment, education, etc. – and the ministerial heads of the major departments are in the Cabinet.

In the UK system of parliamentary government, the ministers are appointed from within Parliament and are accountable to Parliament, and thus (indirectly) to the electorate, for the policies of the government and the actions of government departments.

key terms

Crown

The permanent, abstract institution which embodies the supreme power of the state in the UK, culminating in the monarchy

Cabinet

Combined heads of executive policy departments and team of senior policy-makers

civil servants

Permanent, impartial, non-elected career administrators and officials of the government

Question

What steps might citizens take if they felt that they had been unfairly treated by a government department? *(20 marks)*

Example of a government department and its ministers

Home Secretary Charles Clarke MP
The Home Secretary has overall responsibility for the work of the Home Office,
civil emergencies, security, terrorism, expenditure and Civil Renewal

Minister of State for Policing, Security and Community Safety
Hazel Blears MP will be supported by Paul Goggins MP
- Police
- Counter terrorism
- Crime reduction (including violent crime, guns, knives)
- Anti social behaviour
- Community safety and active citizenship

Minister of State for Criminal Justice and Offender Management
Baroness Scotland QC will be supported by Fiona Mactaggart MP
- Youth justice
- Home Office input into government policy on young people
- Sentencing policy
- Domestic violence

Minister of State for Immigration, Citizenship and Nationality
Tony McNulty MP will be supported by Andy Burnham MP
- Immigration
- Asylum
- Nationality, naturalisation and citizenship

Parliamentary Under-Secretary of State
Paul Goggins MP
- Serious and organised crime
- Drugs
- Asset Recovery Agency
- Security Industry Authority
- Public order, sex offences, roads policing, animal extremism, internet crime, child pornography and football
- Voluntary and community sector, community cohesion, faith and race equality

Parliamentary Under-Secretary of State
Fiona Mactaggart MP
- Criminal Justice system including race equality, victims and witnesses, inspection and IT
- Criminal law (including homicide, fraud, corruption, corporate killing and memoirs)
- NOMS casework and restorative justice
- Mental Health Act
- Criminal injuries compensation
- Prostitution
- Correspondence champion

Parliamentary Under-Secretary of State
Andy Burnham MP
- ID cards and passports
- Forensic Science Service
- Refugee integration
- E borders
- Extradition and judicial co-operation
- Criminal Records Bureau
- Home Office research and science
- Better regulation
- Design and Green Minister

The Home Office: ministers and responsibilities (June 2005)

key terms

monarchy
The institution of hereditary rule by a royal family

monarch
The individual person upon whom the Crown is conferred

royal prerogative
The formal powers of the Crown

absolute monarchy
A hereditary head of state with total political power

constitutional monarchy
An impartial (non-party political), largely symbolic, hereditary head of state whose powers are exercised by, and on the advice of, ministers, in theory subordinate to the will of Parliament, the people and the rules of the constitution

■ The monarchy

The Crown is the permanent, abstract institution which embodies the supreme power of the state. It is the formal head of all three branches of government – legislature, executive and judiciary – and all acts of state are done in the name of the Crown. The **monarchy** is the institution of hereditary, royal rule (as opposed to a republic, which is usually headed by an elected president). The sovereign or the **monarch** is the individual person upon whom the Crown is conferred. In the UK, succession to the throne is determined by the Act of Settlement 1701; this states, for example, that male heirs take precedence over females, and that the monarch is not allowed to be, nor to marry, a Roman Catholic – outdated and offensive rules, according to some critics.

The **royal prerogative** is the term given to the formal powers of the Crown. They are part of common law, and in theory are substantial. They include: the appointment and dismissal of the Prime Minister; other powers of patronage; the opening and dissolving of Parliament; approval of statute law; the declaration of war and signing of treaties. However, the UK no longer has an **absolute monarchy**, but a **constitutional monarchy**: an impartial (non-party political), largely symbolic head of state whose powers are exercised by, and on the advice of, ministers, in theory subordinate to the will of Parliament, the people and the rules of the constitution. Most of the powers listed above have either passed to the PM

Queen Elizabeth II

and other ministers or are governed by strict convention. The monarch, therefore, has very little personal power. This is meant to 'democratise' the powers of the Crown and to keep the monarch out of political controversy. In the nineteenth century, therefore, Bagehot classed the monarchy as a 'dignified' rather than 'efficient' part of the constitution, with much symbolic and ceremonial authority but little real power. Except in times of constitutional crisis, he said, 'The Queen reigns, but does not rule.'

Crown immunity

The monarch, in her private capacity, is above the law. The legal immunity conferred by the royal prerogative may also extend to institutions and servants of the Crown such as ministers and intelligence agents. Since this puts them, too, above the law, it is sometimes controversial.

Case for the monarchy

As the actual powers of the monarchy have declined, its symbolic and ceremonial functions have increased. The monarch is an impartial head of state, and thus a symbol of national unity, stability and continuity. As the head of the Church of England she promotes Christian morality and family life. The UK monarch is also head of many Commonwealth countries; she promotes good international relations and trade, while the pomp and ceremony of royal pageantry is good for tourism. The link with the Crown – royal assent, prerogative, etc. – lends authority and legitimacy to Parliament and government. The present Queen has lengthy experience and exceptional knowledge of UK and international politics, which may be a valuable source of advice to governments and Prime Ministers. She does her job conscientiously and competently, and both monarch and monarchy are currently quite popular.

analyse this

The royal prerogative

The conventional view of the royal prerogative is that, following the Glorious Revolution of 1688, it was made subject to parliamentary control; and our constitution, based on parliamentary government under the rule of law, dates from that time.

The fact is that the royal prerogative is alive and well and living, for the most part, in 10 Downing Street. Prime ministerial (and ministerial) use of the royal prerogative allows them to bypass parliamentary, and often judicial, control – especially where 'national security' is invoked. Examples have included: ministers trying to withhold information in the court case about 'arms to Iraq' in 1995; MI5 officers being allowed to 'bug and burgle' without fear of prosecution; the government forbidding some civil servants to be members of trades unions; and the Home Office supplying the police with plastic bullets and CS gas.

1 Suggest why the powers of the Crown have not been formally or legally transferred to the Prime Minister and other ministers.

2 Suggest three exceptional circumstances in which the monarch may exercise real power.

3 Since the monarch usually has little real personal power, give reasons why the royal prerogative – the power of the Crown – is still controversial.

Case against the monarchy

Approval of the symbolic role of the monarchy is a conservative view which favours the *status quo* and fears progressive change. The institution of the monarchy has an ideological role in promoting social class hierarchy, hereditary privilege, snobbery and deference, and its existence reduces UK citizens to mere subjects. It is also outdated to have one established church in the modern, multicultural age. Heredity is no guarantee of merit, and the aristocracy and patronage perpetuated by the institution of monarchy are undemocratic. 'New' Labour's arguments against hereditary peers should, logically, apply equally to the monarchy. The popularity of the monarchy is said, by critics, to be largely a product of socialisation by the media, which trivialises the royal family and treats it as a soap opera, whilst neglecting any pluralist debate about the institution of the monarchy itself and its impact on the balance of political power in the UK – especially the large powers which it confers upon modern Prime Ministers.

■ The Cabinet

The 20 or so most senior government ministers form the Cabinet, which grew out of the body of policy advisers to the monarch in the eighteenth century. According to current constitutional theory (since Bagehot), we have **Cabinet government**: collective policy-making by a united team of senior ministers with the Prime Minister *primus inter pares* (first among equals). All Cabinet ministers are MPs or peers drawn from Parliament, and most are appointed as heads of major government departments such as the Foreign Office and Treasury. The Prime Minister decides the size and composition of the Cabinet, and allocates portfolios, i.e. departmental responsibilities.

The Ministers of the Crown Act 1937 gives ministers (together with the Opposition Leader and Chief Whip) a special salary, and the Ministerial and Other Salaries Act 1975 sets an upper limit of 22 paid Cabinet members; but the Cabinet's composition, functions and powers are otherwise governed largely by conventions. The two most important of these are the doctrines of **collective** and **individual ministerial responsibility**.

Collective responsibility

This doctrine rests on the assumption that ministers make policy decisions collectively and that they should, therefore, publicly support and defend all government policies, and should be accountable for them to

key terms

Cabinet government

Collective policy-making by a united team of senior ministers with the Prime Minister *primus inter pares* (first among equals)

collective Cabinet responsibility

The convention that ministers make policy decisions collectively and, if ministers disagree so strongly with a policy that they cannot defend it in public, they should resign

individual ministerial responsibility

The convention that ministers should be publicly accountable for all of the actions of their departments, and should resign in the event of serious departmental or personal error

Question

What factors affect the appointment of ministers? *(15 marks)*

The Prime Minister and members of The Cabinet

Parliament and thus to the electorate – for example, through Question Time and votes of censure (no confidence) in the Commons. If ministers disagree so strongly with a policy that they cannot defend it in public, they should resign, as did Cabinet minister Robin Cook in 2003 over the invasion of Iraq. A united front – even if it is sometimes a façade – increases public confidence in the government and gives it strength and stability. More importantly, collective responsibility is central to the principle of the democratic accountability of the whole government to Parliament and, thus, to the voters.

In recent years this convention has been weakening: because of the rise of prime ministerial power, adversary politics in the 1980s and internal party divisions in the 1990s, ministers have often disagreed publicly with government policy but have not resigned over it. For example, in 2004, Cabinet ministers such as Jack Straw made public their opposition to government plans for compulsory national identity cards – but no one resigned (and the plan went ahead regardless, due to its strong support by the Prime Minister and the Home Secretary).

Individual responsibility

This doctrine rests on the assumption that ministerial heads of department are the chosen representatives of the people, while the non-elected civil servants who administer policy within each department are impartial, anonymous bureaucrats merely carrying out political orders. Ministers, not civil servants, should therefore be publicly accountable for all of the actions of their departments, and should resign in the event of serious error.

For example, Education Secretary Estelle Morris resigned in 2002 over her personal failure to meet key policy targets, and Immigration Minister Beverley Hughes resigned in 2004 over policy errors within her department.

However, this convention is also weakening. Conservative Home Secretary Michael Howard, in the 1990s, made a novel distinction between 'policy' and 'operational' responsibilities and sacked top civil servant Derek Lewis, rather than resigning himself over a series of prison crises. Other ministers have, since, copied his example: for example, Labour's Lord Falconer named and blamed civil servant Jennie Page for the failures of the Millennium Dome; and Commons leader, Peter Hain, blamed police operations rather than policy decisions for the breach of Big Ben's security by Greenpeace protesters in 2004. This may undermine the democratic accountability of government ministers and openly embroil civil servants in controversial political matters.

Individual ministerial responsibility also covers personal impropriety – often sexual or financial scandals. For example, Labour's Welsh Secretary Ron Davies resigned in 1998 over sexual impropriety on Clapham Common; and at the end of that year, Peter Mandelson and Geoffrey Robinson both resigned over a large, undeclared loan from Robinson to Mandelson at a time when Mandelson's Trade and Industry department was investigating fellow minister Robinson's personal

" IT WASN'T ME... "

financial affairs. Trade and Industry Secretary Stephen Byers had to resign in 2002 because he had forced his senior civil servant Martin Sixsmith's sacking over a row with his (Byers') personal spin doctor Jo Moore (who, famously, had emailed the department on 11 September 2001 that 'This is a good day to bury bad news'). In 2004, Home Secretary David Blunkett resigned over the fast tracking of his lover's nanny's visa.

All of these ministers, except Estelle Morris, went reluctantly, under sustained pressure from the media, party, public opinion and therefore ultimately also from the PM.

It is significant that ministers resign far more frequently over personal indiscretion (since there is no one else to blame) than over departmental error; although the latter seems, constitutionally, more important.

■ The Prime Minister

Tony Blair

By convention, the monarch chooses, as Prime Minister, the leader of the majority party in the Commons. The first Prime Minister in the modern sense is usually said to be Sir Robert Peel, who held office after the 1832 Reform Act which established the principle of executive accountability, through Parliament, to the electorate.

The powers of the Prime Minister derive from the royal prerogative and rest entirely on convention, not law. They include:

- huge powers of patronage, including the appointment and dismissal of all ministers and allocation of departmental responsibilities; appointing top civil servants, judiciary, clergy, etc.; awarding peerages, honours and titles

- deciding the structure of government – for example, creating, merging or splitting departments

- deciding the agenda for Cabinet meetings, chairing Cabinet meetings, and summing up decisions reached in Cabinet (without a vote)

- deciding the number, composition and terms of reference of **Cabinet committees**; and PM may chair important Cabinet committees personally

- co-ordinating government policy

- political head of the civil service, ultimately responsible for their numbers, duties and conditions of work

- representing the government and country at international summits

- deciding the date of the general election within the five-year term

- deciding the timetable of government legislation in the Commons – a function usually delegated to the Leader of the House, a senior Cabinet minister

- leader of the party (this role differs somewhat within different parties)

- communicating government policy and advice to the monarch through weekly meetings.

key term

Cabinet committees

Small sub-groups of ministers, chosen by the Prime Minister, to aid policy-making

UK Prime Ministers 1945–2005

1945–51	Clement Attlee (Lab.)
1951–5	Sir Winston Churchill (Cons.)
	Resigned 1955; new PM Eden called and won election.
1955–7	Sir Anthony Eden (Cons.)
	Resigned over ill-health and Suez.
1957–63	Harold Macmillan (Cons.)
	Resigned 1963. No general election.
1963–4	Sir Alec Douglas-Home (Cons.)
1964–70	Harold Wilson (Lab.)
	Majority of 4. Re-elected 1966.
1970–4	Edward Heath (Cons.)
1974–6	Harold Wilson (Lab.)
	Feb. 1974 minority government.
	Oct. 1974 election – majority of 3.
	Resigned March 1976 – no general election.
1976–9	James Callaghan (Lab.)
	1977–9 Minority government. 'Lib–Lab Pact'.
	Defeated on vote of censure in Commons.
1979–90	Margaret Thatcher (Cons.)
	Resigned 1990. No general election.
1990–7	John Major (Cons.)
	Lost his majority by 1997.
1997	Tony Blair (Lab.)
	Record 179 majority. Re-elected 2001 and 2005.

talking point

UK voters do not elect the Prime Minister. In a general election, voters elect individual constituency MPs – usually on the basis of a party label – to Westminster and, if one party has over 50 per cent of Commons' seats, its leader – by convention – is appointed as Prime Minister by the monarch. This fact becomes clear on the rare occasions when there is no majority party – in which case, the monarch has some real degree of choice of PM, since there is no convention to guide her (for example, in February 1974); and also when the governing party chooses to sack its own leader – and hence also the country's Prime Minister – in mid-term, as the Conservatives did with Margaret Thatcher in 1990.

According to the theory of collective Cabinet government, the Prime Minister is simply *primus inter pares* – first among equals – but a leader who can hire and fire all other ministers is clearly more than that. The conventional list of the PM's powers is extensive and, since the 1960s, many commentators have perceived a trend towards **prime ministerial government** rather than Cabinet government in the UK. However, the real *powers* of a Prime Minister vary considerably according to circumstance; above all, they depend on *authority*.

Cabinet or prime ministerial government?

Former Labour minister Richard Crossman, in the 1960s, was among the first to assert that 'The post-war epoch has seen the final transformation of Cabinet government into prime ministerial government.' He borrowed Bagehot's phraseology to argue that the Cabinet had joined the monarchy in 'dignified impotence'. It is often difficult to assess the real balance of power within the executive because of the exceptional secrecy which shrouds the whole machinery of UK government and policy-making, but commentators point to the following:

Factors enhancing prime ministerial power:

- Party discipline

- PM's office: the increasingly powerful group of political advisers (or 'spin doctors') and civil servants at Number 10

- PM's control of the wider civil service bureaucracy throughout government

- Media: the growing influence of the modern mass media and their increasing focus upon the PM

- The EU: the PM is national leader and policy-maker at the European Council and EU summit meetings

- Consensus politics: when the policies of the two main parties are quite similar, the media and voters focus, instead, upon the personalities and images of the party leaders

- Time: the PM has no departmental responsibilities

- Control of Cabinet committees: Cabinet committees are established by the Prime Minister to enable the Cabinet to deal more efficiently with policy-making. All Cabinet committees are chaired by a senior Cabinet minister chosen by the PM – if not by the PM himself – and have a number of Cabinet ministers, and perhaps civil servants, as members. There are currently around 55 Cabinet committees in total, but their numbers, personnel and powers are decided solely by the Prime Minister. Some are permanent committees while others are set up to deal with particular issues as they arise. Cabinet committees carry out the bulk of Cabinet policy-making work. These (according to writer Peter Hennessy) are the real 'engine room' of UK government. The PM also decides whether they make recommendations to the full Cabinet or actually make policy decisions.

Examples of Cabinet committees:

- Ministerial Committee on the Criminal Justice System (CJS)

- Ministerial Committee on Domestic Affairs (DA)

- Ministerial Sub-Committee on Equality (DA(EQ))

- Ministerial Committee on the Legislative Programme (LP)

- Ministerial Committee on Animal Rights Activists (MISC13)

- Ministerial Committee on the Olympic Games (MISC25)

- Ministerial Sub-Committee on London Resilience (DOP(IT)(R)(LR)).

Source: Cabinet Office, 2004

Prime Ministers have other, informal, sources of policy advice, such as sympathetic pressure groups (for example, for Thatcher, the Adam Smith Institute; and, for Blair, Demos). Critics of prime ministerial power fear that these bodies do not simply advise on policy but help to make policy decisions. Since they are non-elected, and bypass Cabinet government, this may be seen as 'unconstitutional'.

Many key policy decisions since the Second World War are said to have been made by the Prime Minister (usually with the advice and agreement of a few senior ministers, civil servants, policy advisers, etc.) rather than by the Cabinet as a whole.

Key examples of prime ministerial policies are said to include:

- the Budget, nuclear weapons, and intelligence and security, which have never been matters for Cabinet government

- **Thatcher**: the Falklands conflict (1982); abolition of the Greater London and metropolitan councils (1985); the bombing of Libya by US planes from UK bases (1986); the Spycatcher affair (1986–8); the poll tax (1988)

- **Major**: the Gulf 'War Cabinet' (1991)

- **Blair**: Formula One tobacco advertising exemption; the Dome; Amsterdam Treaty; personal veto of Chancellor Brown's plan to increase the top rate of income tax in 1998; appointment of friend and Scottish media owner Gus McDonald as Scottish Industry minister from outside Parliament, contrary to powerful convention; Blair, personally and strongly, backed Bush on the 'war on terror' and invasion of Iraq – despite clear Cabinet divisions on the issue. In a major policy U-turn, Blair decided, in 2004, to promise a referendum on a new EU constitution in the face of strong opposition and media pressure, without any formal Cabinet consultation at all.

Although arguments about prime ministerial government predate Thatcher, her style and image of leadership – variously described as 'strong' and 'authoritarian' – intensified the debate. Ultimately, some of her key Cabinet colleagues, such as Nigel Lawson and Geoffrey Howe, wearied of her autocratic nature and it eventually destroyed her. John

Major's approach was deliberately more Cabinet-oriented, collegiate and consensual but, this in turn, came to be seen as a weakness, and his government became increasingly divided, especially over Europe.

Blair displayed his centralising and disciplinarian tendencies over his 'new' Labour government and party from the earliest days of his premiership, and critics made much of his 'control freakery' – for example, keeping his MPs ruthlessly 'on message' via pagers from the party's headquarters, his reliance on powerful spin doctors such as Alastair Campbell and Jonathan Powell, and his promotion of Blairite loyalists in government reshuffles – what critics called his 'culture of cronyism'.

Suggested reforms
Suggested reforms to curb the powers of modern Prime Ministers include:

- a 'constitutional premiership' – outlining and limiting the powers of the PM (and perhaps also the Cabinet) in law
- election of the Cabinet by the parliamentary party
- transferring the PM's powers of patronage to the Commons or the Speaker
- more political advisers for ministers
- ministers choosing their own senior departmental civil servants
- less power and authority for the PM's spin doctors.

A UK presidency?

The growing emphasis in UK politics and in the media on party leaders' individual personalities, styles and images has led some (for example, Michael Foley) to suggest that UK government is becoming 'presidential'. However, a formal presidential system is based on separation of the executive and legislature; for example, in the USA the President is separately elected by the people, and neither he nor his appointed executive team (also called Cabinet) are allowed to be members of Congress (the US equivalent of Parliament). The President may therefore lack a majority in Congress, and may thus be weaker than a UK Prime Minister – for example, Bill Clinton's Health Bill fiasco and his historic impeachment hearings by the Senate in 1999. An outright 'presidential system' therefore has additional checks and balances which are lacking in the UK system of 'parliamentary government'.

In the looser sense, however, Tony Blair has undoubtedly displayed a more 'presidential' style of leadership than most: i.e. a carefully cultivated and exceptionally personal, populist, 'hands on' style and image, distanced from both his Cabinet and his party. Conservative leader Michael Howard has spoken of 'a trend towards presidency away from parliamentary democracy'.

Examples include: Blair's claiming of a personal mandate for the creation and success of 'new' Labour; his walkabout with his wife Cherie upon his victory in 1997 (and Cherie herself personifying the 'first lady' syndrome – for example, her attendance at the 1999 music Brit Awards); his 'call me Tony' relationship with ministers and officials; his 'people's Princess' speech on the death of Diana; his personal intervention in the Northern Ireland and Middle East peace talks; and personal slogans such as the 'third way', etc. A leaked memo from Blair in 2000 said, 'We need eye-catching initiatives . . . and I should be personally associated with as much of this as possible.' Blair visited 22 countries in the three months following the 11 September 2001 attacks on America. In 2002 he launched monthly, live, TV press briefings. The 2003 invasion of Iraq was a supremely presidential act.

On the other hand, however, the case for prime ministerial and presidential government in the UK should not be overstated. All Prime Ministers face real constraints.

Constraints on prime ministerial government

- Authority is the essential precondition of prime ministerial power. It derives from the electorate, the Commons, the Crown and, above all, the party. Unlike a US President, a UK Prime Minister depends upon party support and loyalty (for example Thatcher, who was ousted by her party in 1990 despite having a safe arithmetical majority in the Commons).

- Every prime ministerial power is also a responsibility; if it is misused, the PM may lose authority and even risk losing office: for example, Thatcher over Europe and the poll tax; Major over his failure to control party divisions and 'sleaze'; and Blair over Iraq.

- There are constraints upon the PM's appointment and dismissal of ministers: they should come from Parliament, should represent all regions of the country, should reflect the range of political feeling in the party and retain party support, and they should, preferably, be honest and competent. Such constraints in a parliamentary system contrast with the unlimited patronage powers of a US President which may generate a 'spoils system'. A Prime Minister also must 'be a good butcher' (i.e. be willing to sack incompetent or dishonest ministers when necessary); on the other hand, too many reshuffles suggest prime ministerial misjudgement – after all, she or he appointed them in the first place.

- Cabinet revolts are rare, but significant: for example, against Blair's proposed compulsory national ID cards (2004).

- Backbench revolts: for example, against Blair's top-up tuition fees (2004) which resulted in some government concessions. Also, Blair wanted to support a licensing system for fox hunting but was defeated.

- The Lords: for example, they forced the Labour government to back down over the abolition of the 92 remaining hereditary peers in 2004.

- Pressure groups may be a key constraint: for example, the Countryside Alliance frightened Blair's government off banning fox hunting for many years.

- The EU is clearly a growing constraint on the policy-making power of any PM (for example, the beef ban) and may also affect his or her authority if relations are clumsy (for example, Thatcher).

- The media and civil service may be a hindrance as well as a help, but a Prime Minister's effective power at any time depends on a wide variety of circumstances: personality and charisma, health and energy, size of majority, length of time in office and proximity of a general election, the state of the economy, international events (such as war), popularity and competence of the Opposition (especially their Leader), etc. When former PM Harold Macmillan was asked what was his biggest challenge, he famously replied, 'Events, dear boy, events'. For example, Blair unexpectedly had to delay the 2001 general election because of the foot-and-mouth crisis.

- A Labour Prime Minister used to be subject to additional party constraints, such as the National Executive Committee and annual conference, but these have been increasingly weakened and sidelined under Blair. Also, Labour Shadow Cabinets are elected by fellow Labour MPs, and will expect ministerial offices in a new government – but they can fairly quickly be reshuffled.

To quote former Prime Minister Herbert Asquith: 'The office of the Prime Minister is what its holder chooses and is able to make of it.' This stresses the flexibility of prime ministerial power, but also its limitations.

In sum, to expect or assume either Cabinet government or prime ministerial government, in any literal sense, may be too simplistic. The tasks of modern government are too many for a group of 20 or so busy (and more or less temporary) ministers – never mind one person. Policy-making is a pluralist process, dispersed throughout what Madgwick calls 'the central executive territory' – though the diverse groups of ministers, civil servants, advisers and experts involved may often be directed or even dominated by the Prime Minister. The key problems arising from this process are:

- the secrecy surrounding the policy-making process

- the fear that PM-dominated policy-making may produce unbalanced or ill-judged policies, unchecked by Cabinet or Commons (given the strength of party discipline)

- the fear that policy decisions are made by non-elected, unaccountable groups and individuals

- the perceived decline in ministerial accountability to Parliament and to the voters.

key terms

civil service neutrality

As permanent, non-elected, career officials who serve under successive governments of any party, civil servants should not let political or personal bias influence their work (though they are allowed to vote)

civil service anonymity

Civil servants should not be publicly accountable for the work of the department; the minister in charge is answerable to Parliament and public for government policy and administration, according to the convention of individual ministerial responsibility

■ The civil service

Civil servants are non-elected administrators and officials of the government. There are around 500,000 of them, and they form a hierarchy within each government department. At the top are the higher civil service – the Permanent Secretaries and other 'mandarins' (as they are often called, after the Chinese bureaucrats of old). Their functions include: giving information and policy advice to ministers, preparing policy papers and speeches, keeping the ministers' official diaries and dealing with correspondence, organising and minuting meetings, anticipating parliamentary questions and preparing answers for ministers, consulting with outside interest groups, and running the departments. Further down the ladder are the administrative and clerical officials who administer the policies of government in Whitehall and around the country.

As permanent, non-elected, career officials who serve under successive governments of any party, civil servants are required to be **neutral**, i.e. they should not let political or personal bias influence their work. Civil servants are also not supposed to have policy-making power, although their advice may legitimately influence ministers' decisions. Therefore, civil servants are also meant to be **anonymous**, i.e. not publicly accountable for the work of the department; the minister in charge is answerable to Parliament and the public for government policy and administration, according to the convention of individual ministerial responsibility.

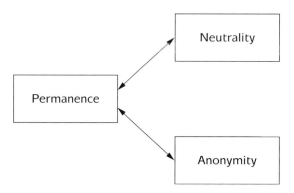

Civil service conventions

The New Right Conservative government under Thatcher sought to 'roll back the frontiers of state' and 'cut the bureaucracy' in accordance with its *laissez-faire* economic philosophy and its wish to cut public spending. Civil service numbers were reduced in the 1980s by over 100,000 (the 'new' Labour government, in 2005, similarly proposed cuts of up to 40,000 civil service jobs).

Also under Thatcher's government, politically sympathetic businessmen and industrialists were brought in to devise ways of making the civil service more efficient and management-minded. For example, Sir Robin Ibbs

key term

executive agencies

Organisations of civil servants, structurally separate from the departments and headed by a chief executive but still, in theory, subject to ministerial responsibility

of ICI introduced the structural separation of the higher civil service – the policy advisers – from the administrators, who were to be devolved into semi-autonomous **executive agencies** headed by chief executives with considerable freedom and flexibility of management. This reform was called 'Next Steps'.

Criticisms of these proposals centred mainly upon fears of loss of political (ministerial) accountability for policy administration.

There has, indeed, been some blurring of the question of political responsibility. One prime example was the 1990s' Conservative Home Secretary Michael Howard who sacked the chief executive of the prison service, Derek Lewis, over a series of prison crises rather than resigning himself, by asserting a novel constitutional distinction between 'policy' and 'operational' decisions. Many other ministers have since followed his example. Under Blair's government, Lord Falconer passed the blame for the Dome to civil servant Jennie Page; Defence Secretary Geoff Hoon blamed his officials for not telling him about reports of prisoner abuse in Iraq; and Commons leader, Peter Hain, blamed police operations rather than policy decisions for the breach of Big Ben's security by Greenpeace protesters in 2004. They all, therefore, successfully resisted pressures to resign. This is, arguably, unconstitutional.

Questions

True or false?

1 Parliament can abolish the monarchy at any time.

2 The monarch, in her personal capacity, is above the law.

3 The modern monarch has no political power.

4 There are approximately 100 members of the government.

5 Some ministers are wholly unelected.

6 The Cabinet has been described as 'the real engine room' of British government.

7 The Prime Minister is not elected as such.

8 The monarch's choice of Prime Minister is based on convention, not law.

9 Assertions of 'prime ministerial government' began in the 1980s with Thatcher.

10 Civil servants should be neutral and therefore cannot vote.

Civil service power and influence

As non-elected officials, civil servants may influence ministers' policy decisions but they should not, in theory, have power themselves. However, critics such as writer Peter Kellner argue that civil servants derive power from many sources, such as:

- their large numbers, compared with ministers

- their permanence, compared with ministers

- their experience and expertise

- their network of inter-departmental committees, which parallels the Cabinet committee network

- their effective control of the administrative processes

- their close involvement in national security and intelligence matters

- their extensive powers of patronage over thousands of titles and appointments which are nominally the responsibility of the PM

- UK membership of the EU, which has necessitated much more preparation and co-ordination of policies by officials.

Sample AS answer

> Distinguish between the power and authority of ministers and civil servants. *(15 marks)*
>
> Power is the ability to do, or make others do, what you want regardless of consent. Authority implies legitimacy based on consent and respect.
>
> Ministers derive their authority from party, Parliament, PM and conventions, which give them the rightful power to make policy decisions and to run their departments. This should be enhanced by their civil servants and political advisers. However, ministers' power and authority may be constrained by backbench revolts (for example, second VAT rise in 1996), the Lords (for example, abolition of the hereditary peers), the courts (for example, *ultra vires* rulings), pressure groups (for example, the farmers), the media (for example, the Blair/Brown 'feud'), by the state of the economy and by international events such as Iraq.
>
> Civil servants in theory have no policy-making power, being permanent, neutral and anonymous Crown servants. However, critics such as Kellner have suggested that they derive power from their sheer numbers, permanence, experience and expertise, patronage and their role on committees and in the EU. This can be bolstered by the secrecy of the UK political system. Civil servants do have legitimate authority to advise and administer policy, deriving from their appointment and promotion by the Prime Minister on the basis of meritocratic examination and assessment. They may lose authority and even be sacked if they are perceived by government as a political challenge, for example Martin Sixsmith.

Politicisation of the civil service

Critical commentators argued that senior officials were 'politicised' under the Thatcher governments to act – against their constitutional neutrality – in support of the Conservative governments of the 1980s. For example: the close involvement of Cabinet Secretary Sir Robert Armstrong in the Westland affair, and in the Spycatcher case where he spoke for the government in the Australian courts and admitted to being 'economical with the truth'; and the unusual degree of personal interest which Mrs Thatcher took in senior official appointments, with her well-known tendency to ask 'Is he one of us?'

Civil service 'politicisation' was hardly an issue under the Major government but unconstitutional behaviour has continued under Labour. Blair in 1997 issued an order in council which gave his top political advisers or 'spin doctors', Alastair Campbell and Jonathan Powell, civil service status 'except those aspects which relate to impartiality and objectivity' – creating a strange new constitutional (or unconstitutional?) hybrid; and he also gave them direct executive power over the civil service – an example of both politicisation of the civil service and of prime ministerial government. Alastair Campbell, Blair's former press spokesman, then wrote to the civil service press officers and told them to 'raise their game' in selling government stories to the media – a threat to both their neutrality and anonymity. In 2001 it was revealed that a civil servant had asked colleagues, on behalf of DTI minister Richard Caborn, 'to find background/dirt to rubbish' political comedian Mark Thomas. As civil service trade union boss Jonathan Baume said, 'It is unacceptable that the civil service is all too often used as a political football.'

Civil service permanence has also come under threat – note the sacking of Sixsmith. Short-term contracts also now abound in the executive agencies, and both main parties propose major future job cuts. The civil service is no longer a job for life. This could further undermine their neutrality, if they are asked to promote party policy, as they may fear for their jobs and feel obliged to comply.

Questions

Quiz

1 List three significant prime ministerial powers.

2 Define 'Cabinet government'.

3 Which constitutional writer asserted that the UK has Cabinet government?

4 Who said that Cabinet has joined the monarch in 'dignified impotence'?

5 List five (policy) examples of prime ministerial government.

6 List five constraints on a Prime Minister.

7 List five factors which may affect the relationship between the Prime Minister and the Cabinet.

8 Suggest three reasons why a Prime Minister might reshuffle his/her ministerial team.

9 Explain Foley's concept of 'a uniquely UK presidency'.

10 In what sense is the UK *not* presidential?

11 To whom is the executive accountable?

12 List the three key conventions which govern the role of civil servants.

13 Why are civil servants required to be neutral?

14 Why are civil servants required to be anonymous?

15 Suggest three reasons why civil service permanence may be declining.

8

Rights and liberties

■ Law, justice and morality

Laws are the rules of state which – unlike conventions – are enforceable in the courts. There are many different types of law, including: EU law, statute law, common law, case law and delegated legislation.

Broadly, all of these types of law fall under one or other of two headings:

● **civil law**, which concerns disputes between individuals or groups in society. The aggrieved individual (or company, etc.) decides whether to take proceedings, and the aim is compensation

● **criminal law**, which concerns offences against society or state, and the aim of proceedings is punishment. The offence may be the same – for example, assault – but under criminal law, the Crown Prosecution Service (CPS) may take action even if the victim does not desire it. The legal processes are different and are often in different types of courts: for example, county courts and the High Court for civil cases, and magistrates' courts and crown courts for criminal cases.

The rule of law

This phrase was coined by the constitutional writer A.V. Dicey (1885). The concept, which seeks to equate law and justice, is said to be central to any constitutional democracy. However, it is best seen as a statement of an ideal (or as a list of ideal principles), to which many legal systems may aspire; but, in the UK and other countries, all of its key principles are often breached in practice.

Principles and breaches of the rule of law

● *Legal equality*: everyone, including government, should be equally subject to the same laws.

   Exceptions: parliamentary sovereignty; the capacity of any UK government, through Parliament, to rewrite the law and even to legalise its own, previously illegal, actions; the legal immunities of diplomats,

MPs, etc; the costs of litigation – 'The law, like the Ritz Hotel, is open to all' (Lord Justice Darling); legal immunity orders (for government and the MI5, for example); internment (imprisonment without charge or trial) of foreign terror suspects.

- ***Legal certainty**:* there should be a clear statement of people's rights and duties under the law.

  Exceptions: the sheer quantity and complexity of law; retrospective (backdated) law – for example, a retrospective increase in the penalty for terrorist hoaxes from six months to seven years (2001) and the retrospective abolition of the double jeopardy rule (2003).

- ***Just law**:* justice should be an end in itself, with no arbitrary law or government. There should be fair, consistent and open court procedures.

  Exceptions: inconsistent sentencing – for example, a life sentence for one rapist and a £500 fine for another within the same month in 2004; secret trials proposed for terror suspects; internment of foreign terror suspects; alleged police bias – for example, in racial cases such as Stephen Lawrence.

- ***Innocent until proven guilty**:* no one should be subject to legal penalty unless she or he has broken the law.

  Exceptions: internment; remand before trial; effective removal of the right to silence in the Criminal Justice Act 1994; 'trial by media' – for example, the *Daily Mail* (1997) printing the names and pictures of five unconvicted men as 'murderers' of black teenager Stephen Lawrence; the 'sus' laws (laws of suspicion) under which a person may be convicted and imprisoned simply for being suspected of being likely to commit a future crime.

- There should be an **independent and impartial judiciary**.

  Exceptions: lack of separation of powers – for example, the Law Lords; political patronage in judicial appointments; alleged judicial bias – for example, the serious miscarriages of justice in the 'numbers cases' of the 1980s where the 'Guildford Four' and 'Birmingham Six' were wrongly imprisoned for up to 17 years; and Lord Hutton's inquiry into the death of Iraq weapons inspector Dr Kelly which, said critics, 'whitewashed' the government.

Something is 'legal' if it is in accordance with the law of the land; whereas something is 'just' if it is deemed fair and equitable. The idea of the rule of law seeks to equate law and justice, but sometimes the law may be regarded as unjust: for example, the poll tax, legal immunities of diplomats, legal tax avoidance, retrospective (backdated) law, internment , the high costs of litigation, etc. Conversely, an action may be seen as 'just', though illegal: for example, personal retribution – 'an eye for an eye'; breaking the law to prevent a greater crime; the Robin Hood principle (stealing from the rich to give to the poor); illegal political protest,

The Birmingham Six

for example, cannabis 'smoke-ins' in Hyde Park; 'just' violence against an 'unjust' state (one man's 'terrorist' is another man's 'freedom fighter'), etc.

Similarly, an action that is deemed 'moral' – ethically right and proper – may be illegal: such as 'draft-dodging' (refusing conscription into the army, for example on religious grounds); anti-nuclear protests such as trespassing in nuclear bases; euthanasia ('mercy killing'); Sikhs refusing to wear motor-cycle helmets in place of their turbans, etc. Or an 'immoral' action may be legal: for example, suicide, adultery, divorce or abortion.

The Robin Hood principle

analyse
this

All three concepts – law, justice and morality – are subjective; even whether an action is legal or illegal is often a matter of debate between senior judges, as the divisions among the Law Lords over the extradition of Chile's former dictator General Pinochet (1998) demonstrated. However, perceived conflicts between law, justice and morality are sometimes used to justify civil disobedience: deliberate, peaceful law-breaking as an act of public, political protest. Some examples are: public refusals to pay the poll tax and council tax; cannabis 'smoke-ins' in Hyde Park; the obstruction by the pressure group Greenpeace of nuclear waste discharges into the North Sea, its occupation of the Brent Spar oil platform and its 2004 protest on Big Ben against the invasion of Iraq; the freeing of animals from research laboratories by the Animal Liberation Front; the Newbury bypass protesters; anti-capitalist demonstrators; and anti-Bush demonstrators in 2003. In 2004, two men from Fathers4Justice threw purple flour bombs at the Prime Minister from the public gallery in the Commons during PMQT. Finally, thousands of fox hunters say that they will defy the law when hunting is banned in England.

A fox hunt

1 Find (in the media) further recent examples of civil disobedience by pressure groups or individuals.

2 What arguments were used to justify the action in each case?

3 List three general arguments for, and three arguments against, civil disobedience.

■ **The courts**

The civil and criminal courts in England and Wales are summarised in the diagram below.

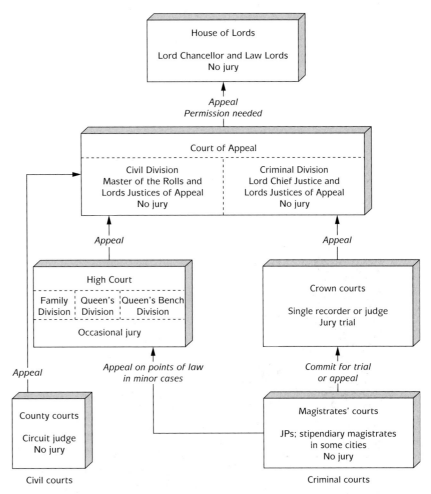

The civil and criminal courts in England and Wales

Besides the UK courts, the UK is a member of two separate European courts:

● ***the European Court of Justice (ECJ) at Luxembourg***: this enforces European Union law, for example on the world-wide beef ban, the 48-hour maximum working week, against the UK's discriminatory retirement ages for men and women, pollution of UK beaches, etc.

● ***the European Court of Human Rights (ECHR) at Strasbourg***: this is *nothing* to do with the EU. It pre-dates the creation of the EU. It enforces the 1950 European Convention for the Protection of Human Rights, ratified by 40 countries including the UK. However, its rulings are not formally binding in the way that EU law is: for example, in

1990 the ECHR ruled illegal the detention without charge of three men for over four days under the UK Prevention of Terrorism Act; but the UK government said that it would simply ignore the ruling.

The ECHR has ruled against UK governments on phone tapping by government agencies, corporal punishment in state schools, torture of prisoners in Northern Ireland, press censorship, discrimination against women, gays and ethnic minorities, and many other matters. In April 2002, the ECHR refused to allow Diane Pretty's husband the legal right to help her to die. In 2004, the court ruled that the UK's blanket ban on votes for prisoners was a breach of free elections, free expression and anti-discrimination laws. UK governments have lost more cases at Strasbourg than have any other governments, largely because, until 2000, the UK had no domestic Bill of Rights and did not enforce the European Convention in its own courts; and also because much UK government action is still based simply on convention rather than on law.

However, the Labour government enshrined the European Convention into UK law as the Human Rights Act 1998, and it took effect in the year 2000. This has reduced the number of UK cases which go all the way to the ECHR.

The courts and Parliament

Parliament is sovereign; the UK courts therefore cannot challenge or veto the law of Parliament; they can only interpret and enforce statute law as it is written.

However, EU law takes precedence over UK law and, where they conflict, UK courts are required to enforce EU law. This was established by the Factortame case of 1990 (about the rights of Spanish trawlers to fish in UK waters, contrary to the UK Merchant Shipping Act 1988). Parliament remains technically sovereign in that it could pass a law expressly overriding European law or, indeed, it could withdraw from the EU altogether – but this is unlikely in practice.

Secondly, Parliament's law may be unclear or ambiguous; in a test case, the judges must interpret the law precisely, which can allow a very 'creative' judicial role amounting effectively to 'law-making' by the judges. This is called **case law**. In 2004, for example, the UK courts gave some protection to the model Naomi Campbell's right to privacy, and to the right of anonymity for Maxine Carr (former girlfriend of Soham murderer Ian Huntley). The courts and Parliament may clash when the courts interpret a statute in a way which Parliament did not intend. Parliament may then, of course, rewrite the law; it can thus 'legalise illegality' or set aside court decisions.

The new UK Bill of Rights (Human Rights Act) has undoubtedly extended the role of the UK judges; but it expressly maintains the principle of parliamentary sovereignty and says that the judges cannot set aside parliamentary statutes when they conflict with the Human Rights Act; the judges can only point out such conflicts and leave it for Parliament to

key term

case law

Judicial interpretation of the law in test cases which sets a precedent for future, similar cases

resolve them, or not. In other words, the UK Human Rights Act has no superior status – it is not entrenched in the way that the American Bill of Rights is.

The courts and the executive

Administrative law is the whole package of laws which apply to government and other public bodies. There is no distinct body of administrative law or courts in the UK (unlike France, for example). However, the ordinary courts may hear civil or criminal actions against central or local government members or departments. They may declare the orders or actions of a minister or department to be *ultra vires*, i.e. beyond their legal powers – either because of what was done or because of the way in which it was done.

Court rulings against governments – **judicial review** or *ultra vires* – have risen in the UK from under 1,000 per year in the 1980s to around 5,000 per year now. Examples of UK court rulings against Labour since 1997 are: the *domestic* ban of beef (not to be confused with the EU case); against the secret extension of GM crop research; and against NHS restrictions on the prescription of Viagra. The Home Office has repeatedly been ruled illegal over the denial of accommodation and basic subsistence to destitute asylum seekers. In 2004, the courts ordered the Home Secretary to release a Libyan Belmarsh internee (known only as 'M'); and then to place another internee (known as 'G') under house arrest – a decision which then Home Secretary David Blunkett controversially described as 'bonkers'. The Law Lords then ruled that the internment of foreign terror suspects generally was contrary to both UK and European human rights laws.

However, any central government usually has a majority in a sovereign Parliament. Therefore, if it is ruled illegal by the courts, it may use Parliament to rewrite the law and so legalise itself. The government may even backdate the rewritten law so that the government was never technically illegal – so-called 'retrospective law'.

Retrospective law may also apply to ordinary citizens. In 1998, retrospective government legislation stopped tax exemption for overseas earners (which prompted the Rolling Stones to cancel their UK tour). After 11 September 2001, the government hastily imposed a retrospective increase in the penalty for terrorist hoaxes from six months to seven years. They also abolished the double jeopardy rule, to take effect retrospectively.

The courts' control of central government is therefore limited, and is bound up with the issue of parliamentary sovereignty. It is also debatable how far non-elected and, arguably, unrepresentative judges *should* control 'democratic' public bodies.

Nevertheless, such cases of judicial review continue to rise: perhaps because the judges are less 'executive-minded' nowadays; or because citizens are increasingly aware of their legal rights against government; or, perhaps, because governments are increasingly careless about obeying the letter of the law.

key
terms

administrative law

The law as applied to executive and administrative bodies, especially government

judicial review

Court rulings on government policies and actions

Question

What are the main features of judicial review in the UK, and how effective is the process? *(20 marks)*

key terms

judicial independence

The freedom of judges from the influence of the executive or legislative branches of the state

judicial neutrality

The absence of political or personal bias amongst judges

■ The judges

There is a hierarchy of judges in UK courts, from magistrates or Justices of the Peace (JPs) who are lay-people rather than trained lawyers, through recorders (part-time judges) and judges in the crown courts, up to the most senior judges (Law Lords) in the House of Lords.

The independence and impartiality of the judiciary

According to the rule of law, justice should be an end in itself, and judges should not be subject to political pressure from the legislature or executive, nor should they be partial or prejudiced in their interpretation or enforcement of the law.

To these ends, there are certain rules and principles in the UK legal system:

- The judiciary should be separate from the other branches of government, in accordance with Montesquieu's principle of the 'separation of powers'.

- Judicial appointments should be based on merit, not on political patronage.

Question

Explain the difference between judicial independence and judicial neutrality. *(5 marks)*

A UK judge

- Senior judges have security of tenure: under the Act of Settlement 1701, they can only be removed from their jobs by a vote in both Houses of Parliament (which has never yet happened).

- Judges receive salaries which are fixed by a formula and are not subject to political debate in Parliament.

- Judges' decisions should not be questioned in Parliament.

- Judges' remarks in court (like those of lawyers, witnesses and jury members) are not liable to legal actions for damages.

However, many commentators, such as Griffith, question how far judges are, or can be, 'non-political'. This concept has at least four dimensions: separation of powers; freedom from external political pressure; lack of personal or political prejudice; and lack of involvement in any political role.

Judges are often said to be unavoidably 'political', in one sense or another, for the following reasons:

- Judges' social background – top judges are 97 per cent male, public school and Oxbridge educated – their above-average age, and the nature of their legal training (still steeped in nineteenth-century Victorian values) may combine to foster a conservative, if not Conservative (i.e. party political), outlook. Judges' comments especially on class, race and gender have often caused controversy. In 1998 the government declared that new judges (as well as police and prison officers) must declare Freemasonry membership. On the issue of personal interest or bias, there was an unprecedented case in 1998 where the Law Lords overturned their own previous ruling in favour of the extradition of former Chilean dictator General Pinochet for war crimes, because of the undeclared connection of one of the Law Lords, Lord Hoffman, with a relevant pressure group, Amnesty International.

- Overlaps between judiciary, legislature and executive: for example, the Law Lords – and, for centuries, the office of Lord Chancellor. Former Labour Lord Chancellor Lord Irvine was involved in controversy in 2001 when he asked Labour-supporting lawyers to donate £200 or more to the party – the so-called 'cash for wigs' affair – since he was in a position to promote the lawyers to judicial posts (or not). Importantly, however, the government is in the process of abolishing the office of Lord Chancellor, creating an independent commission for recommending appointments of senior judges, and establishing what they call a separate 'supreme court' (which simply means removing the Law Lords from the House of Lords). This will enhance judicial independence to some extent.

- 'Judges are part of the machinery of authority within the state and as such cannot avoid the making of political decisions.' (Griffith) Also as 'part of the state', judges may have a particular view of the 'national interest'; in cases of dispute between state and citizen, they may 'show themselves more executive-minded than the executive' (Lord Atkin) – especially on issues of national security and official secrecy such as the banning of trade unions for some civil servants in the 1980s, and also in key industrial disputes such as the 1984/5 miners' strike.

- Judges must review executive actions under administrative law – an unavoidably 'political' role whichever way they rule – for example, the Labour government being ruled illegal over internment in 2004.

- The Law Lords have also been given the politically fraught task of ruling on any conflicts between the Scottish and Westminster Parliaments.

- Commissions of inquiry are appointed by the Prime Minister and usually headed by senior judges (for example, the Scott Inquiry into arms to Iraq, Macpherson Inquiry into the Stephen Lawrence affair, Hutton Inquiry into the death of Dr Kelly, etc.). Whatever their findings, they will be perceived as political.

- Judges must enforce parliamentary statutes which sometimes seem overtly party political: for example, the anti-trades union laws of the 1980s and 1990s, the council tax capping legislation, etc.

- Marxists such as Ralph Miliband argue that the whole legal system in a capitalist country like the UK is necessarily class-based, and that judges are – unavoidably – part of the political 'superstructure' which protects private property and profits for a minority bourgeois (capitalist) ruling class.

The 'political' nature of the judiciary, in the broad sense, is both enhanced and highlighted by the 'judicial creativity' of case law. For example, in 2000, the Appeal Court ruled that the force-feeding of Moors murderer Ian Brady should continue, against his wish to die; and also that an operation to separate Siamese twins should go ahead although it would mean the certain death of one twin to save the other. In 2004 the courts, controversially, granted Maxine Carr (former girlfriend of the Soham girls' killer Ian Huntley) the right to keep her public identity secret for life; and the terminally ill Diane Pretty lost her appeal to the Lords on allowing her husband to help her to die. All significant examples of judicial review – court rulings on government policies – are also 'political' case law.

The other side of the coin of judicial 'independence' is judicial unaccountability. Election of judges, either by the general public or by an electoral college of lawyers, is therefore sometimes suggested. Note, however, that this would very likely make judges more, rather than less, political. Appointment by a genuinely independent commission is, perhaps, preferable.

key terms

rights

Entitlements, for example to some kind of freedom or equality or security

natural rights

Those rights to which, according to some philosophers, everyone is entitled simply by being human

civil rights

Those rights granted to citizens in law by a particular state

■ Civil rights and freedoms

Rights are entitlements – for example, to some kind of freedom or equality. **Natural rights** are those to which, according to some philosophers, everyone is entitled simply by being human; **civil rights** are those granted to citizens in law by a particular state or government, and they may differ widely from one society to another.

Different political ideologies adopt different views on rights and freedoms. Liberals tend to stress positive individual rights and freedoms which should be enhanced by state action if necessary – for example, the right to own private property, and the freedom from sexual or racial discrimination, protected by law. Socialists tend to stress collective rights (such as the freedom of assembly, or of industrial action for trade unions), and economic, political or social equalities (such as the right to employment, housing and a decent standard of living); and socialists are (more or less) opposed to private property.

Freedom and equality may conflict; for example, the freedom to choose between private or public health and education (a liberal tenet) may conflict with the goal of equal access to health care and equal educational opportunities (a socialist tenet). Similarly, progressive taxation in pursuit of greater economic equality or welfare (which means that wealthy people pay more income tax than poor people) may conflict with the freedom of individuals to spend their own money as they wish.

Conflict may also arise between individual and collective freedoms: for example, the collective right to strike against the individual's right to strike-break was a source of acute conflict within mining families and communities during the bitter 1984–5 coal dispute.

Law, by its nature, may both enhance and constrain freedom: for example, it may protect the individual against violence, theft or discrimination, but it also limits individual freedom of action in those spheres. Is discrimination – sexual, religious, racial, ageist or fattist – an individual right or a social wrong?

Some laws in the UK are often seen as excessive constraints on individual or collective freedoms, and this view is sometimes used to justify civil disobedience. For example, the Police Act 1997 gave the police extensive powers to enter private premises, plant bugs, inspect files, etc. with no external authorisation; and the 1998 anti-terrorism laws allow individuals to be convicted of belonging to terrorist organisations purely on the

talking point

The 1984–5 coal miners' strike tore many families apart. Hundreds of couples divorced because striking miners were no longer earning a wage and could not support their families; fathers and sons – or even brothers – were sometimes on opposite sides of the dispute; and, when some strikers gave in and went back to work earlier than others, they were shunned by their communities, sometimes for years.

opinion of a single police officer. The Terrorism Act 2001 allowed some foreign nationals to be detained indefinitely without any charge or trial and by 2005 some had been interned for three years. The UK is the only country to have opted out of part of the European Convention on Human Rights in order to introduce these measures. Even the Conservatives – usually strong law and order advocates – described this law as 'needless totalitarianism'. The policy was eventually ruled illegal. Labour Prime Minister Blair and Home Secretary Charles Clarke are also pressing ahead with compulsory national identity cards despite substantial Cabinet, parliamentary and public opposition.

talking point

Source: www.bbc.co.uk 2005

Compulsory national identity cards: What are the arguments?

For identity cards

The government and supporters of the scheme argue that identity cards are important because they believe they will:

- **prevent illegal immigration:** Lack of a card allows illegal immigrants to arrive and disappear
- **prevent illegal working:** They give employers a secure way of knowing if people are actually allowed to work. It'll be easier to prosecute employers who break the law
- **aid anti-terrorism measures:** It'll be harder for terrorists and organised crime rings to use false and multiple identities
- **tackle identity theft:** They'll help protect against identity theft
- **reduce benefit fraud and abuse of public services:** They will ensure that public services are only used by those entitled
- **enhance sense of community:** ID cards will create a sense of shared citizenship and belonging.

Against identity cards

Opponents say that identity cards won't improve security. They will:

- **worsen harassment of ethnic minorities:** They'll provide another pretext for stop-and-search, often directed at ethnic minorities
- **have little impact on counter-terrorism:** Sophisticated terror networks would soon be able to produce counterfeit cards or papers enabling people to get legitimate cards
- **have little effect on illegal working:** Employers who are already willing to break the law won't be put off by identity cards
- **lead to 'function creep':** The functions of the card will grow over time as it stores more personal information. More people could demand to see it, effectively making it compulsory to carry one
- **lead to loss of privacy:** There will be a massive database containing an unprecedented amount of personal information on people
- **be costly and impractical:** There is scepticism about the cost and operability of the scheme, as well as the government's ability to manage the technology.

analyse
this

Consider the following list of rights and freedoms.

➡ The right to life

➡ The right to death

➡ Freedom of assembly

➡ Freedom of movement

➡ The right to strike

➡ Freedom of speech

➡ Freedom of information

➡ Freedom of the media

➡ The right to privacy

➡ Freedom of religious conscience

➡ Freedom from arbitrary arrest or imprisonment

➡ Freedom from discrimination

➡ Legal equality

➡ Political equality

➡ Equal educational opportunities

➡ The right to work

➡ The right to housing.

Note: Consider, for example, the laws or practices on:

> murder; abortion; euthanasia; treason and sedition; libel and slander; official secrets; obscenity and pornography; internment; remand; the 'sus' laws (suspicion); the costs of litigation; race relations and religious, sexual and age discrimination; immigration and asylum; political and religious 'extremism'; personal privacy; personal morality; homosexuality; age of consent; the electoral deposit; a minimum wage; conditions of work; trade union membership; picketing; state and public schooling; corporal punishment; unemployment; homelessness; poverty and welfare.

1 For each of the rights and freedoms listed above, can you list some of the limits which currently exist in UK law and practice?

2 What limits, if any, do you think there should be on each, and why?

3 Do some rights conflict with others?

Case against saying that 'judges protect civil liberties'

Examples include: 'numbers cases' prior to release (1970s and 1980s); ban on trade unions at GCHQ (1984); miners' strike cases (1984); government secrecy upheld by judges in Tisdall and Ponting cases (1985); eight men imprisoned for private and consensual acts of sado-masochism (1991); two Rastafarian parents imprisoned for refusing insulin to diabetic daughter on grounds of religious conscience (1993); Lord Chancellor pressured judges to cut employment tribunal appeals in order to save government money (1994). Also: in 1999 an elderly, arthritic cannabis smoker (Eric Mann) was jailed for a year, despite the introduction of medical trials for the use of cannabis in the same year. In 2000, the courts refused Moors murderer Ian Brady's right to die after he had been on a hunger strike and force-fed for four months. In 2001 they refused Diane Pretty's appeal for her husband to be allowed to help her to die. In 2003 the UK courts ruled that evidence obtained through torture in other countries may be admissible.

Case for saying that 'judges protect civil liberties'

Examples include: Labour ruled illegal since 1997 on the domestic ban on beef on the bone, the extension of GM crop research, NHS restrictions on prescription of Viagra, the detention and deportation of some asylum seekers and the arbitrary fining of lorry drivers for carrying stowaways. Also: in 2004, the UK courts gave some protection to the model Naomi Campbell's right to privacy, and to the right of anonymity for Maxine Carr (former girlfriend of Soham murderer Ian Huntley). In the same year, the Law Lords ruled that internment was illegal. In 2005 they upheld a Muslim school pupil's right to wear strict Islamic dress.

Note that these and many other cases may raise complex and conflicting civil liberties issues for all of those involved.

'New' Labour authoritarianism on law and order

'New' Labour has passed 16 Criminal Justice Acts since it came to power in 1997. Examples include: reducing the age of criminal liability and extending abolition of the right to silence to 10-year-olds; curfews for under-10s and electronic tagging of 10-year-olds; the first prison for 12–14-year-olds was opened in Kent in 1998; and the retrospective abolition of the double jeopardy rule. The UK now has more CCTV cameras per head of the population than any other country in the world; and it has a record 140,000 police officers. The prison population is a record 76,000, and female prisoners have increased by 200 per cent since the 1990s. New and draconian anti-terrorism laws were passed in 1998, 2000 and especially 2001. Under these laws, over a dozen foreign 'terror suspects' were detained in the UK for three years without any charge or trial, i.e. internment; and the UK was the only country to have opted out of part of the Convention on Human Rights in order to introduce these measures. The UK government is pressing ahead with compulsory national ID cards despite substantial parliamentary and public opposition.

A Bill of Rights for the UK (the UK Human Rights Act 1998)

In the UK, until the enforcement of a domestic Bill of Rights in 2000, few rights were guaranteed in law; such rights as citizens had tended to be negative, i.e. they were allowed to do something if there was no law against it. The Human Rights Act 1998 incorporated the European Convention on Human Rights into UK law, and it came into force in 2000 after UK judges had undergone relevant training. However, in cases of conflict between the Bill of Rights and ordinary parliamentary statute, the judges are required to enforce statute (to maintain the concept of parliamentary sovereignty); they can only point out any such conflicts to Parliament for possible action (or not). The Bill of Rights also has sweeping exemptions 'In accordance with the law and the necessity for public safety, prevention of disorder or crime, protection of public health or morale or rights and the freedoms of others'. It is therefore much weaker than, for example, the US Bill of Rights – but it has prompted more 'rights awareness' in the drafting of laws, in judicial interpretation of those laws and, increasingly, amongst the general public – and even the politicians.

Question

Argue for and against the incorporation of the Human Rights Act into UK law.   *(20 marks)*

Rights under the European Convention on Human Rights

Rights under the European Convention on Human Rights are covered in the following conventions and protocols.

Conventions

- Article 2: Right to life
- Article 3: Freedom from torture or inhuman or degrading treatment or punishment
- Article 4: Freedom from slavery or forced labour
- Article 5: Right to liberty and security of person
- Article 6: Right to a fair trial by an impartial tribunal
- Article 7: Freedom from retroactive criminal laws

- Article 8: Right to respect for private and family life, home and correspondence
- Article 9: Freedom of thought, conscience and religion
- Article 10: Freedom of expression
- Article 11: Freedom of peaceful assembly and association, including the right to join a trade union
- Article 12: Right to marry and found a family
- Article 13: Right to an effective remedy before a national authority
- Article 14: Freedom from discrimination

Protocol 1

- Article 1: Right to a peaceful enjoyment of possessions
- Article 2: Right to education; and to education in conformity with religious and philosophical convictions
- Article 3: Right to take part in free elections by secret ballot

Protocol 2

- Article 1: Freedom from imprisonment for debt
- Article 2: Freedom of movement of persons
- Article 3: Right to enter and stay in one's country
- Article 4: Freedom from collective expulsion

UK cases heard by the European Court of Human Rights have included:

- illegal imprisonment of poll tax non-payers
- corporal punishment in state schools
- press censorship – for example, in the *Sunday Times* thalidomide drug story and the Spycatcher cases
- phone tapping by government agencies
- retrospective seizure of drug dealers' assets
- prisoners' conditions and treatment in the UK and torture of prisoners in Northern Ireland
- birching of criminal offenders in the Isle of Man
- discrimination against homosexuals in Northern Ireland
- discrimination against women, ethnic minorities and immigrants
- the rights of workers against closed shops.

Question

To what extent are civil liberties protected in the UK?　　*(30 marks)*

talking point

- **Corporal punishment** refers to the beating of students (which is, incidentally, still allowed in some UK private schools, although the ECHR has banned it from all state schools).

- **Capital punishment** means the death sentence. Students often confuse these terms in exam answers!

Questions

True or false?

1 The UK courts can rule Parliament illegal.

2 The UK courts can rule government illegal.

3 Parliament can backdate the enforcement of a new law to take effect before it was actually passed.

4 Parliamentary sovereignty is, itself, merely a convention.

5 Parliamentary privilege means that MPs have certain legal immunities.

6 The European Court of Human Rights is the court of the European Union.

7 A government minister appoints the top judges.

8 Attempting suicide is illegal.

9 The prosecution always opens a court case.

10 A unanimous decision by the jury is necessary for a guilty verdict.

9

Local government and devolution

■ Local government

Local government entails the election of local people to run local services such as education, housing, rubbish collection, social services, planning and transport, leisure and recreation, police, etc. The structure of local government in the UK is a little bit complicated and, at the same time, local councils do not have very much real power in the UK's centralised system. These two points help to explain why voter turnout for local elections is usually low.

Local government is a mixture of single-tier and two-tier local authorities. It has been reorganised frequently by central governments through parliamentary statutes over the last 40 years – partly in a search for greater efficiency and accountability, but also sometimes for less laudable motives of party interest and political control.

The structures and major functions of local government

There are almost 500 local councils or 'authorities' in the UK, which have two main structures: single-tier and two-tier systems. This situation is further confused because of the wide range of names that these councils can have.

The single-tier system
The single-tier system exists in all of Scotland, Wales, Northern Ireland and parts of England. It means that one all-purpose council has responsibility for all local authority functions. It includes:

- unitary councils, such as Bristol City Council

- metropolitan councils, such as Birmingham City Council

- the 33 London boroughs, such as the London Borough of Lewisham.

Single-tier, or unitary, councils can be given different names such as county borough councils, county councils or city councils, but they are all the same thing.

The two-tier system

The rest of England, covering mostly rural areas, has a two-tier system with responsibilities divided between large county and smaller district councils. There are 34 large county councils, such as Buckinghamshire County Council, and 238 smaller district councils, such as Aylesbury Vale District Council.

Again, county and district councils can have different names. Some district councils, for example, are called city councils. Small wonder that voters get confused.

Parish and community councils

In addition to unitary, county and district councils, local areas are also represented by parish and community councils. These cover very small areas and do not have much formal political power, but they can be quite influential at a very local level.

The main areas of responsibility for local government

The list below gives the main areas of responsibility for each type of council. Some of the responsibilities may overlap, with housing being under a county council in one area and a district council in another.

Unitary (single-tier) councils

- Social services
- Education
- Housing
- Libraries
- Transport (except the London boroughs)
- Planning applications and development
- Leisure, recreation and the arts
- Environmental health
- Highways
- Waste collection
- Revenue collection

Two-tier councils

County councils

- Social services
- Education

- Libraries
- Transport (public and planning)
- Leisure, recreation and the arts
- Highways
- Fire and emergency services
- Refuse disposal

District councils

- Housing
- Planning applications and development
- Leisure, recreation and the arts
- Environmental health
- Waste collection
- Revenue collection

Parish, community and town councils

- Community centres
- Allotments
- Cemeteries and churchyards
- Clocks
- Commons, open spaces and playing fields
- Street lighting
- Litter
- Parking places

- Public lavatories

- Road verges

- Seats, shelters and signs

Police and fire services are run separately – but they do have local councillors on their governing bodies and their civilian employees are often employed by one of the nearby local councils.

The Greater London Authority (created in 2000) is responsible for London-wide strategic issues such as transport, but day-to-day services are still run by the local borough councils.

talking point

Why go to your local council?

Councils are responsible for a wide range of services covering many areas of local life, from education and housing to local planning. So for lots of problems and issues, your council is the place to go for help.

You should contact your council or your councillor if you want to:

- Influence council decisions

- try to reverse decisions that have already been made

- access services

- complain about services

- seek council support or permission for an event.

Ways to get in touch

Write to your councillor
This is the most common way of contacting councillors. Make sure you plan your letter carefully, clearly setting out your argument. Research your councillors and see if you can take advantage of any special interests they may have. You can get the letter to them by addressing it care of the council headquarters, or you can send it to their home addresses.

Councillors' surgeries
All councillors have a duty to represent the people who live in their local areas or 'wards'. Many hold 'surgeries' on a regular basis, when people can come to discuss local issues. Again, you will be able to get details of surgeries from your council and probably from their website.

Council meetings
All council meetings are open to the public unless they are classed as 'exceptional'. All council cabinet meetings where important decisions are due to be made must be held in public. You may be able to speak at some of these meetings and you should consult your council about which meetings are open to the public and which you can speak at. Quite often this information is available on council websites or you can contact the committee clerk. Members of the public have no automatic speaking rights at council meetings. You

talking point

will have to ask for leave to speak in advance from your council committee services section.

A local council meeting

Public question time
Many councils hold a public question time. This is a forum where any member of the public can ask questions of those councillors who make any decisions. They are generally held every few months and the details of each session will be advertised beforehand.

Public consultations
Public consultations are carried out by councils to consider the views of the local community. If the planning and decision-making process for your particular issue is at an early stage, this is a very useful way of airing your views.

There are currently around 20,000 county, district and borough councillors. They are elected for fixed four-year terms to small local areas known as 'wards' (rather than 'constituencies', which MPs represent). In London, all borough seats are contested together every four years. In the 36 metropolitan (big city) boroughs, one-third of the seats are contested each year, with county council elections in the fourth year. The non-metropolitan district and unitary councils choose either method!

Councillors are part-time and are paid expenses and attendance allowances only; they therefore tend not to be socially typical of the electorate, many of whom lack the time or money for local political involvement. Only around 25 per cent of councillors are women. (However, this is higher than the 19 per cent of women MPs at Westminster.) Councillors are usually party political like MPs, but there are many more independents (around 15 per cent), and there are many 'hung' councils where no single party has an absolute majority.

The table below shows the results of the 2004 local government elections, where 166 (out of about 500) councils were up for election. It illustrates how pluralist local government is, compared with Westminster.

These were the worst local election results in Labour's recent history; they slipped to third place in terms of share of the vote – the first time a governing party has ever done so in local elections. They took place on the same day – 'Super Thursday' (10 June 2004) – as the elections for the European Parliament, where both main UK parties did badly. However,

2004 local government elections (166 councils)

Party	Councillors			Councils		
	Gain	Lose	Total	Gain	Lose	Control
Conservative	339	56	1,714	13	0	51
Labour	84	563	2,250	7	15	39
Liberal Democrat	248	111	1,283	2	4	9
Plaid Cymru (PC)	17	45	172	0	2	1
Residents Association (RA)	17	3	37	0	0	1
Green Party	10	1	24	0	0	0
Liberal Party	2	2	20	0	0	0
British National Party (BNP)	7	3	13	0	0	0
Independent Kidderminster Hospital and Health Concern (IKHH)	0	8	8	0	0	0
UK Independence Party (UKIP)	2	3	2	0	0	0
Other	104	95	556	0	2	3
No overall control	0	0	0	17	16	62

Small earthquake

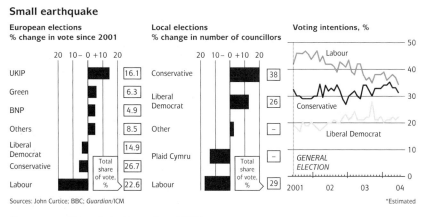

Sources: John Curtice; BBC; *Guardian*/ICM

European and local elections, June 2004

Source: *The Economist*, 14 June 2004

Question

What are the functions and powers of a local councillor? *(15 marks)*
How do they differ from those of an MP?

local and European elections provide the electorate with a chance to cast a 'protest vote' (often for minority parties, especially in PR electoral systems) which largely evaporates when it comes to the general election.

Local government is advised and administered by appointed officials who are full-time, paid and permanent. As with the central civil service, the distinction between advice, administration and policy-making between politicians and civil servants may be blurred, and the local officials are sometimes accused of having power without public accountability. The issue of 'politicisation' of these officials is, perhaps, even stronger at local than at national level.

Local government finance

Local government spending (for example, on building and running schools, council housing, roads, and providing services like homes for the elderly, parks and gardens, plus the administrative costs of local government itself) totals around £40 billion – nearly 10 per cent of all UK public expenditure.

Capital spending – for example, on new roads – is financed by borrowing from central government and banks, etc., and by selling assets such as land.

Revenue (day-to-day running costs, wages, etc.) is financed by:

- *grants from central government*: these have increased to provide over 60 per cent of local revenue, together with increasing central control of the council tax system (see below)

- *public payments for services*: for example, council house rents

- *local taxation*: until 1989–90, local rates were levied on business and domestic properties. These were replaced (by Thatcher's Conservative government) by the community charge or 'poll tax' – a flat-rate charge paid by every adult, unconnected with property or income. This measure was highly controversial because it was unrelated to voters' ability to pay. It sparked a widespread campaign of civil disobedience (illegal non-payment), culminating in a violent anti-poll tax demonstration in London in 1990. It was one of the issues that helped to bring down Margaret Thatcher as Prime Minister in 1990; and her successor, John Major, was quick to replace the poll tax with a banded property tax per household – the 'council tax'.

Like the poll tax, the council tax may be 'capped', i.e. central government can impose a ceiling on the maximum levied by each local council, which contradicts the principle of local responsibility and accountability for spending levels. This also undermines the mandate of local authorities, and some councillors have said that, if capped, they could not then afford to provide mandatory (compulsory) local services. Capping is also perceived by critics as being motivated by party politics.

In the face of well-publicised pensioners' protests against the council tax, the Labour government is reviewing the system. It is even considering the Liberal Democrats' alternative proposal of a local income tax system.

● **uniform business rate**: this has replaced business rates, which have been removed from local authority control. The uniform business rate is centrally fixed and collected, then redistributed to local councils in the form of grants. There is, therefore, still a strong element of central financial control.

Controls on local government

● **Parliament**: local authorities are created by statute, and all powers must be granted by law.

Royal Borough funding of total expenditure 2004–5

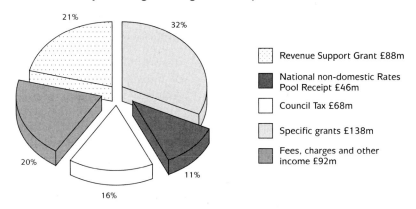

Royal Borough total net expenditure 2004–05

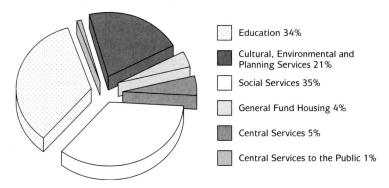

Local government finance – an example

Source: Royal Borough of Kensington and Chelsea, 2004/2005

- **Courts**: just as with central government, the courts may rule local authorities *ultra vires*, i.e. acting beyond their legal powers.

- **Local quangos**, such as the (unelected) Regional Development Agencies, which are given resources and powers by central government, diverted from or in competition with elected local authorities.

- **Central government**: intervenes to control overall public spending – hence, for example, compulsory competitive tendering of some local services (this means that local councils are legally obliged to invite and accept competitive bids from private companies for the running of public services such as rubbish collection). This is also to ensure consistency of standards across the country, for eample in education; and to co-ordinate local functions such as planning. Methods include:

  - financial control: grants, audits, capping, powers of veto over capital spending projects, etc.

  - ministerial approval – required in many policy areas, such as education

  - inspection by the relevant central department – for example, police, fire, education

  - appeals against local authority action – for example, to the Environment Secretary against planning decisions

  - inquiries set up by central government into local councils

  - the Commissioners for Local Administration – three local ombudsmen established in 1972 – who investigate public complaints of maladministration against local authorities

  - removal of local authorities' specific powers – 'default' – or, through parliamentary legislation, whole local authorities can themselves be abolished.

Dame Shirley Porter

It may be argued that all of this undermines local democracy and the mandate of local authorities. However, local elections are often about national parties, policies and issues; and the voter turnout is usually low – around 30–40 per cent – perhaps, of course, precisely because local councils are seen as weak and insignificant. Local government may be even more prone to sleaze and corruption than central government and, therefore, in need of strict external control. For example, in the 1980s, Westminster council was embroiled in the 'homes for votes' scandal: this involved the targeting of council house sales to increase potential Conservative voters in key marginal areas, at a cost to the public purse of over £20 million. The district auditor in his report condemned the policy as 'disgraceful and unlawful gerrymandering'. Protracted legal proceedings followed, until 2004, when the former Conservative Westminster council leader, Dame Shirley Porter, finally paid £12 million of her substantial personal wealth in partial settlement of the dispute.

analyse
this

'Gerrymandering' usually means the redrawing of constituency boundaries for party political advantage. (The word comes from a corrupt nineteenth-century US governor, Elbridge Gerry, who created an electoral district shaped like a salamander, where his voters were located in the tail.)

Former electoral district	New electoral district

1 Explain the term 'gerrymandering'.

2 Since UK local councils do not have the power to reshape voting boundaries, what did the Westminster council do instead?

3 Under 1980s' statute law, local councillors can be 'surcharged' – that is, they can be held personally responsible for the financial losses of their councils through corruption or incompetence. Thus they must repay those losses from their own pockets. Do you think that MPs and government ministers should have the same personal, financial liabilities? Why/not?

London

The 1997 Labour government promised to introduce an elected London council and mayor and, in 1998, a local, single-question referendum on this proposal produced a two-thirds majority in favour. The nature of the referendum was, however, controversial because many voters wanted a council but not a mayor, or vice versa, but they were not given the choice. Voter turnout was only 34 per cent. The new Greater London Authority (GLA) was the first local council to be elected (in 2000) on a system of proportional representation (AMS).

In the first process of selecting a London mayoral candidate, Labour tried unsuccessfully to exclude the left-wing candidate Ken Livingstone – a

2004 GLA elections

Party	No. of seats	Change from 2000
Conservative	9 seats (all constituency)	0
Labour	7 seats (5 constituency and 2 top-up)	-2
Liberal Democrat	5 seats (all top-up)	+1
Green	2 seats (all top-up)	-1
UKIP	2 seats (all top-up)	+2

move widely criticised as a 'stitch up'. Meanwhile, the Conservatives' chosen candidate, Jeffrey Archer, was forced to stand down when he was charged and then jailed for perjury and perverting the course of justice. Steven Norris was chosen instead.

Ken Livingstone quit the Labour Party and won the mayoral election as an independent candidate. By 2004, he looked very likely to win again, so Labour took him back into the party and ditched their own previous candidate. Opposition parties criticised both Labour and Livingstone for being opportunist rather than principled. It suited Labour to back a winner (when they were doing badly in other elections at the same time) and it suited Livingstone to have the political and financial support of central government for the next four years. Sure enough, he won 36 per cent of first preference votes – 11 per cent higher than Labour's score in the London assembly election – and he won a clear majority on second preferences.

London's mayoral election results, 2004

Name	Party	1st pref-erence votes	%	2nd pref-erence votes	%	Final votes
Livingstone	Labour	685,541	35.7	250,517	13	828,380
Norris	Conservative	542,423	28.2	222,559	11.6	667,178
Hughes	Liberal Democrat	284,645	14.8	465,704	24.3	n/a
Maloney	UKIP	115,665	6	193,157	10	n/a
German	Respect	61,731	6.2	63,294	3.3	n/a
Leppert	BNP	58,405	3	70,736	3.7	n/a
Johnson	Green	57,331	2.9	208,686	10.9	n/a
Gidoomal	Christian People's Alliance (CPA)	41,696	2.2	56,721	2.9	n/a
Reid	International Working Class Action (IWCA)	9,542	0.5	39,678	2.1	n/a
Nagalingam	Independent	6,692	0.4	20,391	1.1	n/a

Note: Second preference votes are only used to elect the mayor if no single candidate receives more than 50 per cent of the vote. The top two candidates then receive the second preference votes from their eliminated opponents.

Ken Livingstone

analyse
this

What a difference a mayor makes

Who cares about local politics?

Few people now recognise the legitimacy of local government, much less stand as councillors or bother to vote in elections. Britain has the lowest election turnouts in the European Union in local elections. Liverpool City Council holds the unenviable record for the lowest election turnout when just 6 per cent bothered to vote in a 1996 by-election. According to the latest British Social Attitudes Survey, just 5 per cent of people could correctly name their council leader.

The government has already accepted the flaws inherent within local governance and has given councils three options for reform: a cabinet style system with a leader; a directly elected mayor and cabinet; or a directly elected mayor and council manager.

Most councils have recognised the problems and have accepted that some form of change is inevitable. Few have accepted that it is time for a more radical solution: that it is time to change the very culture of local politics, to create visibility and transparency with the direct support of a public in touch with its local leadership. That solution is directly elected mayors.

However, local government has already displayed its reluctance for real change. Just four months after the government's proposals were outlined, 75 per cent of council leaders registered their opposition to directly elected mayors. Most leaders cited three main reasons for their opposition: that directly elected mayors would concentrate too much power in the hands of one person; would lead to more corruption; and would 'dumb down' politics, making the personality more powerful than policy. All of these points are misconceptions.

Within most mayoral systems, rigorous checks and balances are in place to ensure the highest standards of probity. Scrutiny committees would have the explicit power to examine any proposals and the full council would have to endorse any policies or budgets before they could be implemented. A directly elected mayor would simply not have the constitutional power to become an 'all powerful dictator'. The opportunity for corruption within such a system of scrutiny, matched by the work of independent auditors and a standards committee, would also be very small.

As for personality politics, there is no evidence that this 'dumbs down' politics – rather the opposite. It creates real electoral competition with individuals able to break free from the constraints of party politics and campaign on more locally driven issues. It gives people a way into politics in a manner they can relate to and so comprehend the issues at stake.

Countries with a long tradition of a mayoral system – such as Germany, Austria, Italy and Australia – have not experienced any of these problems and regularly report high electoral turnouts of 70 per cent and more. These countries demonstrate that directly elected mayors create visible leaders who have significant success in shaping communities and solving long-standing social problems.

The question remains – can local politicians afford to ignore a system that would grant them a powerful new role as a city champion with the backing of a substantial electoral mandate? It is time for councillors to accept that more radical change is needed. It is time for local politicians to open their minds to what the public is telling them or risk losing their democratic legitimacy completely.

Source: K. Day, December 1999, from New Local Government Network: www.nlgn.org.uk, 2004

1 Why were directly elected mayors introduced in the UK?

2 What are said to be the advantages and possible dangers of such a system?

3 What safeguards should be put in place to limit the possible dangers of such a system?

Question

What are the advantages and disadvantages of local government? *(20 marks)*

key terms

legislative devolution

The passing down of limited law-making powers from central to local or regional bodies, with the centre remaining sovereign – i.e. the state remains unitary

federalism

A system of greater decentralisation, where the central and local powers are equal and autonomous, with mutual checks and balances against each other – thus, there is no sovereign centre

separatism

Complete political independence of a territory

The independent Commission for Local Democracy (1995) mourned 'the emasculation of local democracy since the war' which has contributed to low electoral turnouts and reduced representation of local communities. It recommended radical changes to both the structure of local government and its relationship with the centre. The introduction of directly elected local mayors, and also legislative devolution since 1998, has gone some way towards this.

■ Devolution

Devolution means the delegation – passing down – of some **legislative** and/or executive functions of central powers to local bodies, while the national power remains responsible for major national issues such as defence, foreign affairs and macro-economics. The local bodies are subordinate to the central legislature or executive, which can readily retrieve their powers. The system remains unitary because the centre is still sovereign. **Federalism**, on the other hand, entails greater local autonomy. Here the regions allocate certain national powers such as defence and foreign affairs to a central body, and they are in theory equal to it. The local powers have autonomy within their own, defined areas of decision-making. Thus central government cannot increase its powers at the expense of the regions or federal states. The courts arbitrate in cases of conflict. The USA and Australia are examples of federal systems. **Separatism** means complete political independence.

The UK has long had elements of *executive and administrative* devolution in local government, and Scotland and Wales had their own Secretaries of State with Cabinet status. Scotland's legal and educational systems have also long been quite different from those of England. Until 1999 there was, however, no legislative devolution; Westminster was the sole UK legislature since the suspension, in 1972, of the Northern Irish Parliament (Stormont) and the introduction there of 'direct rule' from Westminster because of the growing political conflict in Northern Ireland at that time.

Encouraged by the rise of nationalist feeling in Scotland and Wales, since the 1970s Labour and the Liberal Democrats advocated legislative devolution for Scotland and Wales; and the Liberal Democrats also proposed elected local legislatures for the regions of England. A Labour government in 1977 introduced a Devolution Bill, and held referenda on the issue in Scotland and Wales in 1979. Wales voted against; Scotland voted in favour, but the 'yes' vote amounted to only 32.5 per cent of the total electorate, and the Bill required approval by at least 40 per cent of the electorate (a backbench amendment) so the issue was dropped.

Over the next two decades, support for the Scottish and Welsh Nationalist parties increased, but the Conservative governments of that period were firmly opposed to devolution. In 1997, the Conservatives won no Westminster seats at all in Scotland or in Wales; and Labour came to power with a mandate to hold new referenda on the question of devolution.

Scotland

Scotland held a two-question referendum in September 1997 – 74 per cent voted in favour of a Scottish Parliament and 60 per cent agreed that it should have tax-varying powers of up to 3p in the pound (turnout was 60 per cent). The Scottish Parliament came into being in 1999 with 129 members elected by the Additional Member System: 73 elected by first-past-the-post, and 56 'top-up' MSPs elected from closed regional party lists using the European parliamentary constituencies.

The Scottish executive is responsible for the following policy areas:

- Health

- Education and training

- Local government, housing and social work

- Economic development

- Employment

- Transport

- Law and home affairs

- Police

- Environment

- Energy

- Agriculture, forestry and fishing

- Culture, sport and the arts

- Administration of certain EU laws in Scotland (for example, civil nuclear emergency planning).

Westminster remains responsible for foreign affairs including relations with the EU, defence and national security, macro-economic and fiscal matters, immigration, railways, shipping, airlines, pensions, employment law, broadcasting and telecommunications, and much else. Overall, the Scotland Act lists 19 pages of powers that are reserved to Westminster. In other words, devolution is a fairly limited form of decentralisation.

However, since the Scottish Parliament is elected by PR, this does change the party political balance. Left-wing Labour MP Dennis Canavan quit his party and successfully stood against the official Labour candidate for the Scottish Parliament after being forced off the closed party list for (he claims) being too radical. Left-wing politicians and politics have always been more successful in Scotland than in England, because Scotland has always been more economically disadvantaged.

The Scottish Parliament has voted to abolish tuition fees for Scottish students (the price of Liberal Democrat coalition support); then to repeal Section 28 (which banned the promotion of homosexuality in local government and state schools) just after the House of Lords had blocked its repeal at Westminster; then to support universal free personal care for the elderly; then to ban fox hunting, and the smacking of children; then to reject foundation hospitals for Scotland – all clear examples of a devolved body flexing its muscle in the face of central opposition.

The arrangements for Scotland did not address the 'West Lothian question' (so-called because it was first raised by the MP for that area, Tam Dalyell): that Scottish MPs at Westminster continue to have law-making powers over areas of English policy such as health and education, while English MPs have no such power over Scotland because the Scottish Parliament now legislates on such matters. In 2004, for example, 46 Scottish Labour MPs voted with the Labour government at Westminster to push through top-up tuition fees for England on a total Westminster majority of just five votes – although the Scottish Parliament had already rejected tuition fees for Scotland.

Scotland has also had a disproportionate share of Westminster MPs, of Cabinet ministers and of central government finances across the UK. As English voters became increasingly aware of such imbalances, there were growing calls for fewer Scottish MPs at Westminster, reduced voting rights for Scottish MPs at Westminster, and/or elected assemblies for the regions of England to parallel the Scottish Parliament.

A partial response to these constitutional imbalances was the reduction in the number of Scottish seats at Westminster from 72 to 59 for the 2005 general election). However, critics of the Labour government argue that the government will not contemplate reducing voting rights for the remaining Scottish MPs at Westminster because so many of those MPs are Labour.

In 2004, a test referendum was held in the north-east of England on the proposal for an elected regional assembly – but it was roundly defeated by 78 per cent to 22 per cent (on a quite respectable 48 per cent turnout), probably because the assembly's proposed powers were conspicuously weak.

A final controversy has been the spiralling cost of the new Scottish parliamentary building (Holyrood) from an original estimate of £40 million to over £400 million.

Wales

In Wales, the government held the devolution referendum one week after the Scottish vote in 1997, in the hope of giving the 'yes' side a boost. Despite this, the 'yes' vote scraped a 0.6 per cent majority on only a 50 per cent turnout. Although there has long been a sense of national Welsh culture, centred especially on the Welsh language, there is far less support for political nationalism in Wales than in Scotland because of the perceived economic and political benefits of the union with England. The 60-member Welsh Assembly is therefore much weaker than the Scottish Parliament, with control over the spending of the £8 billion Welsh budget but with no taxation or primary law-making powers.

The Welsh Assembly is also elected by the AMS system, with 40 first-past-the-post and 20 party list members. It operates on the style of a local government committee system, with executive rather than legislative or fiscal powers – in effect, merely taking over the role of the Welsh Office in deciding how Westminster legislation is implemented in Wales, in the following policy areas:

- Economic development
- Agriculture
- Industry and training
- Education
- Local government services
- Health and social services
- Housing
- Environment
- Planning and transport
- Sport and heritage.

In February 1999, the Welsh Labour Party elected its leader for the Welsh Assembly – the Welsh First Secretary. Blair's favoured candidate, Alun Michael, beat the traditionalist, 'people's choice' Rhodri Morgan by 5 per cent, in what some critics saw, again, as a 'stitch up' by the party machine. However, in 2000, Alun Michael had to resign over a funding crisis. Rhodri Morgan – the man whom the Labour leadership had tried so hard to block (just like Ken Livingstone in London) – took over.

The central government's Scottish and Welsh Offices have now been incorporated into a new department of Constitutional Affairs.

According to some critics, devolution in Scotland and Wales has been an example of the Labour government's and Prime Minister's ambivalent attitudes towards power – namely, decentralising only on Labour's own terms and to its own advantage, as far as possible.

However, the 1999 and 2003 devolution elections produced a Labour/Liberal Democrat coalition in Scotland and a minority Labour executive in Wales (which briefly formed a coalition with the Liberal Democrats 2000–3). These arrangements forced some significant policy concessions from Labour, especially in Scotland (for example, on tuition fees, fox hunting, Section 28 and free personal care for the elderly).

The nationalist parties are usually grouped together with the 'others' in UK party analyses – understandably, since over 80 per cent of UK voters live in England, where the Scottish and Welsh nationalist parties do not have a presence. Indeed, as many people live in Greater London as in Scotland and Wales combined. However, the Scottish Nationalist Party (SNP) and Plaid Cymru (PC) are currently the official opposition parties in Scotland and Wales. The nationalist parties are, therefore, now a significant force in UK party politics.

However, in the last (2003) elections for the Scottish and Welsh assemblies, the nationalist parties lost a number of seats – indicating, perhaps, that devolution has helped to dampen down nationalist sentiment in those countries, just as the Labour government hoped that it would.

Scottish devolution election results, 2003 (73 constituencies and 8 regions)

Party	Constituency seats	Regional seats	+/–	Total
Labour	46	4	–6	50
Scottish National (SNP)	9	18	–8	27
Conservative	3	15	0	18
Liberal Democrat	13	4	0	17
Green	0	7	+6	7
Scottish Socialist (SSP)	0	6	+5	6
Independent	2	2	+3	4

Welsh devolution election results, 2003 (40 constituencies and 5 regions)

Party	Constituency seats	Regional seats	+/–	Total
Labour	30	0	+2	30
Plaid Cymru (PC)	5	7	–5	12
Conservative	1	10	+2	11
Liberal Democrat	3	3	0	6
Other	1	0	+1	1

Northern Ireland

At around the same time as the Scottish and Welsh referenda on devolution, but for different reasons – namely, the Northern Ireland peace process – an assembly for Northern Ireland was re-established at Stormont (for the first time since its abolition in 1972), following the peace deal on 10 April (Good Friday) 1998. In May 1998 a rapid referendum on the peace deal was held throughout Ireland and won substantial support:

- Northern Ireland: 71 per cent 'yes' on 81 per cent turnout
- Eire: 94 per cent 'yes' on 56 per cent turnout.

The peace deal provided for a Northern Ireland assembly of 108 seats elected by proportional representation (STV); a 12-member executive chosen from within and by the assembly in proportion to the parties' strength in the assembly (thus, for example, Sinn Fein were guaranteed two seats on the executive). The Northern Irish coalition executive was formed in November 1999; Unionists especially had to adjust to the new realities when former IRA commander Martin McGuinness was appointed Education Secretary.

2003 Northern Ireland devolution results (108 seats)

Party	+/–	Total
Democratic Unionist (DUP)	+10	30
Ulster Unionist (UUP)	–1	27
Sinn Fein	+6	24
Social Democratic and Labour (SDLP)	–6	18
Alliance Party of Northern Ireland (AP)	0	6
Progressive Unionist (PUP)	–1	1
Northern Ireland Women's Coalition (NIWC)	–2	0
UK Unionist (UKUP)	–4	1
Others	+1	1

Since then, however, Stormont has been repeatedly suspended by Westminster because of major policy deadlocks over, for example, the decommissioning of weapons by former 'terrorist' groups in Northern Ireland. This is an example of Westminster's ultimate sovereignty over the devolved bodies.

talking point

It is worth noting that, because of its unique history and political and religious divisions, Northern Ireland has an entirely different – and more pluralist (multi-party) – system than the rest of the UK. This should be mentioned if you are asked in an exam question to assess the nature of the UK's party system.

analyse
this

Summary of devolved powers

Type of devolution	Powers	Scottish Parliament	Welsh Assembly	Northern Irish Assembly
Legislative	The power to pass, amend or repeal laws	✓	✗	✓
Financial	The ability to raise or lower taxes independently	✓	✗	✗
Administrative	The power to run services, allocate funds and organise administration	✓	✓	✓

1 Summarise the differences between the powers of the devolved bodies.

2 Why are tax varying powers controversial?

3 What has been the impact of devolution on the UK political system?

Criticisms of devolution

Some parties have criticised devolution for going too far; for others, it has not gone far enough. In summary:

- **The Conservative Party** were against devolution on principle. They favour politically strong, centralised government and fear that devolution may be the first step down the slippery slope towards the complete break up of the UK. However, largely for political and pragmatic reasons, they will not now reverse it.

- **The Labour Party** favour devolution to different degrees in different parts of the UK, which, critics say, has been a largely self-serving agenda. They have also tried – not always successfully – to control the leaderships of the new institutions. However, they do not favour any greater degree of decentralisation, such as UK federalism.

- **The Liberal Democrats** favour federalism – i.e. greater local autonomy – in a consistent pattern across the whole UK. For them, Labour's programme of devolution has not gone far enough.

- **The nationalist parties (SNP, PC, SDLP and Sinn Fein)** ultimately favour separatism – i.e. the complete independence of Scotland, Wales and Northern Ireland from the UK. However, they are content to accept devolution for the foreseeable future.

A broader list of the advantages and disadvantages of devolution, for exam purposes, would be very much the same as the advantages and disadvantages of local government listed in the answer to the question on page 152 (answer on page 200–1).

Questions

Quiz

1 Suggest two reasons why voter turnout for local council elections is usually low.

2 Explain one way in which the central Labour government has changed the structure of local government since 1997.

3 What was the turnout for the 1998 London referendum on a directly elected local mayor and London authority?

4 Define devolution.

5 How does devolution differ from federalism?

6 Give three distinct legislative decisions made by the Scottish Parliament.

7 Describe the powers of the Welsh Assembly.

8 How do these powers compare with those of the Scottish Parliament?

9 Why is the Northern Irish party system entirely different from that of the rest of the UK?

10 Why might devolution threaten the territorial integrity of the UK?

Questions

True or false?

1 Local councillors are elected for fixed four-year terms.

2 Nationalist sentiment is stronger in Scotland than in Wales.

3 Devolution does not affect England.

4 Scotland separately elects both members to the Scottish Parliament (MSPs) and members to the sovereign Westminster Parliament (MPs).

5 The 'West Lothian question' means that MSPs can vote on English affairs.

10

The European Union

■ History and issues

The (then) European Economic Community (EEC) was formed in 1957 by just six countries: France, Germany, Italy, Luxembourg, the Netherlands and Belgium.

The UK, Denmark and Ireland joined in 1973; Greece joined in 1981; then Spain and Portugal (1986); and Finland, Sweden and Austria (1995). Norway had also planned to join in 1995 but its voters rejected membership in a referendum. Most recently, ten more (mostly former communist) states joined in 2004: Cyprus, the Czech Republic, Estonia, Hungary, Latvia, Lithuania, Malta, Poland, Slovakia and Slovenia. There are now 25 member states in total (455 million people).

The original creation of the EEC was intended to establish a common free market, economic and monetary union and 'an ever closer union among the peoples of Europe'. Thus the visions of a single market and a federal Europe date from the 1950s (not from the 1980s or 1990s, as is sometimes suggested today). These goals were inspired by a desire for lasting peace and security after two world wars; awareness of growing economic and social interdependence and a desire for greater international co-operation between European countries; the advantages of large-scale markets; greater world influence; and the wish to challenge the blocs of the USA and the former USSR. The main economic principle enshrined in the 1957 Treaty of Rome was free trade – the removal of barriers and the establishment of common tariffs and policies (especially in agriculture, fishing, coal and steel) across Europe.

In 1967, the EEC became the European Community (EC). When the Maastricht Treaty came into effect in 1993, this institution became the European Union (EU). The changing labels are clearly illustrative of the broadening and increasingly integrated embrace of the EU.

The EU is a **supranational institution**, i.e. not just an intergovernmental fraternity, but a sovereign power over member states with a body of law that takes precedence over national law.

key term

supranational institution

A sovereign body over member states with laws that take precedence over national law

The changing attitude of the UK towards Europe

The UK initially refused to join in the 1950s for a number of reasons: a sense of superiority and national pride after victory in war; a hankering after lost imperial status; the UK's international status and links with the USA and Commonwealth; a sense of political and geographical difference – an island mentality; xenophobia (and mistrust especially of Germany and France); for the right-wing of the Conservative Party especially, fear of loss of sovereignty and 'national' identity; and for the left-wing of the Labour Party, dislike of the free market capitalist nature of the EEC. By the 1960s, however, it was clear that the EEC was an established success.

The UK eventually joined in 1973, under Ted Heath's Conservative government. When the Labour Party came to power in 1974 they were very divided on the issue, so Prime Minister Harold Wilson held the first (and, so far, only) national referendum in 1975 on the question of staying in the EC. He lifted 'collective responsibility' and allowed his dissident left-wing Cabinet ministers (such as Tony Benn) publicly to divide on the issue. Two-thirds of the UK electorate voted to stay in Europe, thus legitimising Wilson's own support for the EC.

UK elections to the European Parliament were first held in 1979.

talking point

Note that there was no UK referendum on joining the EU – only on staying in it. This is a common source of confusion – and sometimes criticism.

The issue of sovereignty

The question of sovereignty is multi-dimensional.

key term

qualified majority voting (QMV)

A weighted system of voting (according to countries' population sizes) used in the EU Council of Ministers where several member states must vote together to block a decision, across a growing range of policy areas

The main issue since 1973 has been Parliament's *legal sovereignty*, which has been effectively negated (overruled) by the primacy of EU laws and treaties. Even on entry in 1973, the UK Parliament had to accept 43 volumes of existing EU legislation. This loss of sovereignty to Europe has since increased, with the growing scope of European intervention and with reforms of European voting procedures. The most important reform was the change from unanimous voting in the EU Council of Ministers – i.e. any one country could effectively veto any policy – to **qualified majority voting (QMV)**, under the Single European Act 1986 (introduced, ironically, by the Eurosceptic Prime Minister Margaret Thatcher), where several countries must now band together to veto a policy, on a growing range of issues.

For example, in 1993 the UK had to introduce a maximum 48-hour working week (which was good for UK workers). Over 50 per cent of UK legislation now originates from the EU. No other continental country has (or had) parliamentary sovereignty, because they all have written

'I can finally pay off my student loan!'

constitutions and supreme courts; therefore this issue matters more to the UK. However, observers might be forgiven for being sceptical about UK governments' expressed concerns about the loss of sovereignty to Europe, since the elective dictatorships of some recent UK governments have done more than Europe ever has to undermine Westminster's real power, from within.

- UK governments are generally more concerned about their own loss of national sovereignty, i.e. their ability to pursue their own policies without external interference. From another perspective, however, the primacy of EU law has curbed the dangers of elective dictatorship, of a single-party majority UK government within a sovereign Parliament. The European Court of Justice has protected many civil liberties of UK citizens against UK law, for example in relation to retirement ages, workers' hours and holiday entitlements, food and water standards and pension rights of part-time workers.

- Economic sovereignty has become an important issue especially with the creation of the single European currency. However, this has actually long been undermined in the UK by foreign ownership of businesses and industries, and especially by the UK's dependence on the health of the US economy – apparently with little hostility from the traditional right wing Eurosceptics. Moreover, the Labour government's granting to the Bank of England of independent control of interest rates (immediately after the 1997 general election) was a willing surrender of a key economic power which brought the UK into line with one of the conditions for joining the euro.

- The political sovereignty of the electorate has, arguably, been undermined by the 'democratic deficit' created by the EU: namely, that the only directly elected EU institution – the EU Parliament – is also the weakest. However, the EU Parliament is rapidly gaining political strength; it has given UK voters an added tier of democratic representation (via pure PR); and the issue of Europe did set the precedent, in the UK, for the holding of referenda on major constitutional issues.

A more positive view of EU membership argues that national governments benefit from pooling sovereignty to achieve policy goals which would be unattainable alone; and that EU decision-making helps to strengthen national governments by reducing the impact of domestic constraints.

Questions

1 Define the concept of sovereignty. *(5 marks)*

2 Outline two ways in which the EU has limited UK sovereignty. *(10 marks)*

■ The institutions of the European Union

The Council of Ministers

The Council of Ministers is the ultimate EU policy-making body, and comprises the Foreign Ministers of each member state (with other ministers in topic sub-committees when appropriate). Before 1986, Council voting had to be unanimous on every issue. Since then, QMV on a growing range of issues has meant a loss of power by individual states to Europe.

The European Commission

From 2009, each country will have one Commissioner (currently, some big member states have two), appointed by their respective governments for five-year renewable terms. They are usually former – some critics would say 'failed' – politicians, diplomats or senior civil servants. They present policy proposals to the Council of Ministers, have significant powers of delegated legislation (each year the Commission passes 4,000–5,000 pieces of secondary legislation), they carry out decisions made, administer most of the Union's budget and investigate breaches of the rules – thus they can impose fines on offenders and take member states to the European Court of Justice.

In sum, the Commissioners have significant executive, administrative and even legislative powers. Since they are not elected, this annoys Eurosceptics.

Each Commissioner has a small team of personal advisers and officials appointed by the Commissioners themselves, which allows scope for 'cronyism'.

talking point

Brussels bureaucrats

The Commission has a civil service of about 18,000. Although the EU is frequently criticised for being overly bureaucratic, this is remarkably small and generally efficient by comparison with the bureaucracy of some member states (for example, the UK's Ministry of Defence alone has 116,000 civil servants).

However, in 1999 the Commission's officials were at the centre of a major scandal about fraud, corruption, nepotism and cronyism, in which three or four of the Commissioners – notably France's Edith Cresson – were also implicated. The EU Parliament came close to sacking all 20 Commissioners (because it lacked the power to dismiss individuals). Following the publication of a highly critical independent report which concluded, 'It is difficult to find anyone who has even the slightest sense of responsibility', all 20 European Commissioners resigned – an unprecedented crisis in the history of the EU. Most, however, were promptly reappointed by their national governments (though not Cresson, who was charged with corruption).

The European Council

The European Council, established in 1974, is made up of the heads of each government, and meets twice a year in so-called European Summit meetings – for example, the Maastricht Treaty was signed by John Major at a European Council meeting in December 1991, with opt-outs on the single currency and Social Chapter; and in 1997 Tony Blair signed the Amsterdam Treaty by which the UK signed up to the EU Social Chapter. Some summits have weighty programmes about, for example, Nato's bombing of Serbia, the invasion of Iraq or EU enlargement. Other summits, however, may be little more than media events.

The European Parliament

This is the only directly elected body of the EU but it has, arguably, relatively little power (however, see below). It has 732 seats, of which the UK has 78. Germany (the biggest country in the EU) has 99. Other countries have fewer seats in rough proportion to their populations, ranging down to Malta with five seats.

MEPs are elected every five years (the last elections were in June 2004). The Labour government changed the UK electoral system for Euro-elections from first-past-the-post to the closed party list system, a form of pure PR where the party leaders, rather than the voters, choose the MEPs to fill the seats. The obvious criticism of this system is that the voter has no say in who are the actual MPs, who are likely to be loyal party placemen. The House of Lords rejected the closed list system for EU elections a record six times, but the government in the Commons pushed it through nevertheless. By 1999, some independent-minded and popular MEPs – for example, Labour's Christine Oddy (Coventry and North Warwickshire) – were pushed so far down the party lists as to be

The European Parliament

effectively deselected by the leadership, with the voters having no say in the process.

The Parliament is a forum for debate; it is consulted on major policy issues and can suggest amendments which the Commission often accepts; it can veto certain forms of legislation; can modify or reject the EU budget (as it did five times in the 1980s); can investigate public complaints of European maladministration (with an EU Ombudsman since Maastricht); can veto EU Commissioners' appointments; and can, in theory, dismiss the entire Commission by a two-thirds majority – never yet done, but it was pressure from MEPs which forced the Commission's collective resignation in 1999.

The European Parliament's profile is fairly low and many voters are apathetic or cynical about it. In the 2004 elections turnout reached a record low, with just 45 per cent of EU voters casting ballots. It was especially low for many of the ten new member states, which averaged a mere 26 per cent. The lowest turnout was in Slovakia, where fewer than 17 per cent cast their votes. Turnout in the UK was 38 per cent.

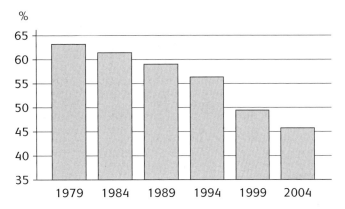

Voter turnout in EU elections

Source: European Parliament

The whole European Parliament commutes each month between Brussels and Strasbourg, at a cost to European taxpayers of £132 million per year. France will not agree to it staying permanently in Brussels.

The European Court of Justice (ECJ)

This comprises judges appointed by member states for six-year renewable terms, and is based in Luxembourg. It interprets and enforces EU law, which takes precedence over national law. UK courts are obliged to refuse to enforce Acts of Parliament which contravene European law (a principle established by the 1990 Factortame case about fishing rights in UK waters).

analyse
this

Europe's Cinderella or Ugly Sister?

The European Parliament (EP) is perhaps the most misunderstood and, mainly in Britain, probably most reviled institution in the European Union.

It seems to be in the news solely when there are expense scandals or when someone takes a shot at it for being an expensive and pretentious talking shop.

In fact, it has acquired a significant amount of power over the last 20 or so years so that it now stands as a co-equal to the Council of Ministers, that is the member states, in making decisions about many European laws.

This power of 'co-decision', as it is called in eurospeak, means that, largely unnoticed by most of the populations which vote in its members, it can make or break many pieces of legislation which affect the ordinary lives of European citizens.

It stands to gain even more powers from the new European constitution as co-decision is spread to more policy areas.

Some examples illustrate how and why the Parliament now counts.

➡ Working time directive. This introduces limits on the hours employees can be made to work, and regulates rest periods, annual leave and night work.

➡ Cosmetics directive. This regulates what industry can do to test cosmetics on animals, and bans animal testing of cosmetics after 2009.

➡ Takeovers directive. This establishes standard EU rules on takeover bids, and restricts the tactics companies can use to avoid foreign takeovers.

➡ GM food regulation: This governs the amount of GM products allowed in food and the labelling required to alert the consumer.

It affects the food you eat, the air you breathe, your workplace, your health and safety and your environment.

Quite often the European public is unaware that laws passed by their national parliaments began life in Brussels.

In the UK, the government has begun introducing a plan to ban age discrimination in the workplace – without widely advertising the fact that it stems from an EU directive.

'When it is seen as a good-news thing, they want to claim credit for it,' says Kirsty Hughes, of the Centre for European Policy Studies.

'If it is something controversial, they blame it on Brussels.'

The struggle for recognition by the European Parliament has been a long one. It is not over yet. Somehow it has not overcome its poor image to be accepted for what it wants to be – a democratic workhorse at the heart of the European Union.

Source: adapted from an article by Paul Reynolds,
News Online world affairs correspondent;
http://news.bbc.co.uk, June 2004

1 What are the merits and demerits of the UK's voting system for the EU Parliament?

2 Suggest reasons why the turnout for EU elections is so low.

3 Should the European Parliament have more or less power than it has now?

Questions

1 What are the powers of the European Parliament? *(20 marks)*

2 Does the European Parliament need reform? *(20 marks)*

EU decision making – a summary

At its simplest: the Commission makes a proposal; the Parliament offers its opinion and agreement; the Council of Ministers makes a decision; the Court of Justice interprets and enforces the decision; the member countries administer the decision.

■ The impact of the EU on UK political parties

Membership of the EU has profoundly divided the two main UK political parties: Labour especially in the 1970s and the Conservatives especially in the 1980s and 1990s. Left-wing Labour MPs have always been hostile to the EU which they perceive as a free market 'capitalist club'. The 'new' Labour government is now much more Europhile (pro-European), and is currently making preparations to join the euro.

The Conservatives, under Margaret Thatcher, became increasingly suspicious of the EC in the 1980s as they saw it extending beyond a free trade community to a supranational political power (which, in fact, it always was). Since 1990, divisions within the Conservative Party over Europe were primarily responsible for: Thatcher's prime ministerial defeat in 1990; the temporary withdrawal of the whip from several Conservative Eurorebels which eradicated John Major's small majority; John Redwood's leadership challenge against Major in 1995; the defection from the Conservative Party of pro-European MPs to the Liberal Democrats or Labour, such as Robert Jackson in 2005; and the defection of some anti-Europeans to increasingly influential Europhobic parties such as the UK Independence Party (UKIP).

The current Conservative leader, Michael Howard, is a Eurosceptic who wants to remain 'in Europe, but not run by Europe'. The party's current

UKIP wants complete withdrawal from the EU

policy on joining the euro is 'never'. They favour a referendum on the EU constitution because they believe that the UK electorate will vote 'no'. This is a rather opportunist position, because, philosophically, Conservatives oppose referenda in principle (the UK Parliament should be sovereign) and have never held one in practice.

Of the three main parties, only the Liberal Democrats are fully committed to the development of a federal Europe.

Euroscepticism in the UK has also generated the creation of some minor parties: most notably UKIP, which dented the main parties' vote especially in the 2004 EU elections. UKIP more than doubled its 1999 vote to take 16 per cent of the vote, in so doing pushing the Liberal Democrats into fourth place. Labour's vote fell 6 per cent to 23 per cent, their worst share of the vote since 1918. The Conservatives got more votes – 27 per cent – but that was still their lowest share of any nationwide election since 1832.

UKIP seeks complete withdrawal from the EU. Former UKIP MEP Robert Kilroy-Silk said he wanted to 'wreck' the EU Parliament by exposing the waste, corruption and the way 'it's eroding our independence'; but he then quit UKIP in 2005 because it would not elect him as party leader.

The Greens (left-wing Eurosceptics) held their two UK MEPs with 6 per cent of the total vote.

EU parliamentary elections (UK), 2004

Party	Vote		MEPs	
	+/–	%	+/– Seat change*	Total
Conservative	−9.0	26.7	−8	27
Labour	−5.4	22.6	−6	19
UKIP	+9.2	16.1	+10	12
Liberal Democrat	+2.3	14.9	+2	12
Green	0.0	6.3	+2	2
BNP	+3.9	4.9	0	0
Respect	+1.5	1.5	0	0
SNP	−1.3	1.4	0	2
PC	−0.9	1.0	0	1
SSP	0.0	0.4	0	0
Other	+3.2	4.6	+1	3

* Seat change is adjusted to allow a direct comparison with the results from the 1999 election.

key terms

subsidiarity

The principle (enshrined in the Maastricht Treaty) whereby decisions should be taken 'at the lowest possible level' compatible with efficiency and democracy – i.e. encouraging decentralisation down to member states

■ Key events in the development of the EU

The Single European Act (SEA) 1986

The SEA developed the idea of a single European market with a commitment to advancing economic integration. The Single European Market officially came into being on 1 January 1993, establishing the 'four freedoms' of movement for goods, capital, services and persons, although the UK refused to scrap frontier controls over the movement of persons.

The Maastricht Treaty 1992

The Maastricht Treaty created a European Union with common citizenship, and set out a timetable and procedure for creating a single currency.

The process of ratification in the UK House of Commons was very fraught and was only achieved when John Major made the issue a vote of confidence for his government. He also ensured the deletion of every reference to federalism ('the F-word') from the treaty, because the word 'federalism' has been used, inaccurately, by Eurosceptics to imply the complete absorption of member countries into a European 'superstate'. In fact, of course, 'federalism' means the ordered division of sovereignty between central and local powers with constitutional guarantees of mutual spheres of autonomy. Thus the Maastricht Treaty established the principle of **subsidiarity**, whereby decisions should be taken 'at the lowest possible level' compatible with efficiency and democracy. This was an attempt to return to member states some power previously lost to Brussels; and Scottish and Welsh nationalists argued that it also implied greater devolution of power within the UK.

The single currency

The Maastricht Treaty bound member states to work towards a single currency (the euro) starting in 2002, with the exceptions of the UK,

The Euro became legal tender in January 2002

Denmark and Sweden, who secured an 'opt-out'. Common interest rates for the participating economies are decided by a European Central Bank based in Frankfurt.

The first stage for each country was to enter its currency into the Exchange Rate Mechanism (ERM) whereby currency values were tied to each other within certain bands of flexibility. The UK joined the ERM in 1990, but was humiliatingly forced out on 16 September 1992 (so-called 'Black Wednesday') when currency speculation on the international financial markets forced the devaluation of the pound below the floor of its ERM band. Conservative Chancellor Norman Lamont eventually – and reluctantly – resigned in 1993 over the UK's fall-out from the ERM.

The Labour government intends to join the euro – subject to a referendum – when its own 'five tests' are met:

● convergence with eurozone

● enough flexibility to adapt

● impact on jobs

● impact on financial services

● impact on foreign investment.

However, these are largely subjective – that is, not easy to quantify precisely. They are, therefore, largely a matter of political assessment.

Case for a single currency
European integration and a truly 'single market' require a single currency; it would enhance Europe's competitiveness against the USA and other major economies; currency transaction costs would be eliminated; the currency speculators would be weakened; business stability and certainty would be enhanced, as would price transparency and hence lower costs for consumers.

Case against a single currency
Practical difficulties in aligning very diverse economies and currencies of member states; loss of national sovereignty; loss of governments' ability to adjust currency values against external shocks; loss of wealth, employment and power from weaker to stronger member countries, including probable domination by the European Central Bank.

The Social Chapter
The Maastricht Treaty also bound member states – except the UK, which again secured an 'opt-out' – to the Social Chapter, an agreement incorporating minimum employment wages and rights, sexual equality, freedom of information and other social improvements throughout the EU. The then Conservative government's main argument against it was that such added constraints and costs on UK businesses would increase unemployment and decrease profits. The Labour government signed up to the Social Chapter in 1997.

Maastricht's other 'pillars'

The two other pillars of the treaty were based on intergovernmental co-operation rather than supranational integration, and also on unanimous voting rather than QMV, therefore the UK government did not feel threatened by them. The Maastricht Treaty's 'second pillar' deals with foreign and defence policy co-operation; the 'third pillar' concerns co-operation on interior and justice affairs, e.g. toughening rules against drug smuggling, terrorism, immigration and asylum seekers from outside Europe, but relaxing restraints against movement of persons within Europe.

The Amsterdam Treaty 1997

This agreement (signed by Blair early in his first term of office) signed the UK up to the Social Chapter and provided for the gradual introduction of common policies on immigration, asylum and visa laws. It also extended QMV to such areas as employment, sexual equality, public health and customs cooperation.

Questions

True or false?

1 Norway is not a member of the EU.

2 The UK held a referendum on joining the EU in 1975.

3 The EU court is the European Court of Human Rights.

4 The EU Parliament is the only directly elected institution of the EU.

5 The Conservative Party seeks withdrawal from the EU.

The Nice Treaty 2000

The aim of the Nice Treaty was to decide how power should be shared out within the European institutions after enlargement to 25 member states in 2004: for example, changing the number of seats in the European Parliament and the size of the Commission, and extending QMV. The result was the EU constitution.

The EU constitution 2004

With the enlargement of the EU to 25 member states, it was agreed that a written EU constitution was necessary, for the first time, to clarify and co-ordinate the rules of procedure. Agreement on the content of the constitution proved difficult, with smaller states (such as Spain and Poland) resisting control by larger states. The UK government, at first, insisted that the new constitutional treaty was simply a 'tidying up exercise'; but, under pressure from the Conservatives, Liberal Democrats and a largely

Eurosceptic press, Blair made a major U-turn in 2004 and accepted the principle of a referendum on the new EU constitution.

The EU constitution creates:

- a new (non-elected) EU President for two-and-a-half-year terms

- a new (non-elected) EU Foreign Minister accountable to member governments

- new powers for national Parliaments to block Commission proposals

- further extension of QMV, with new weighting amongst member states

- a new Charter of Fundamental Rights.

The UK government defended most of its 'red lines' – national vetoes – on tax and economic policy, defence and foreign affairs; but accepted majority voting in areas such as criminal justice and social security in return for the removal of the veto from agricultural and fishing policies.

All change: what the constitution means for states of the Union

European Council President: Position replacing six-month rotating system. President to be appointed for 2½-year terms.

European Council: Leaders of member states meeting quarterly. Decisions by consensus, unless otherwise provided for in constitution.

Council of Ministers: Group of three countries to chair ministerial councils for 18 months, under control of new president.

Minister for Foreign Affairs: Post for security and defence to be appointed by a qualified majority of member states.

European Commission: EU executive, with power to initiate legislation and oversee its implementation.

European Parliament: Enacts legislation jointly with Council of Ministers. Sees powers of oversight doubled in new Constitution to about 80 policy areas. To vote on approving commission president and team. Limited to 750 members. No state to have more than 96 seats or under 6.

Qualified majority voting: 'Double majority' system under which EU decisions would need support of 55 per cent of member states, comprising at least 15 of them representing 65 per cent of population.

Legal standing: Constitution establishes EU as legal body with power to sign international treaties.

Charter of Fundamental Rights: The UK won battle to ensure that charter does not override national laws such as employment legislation.

Source: *The Times*, 21 June 2004

After the new constitutional treaty goes through the UK Parliament, it must be agreed in a UK referendum – which, according to opinion polls, will be difficult.

EU myths

Never let the facts stand in the way of a good story. This is a deeply held principle in the cynical world of journalism, and the EU has long been a victim of it. There are many classic EU myths, and new ones surface all the time. Some of them are based on half-truths, or misunderstandings about the role of different European organisations, or confusion between UK and EU law; and there are many which are complete fantasy and fibs. Perhaps the most famous is the bendy banana myth.

The European Commission's website (www.cec.org.uk/press/myths) provides a lengthy (and fully explained) A–Z list of such myths which, though often amusing, raise serious questions about the integrity of some UK press and politicians.

Questions

1 What are the advantages of European integration?   *(30 marks)*

2 What are the disadvantages of European integration?   *(30 marks)*

"OUTRAGEOUS! THEY'RE GIVING ME MORE RIGHTS!"

The future – a Europe of nation states or a United States of Europe?

The two main UK parties have always been divided on the question of Europe; the Conservatives have become increasingly Eurosceptic since the 1990s, and Labour has had to deal with growing hostility to Europe amongst voters since 1997. By contrast, most other European countries are more pro-EU. It seems likely that the Union will both deepen and widen in the future, and the UK will have to decide whether it genuinely wishes to be 'at the heart of Europe' or to be sidelined and left behind.

However, the EU is not about to become a 'superstate'. The intense national arguments over the drafting of the EU constitution in 2004 demonstrated how much the EU is still a fragmented coalition of self-interested member states fighting to defend their own national interests. And the new constitutional arrangements actually return more powers back to national Parliaments and governments – for better or worse.

Questions

Quiz

Briefly answer the following questions.

1 When was the EEC formed?

2 Where was the treaty signed that created the EEC?

3 Name two European states which are not members of the EU.

4 Give one sentence definitions of the following terms:

   a) Sovereignty

   b) Subsidiarity

   c) Supranationalism

5 Give two reasons why the idea of a more united Europe gained strength in the post-1945 era.

6 Give two reasons why the UK initially refused to join this process.

7 In what year did the UK join the (then) EEC?

8 In what year was the UK referendum on staying in Europe?

9 In what year were UK elections to the European Parliament first held?

10

   a) What is QMV?

   b) When was it introduced?

   c) What impact has QMV had on the balance of power between Europe and individual member states?

11 Why has the left wing of the Labour Party traditionally been hostile to the European Union?

12 Why has the right wing of the Conservative Party been hostile to Europe?

13 Give one argument for, and one argument against, a single European currency.

14 What is the Social Chapter?

15 Why are there 12 stars on the European flag?

Question

Discuss the impact of the European Union on UK political processes.   *(30 marks)*

Answers to questions

■ 1 Political power and participation

Page 2

Power is the ability to dictate others' behaviour through sanctions or coercion. Authority is the ability to shape others' behaviour through consent, respect and support, i.e. authority is rightful, legitimate power, and is a feature of representative democracy.

The nineteenth-century German sociologist Max Weber distinguished three types of authority: traditional (for example, House of Lords), charismatic (for example, Churchill) and legal–rational (for example, MPs). Power may exist without authority (tyranny), or authority without much power (for example, the UK monarchy). Authority tends to generate power, but power may generate authority through indoctrination. Conversely, misjudgement or misuse of power may mean the loss of authority, for example the former Prime Minister Margaret Thatcher's downfall in 1990. In a democracy, power should rest on authority.

Analyse this, page 4

The 'weak' short answers (2 and 3) are not factually wrong. The first is much too short and skimpy; it would be lucky to get one mark. The other is long-winded, repetitive, clumsy and colloquial in style, and it contains unsubstantiated value-judgements; but it would gain 3 marks for factual detail.

Page 8

Democracy can be criticised as a dangerous and inefficient form of government. Political philosophies with a negative view of human nature – such as traditional conservatism and fascism – argue that direct 'people power' is not desirable because it will be exercised in a selfish and irrational way. For example, some Fathers4Justice campaigners have climbed high buildings to publicise their protests, seriously disrupting traffic and endangering the safety of their rescuers in the process.

Such philosophies also argue against representative democracy, on the grounds that voters may be persuaded to vote for unsuitable people who seek power for its own sake, who are clever with words and who know how to appeal to popular emotions (such as Hitler).

'People power' may amount to 'mobocracy' or 'tyranny of the majority', ignoring or suppressing individual and minority views and rights.

'People power' may take illegal or even violent forms – for example, May Day 'anti capitalist' protesters.

Alternatively, the result of 'people power' may be sheer apathy because most people are just not interested enough to take an active part in political decision-making.

All modern and supposedly democratic systems actually amount to rule by a small and powerful minority – a power elite – because most voters are too uninformed, unintelligent or uninterested to take an educated and active part in decision-making.

In representative democracies, elected politicians will favour popular short-term policies for their own political gain, which may actually be contrary to the long-term interests of the voters (for example, politicians may cut taxes and thus damage public services).

Finally, there are practical arguments against 'people power': it may be slow, costly, inefficient, inconsistent, dishonest and prone to corruption.

In summary, there is a view that democracy is the most dangerous and least efficient form of government: one in which the stability of the state is threatened by internal divisions; complex issues are distorted and simplified by self-serving politicians and ignorant voters; difficult decisions are delayed or avoided; and matters of high judgement are reduced to the lowest common denominator acceptable to a majority of the voters at any given time.

Page 10

A pluralist society is one with a diffusion of power amongst many divergent groups. Political pluralism implies a multi-party system and competing pressure groups, and economic pluralism implies competing centres of ownership and control. Genuine pluralism requires: a wide distribution of property and wealth; a distinction between the roles of government, society and individual; and checks and balances between the different sources of power. Although the UK is a multi-party system (for example, there are currently ten parties in the House of Commons), many writers, especially Marxists, for example, Ralph Miliband, question the extent to which power in 'liberal democracies' like the UK is genuinely dispersed and diffused.

Page 13

1   False

2   True

3   False

4   False

5   True

Page 15

1   If a strike by transport workers forces you to walk to school, that involves power because you have been made to do something unwillingly; whereas a persuasive publicity campaign by Comic Relief or Greenpeace is simply influence

2   The ancient Greek city state of Athens in the fifth century BC

3   Switzerland

4   8 per cent

5   Weapons of mass destruction (which undermined the UK government's case for invading Iraq in 2003, since none were subsequently found there)

6   Ten

7   1928

8   UK citizenship allows people the right to vote and obliges them to do jury service if summoned.

9   Belgium, Australia

10 A non-citizen

■ 2 The UK constitution

Page 23

1   What is an uncodified constitution?
    An uncodified constitution is a set of rules by which a country is governed but which is not contained in a single legal document. Instead, the rules derive from many different sources – some written, some not, some with the force of law, some not. This type of constitution is also flexible, that is, it can be changed by the ordinary, parliamentary process rather than requiring a special process such as a referendum. The UK has an uncodified constitution.

2   What are the main sources of the constitution?
    Many – but not all – of the rules of the UK constitution are laws, that is, rules of state which are enforceable by the courts and judges. There are, in turn, several different types of law:

- European Union law (since the UK joined the EU in 1973); this takes precedence over UK law.

- Acts of Parliament (statute law).

- Common law: ancient, unwritten law; for example, the powers of the crown.

- Case law (judge-made law): judicial interpretations of common and statute law, in new court cases, which then set a precedent for future cases.

Other rules of the constitution are not laws, but may still be very important:

- Historical documents and constitutional writings: for example, Magna Carta (1215), and Walter Bagehot's influential book *The English Constitution* (1867). These are not legally binding, but are very influential.

- Conventions: these are unwritten customs which are traditionally regarded as binding, but which have no legal force; for example, the practice that the Queen chooses, as Prime Minister, the leader of the majority party in the House of Commons. Some of the most important rules of the UK constitution are simply conventions, not laws.

3   Why has the UK constitution been criticised?

- The rules are often unclear and uncertain, even unknowable.

- The rules may be contradictory.

- The rules are often too bendable and breakable.

    An uncodified constitution is an ineffective check on the government of the day and thus may allow an overpowerful government to develop (see below).

- An uncodified constitution is an ineffective protector of citizens' rights and freedoms.

Note: topical examples should be given to illustrate all points.

Page 29

1   Principles include: parliamentary sovereignty, the rule of law and representative democracy. Also the unwritten and flexible nature of the constitution and its unitary and parliamentary (versus presidential) nature.

2   Weaknesses include: no clear, easily understood or accessible statement of the powers, functions and duties of the various institutions of the state or government, or of the rights of the citizen; even fundamental and hard-won features of the constitution can be changed relatively easily; the rules can be quite easily broken; an unwritten

constitution is an ineffective check on the government of the day and thus makes 'elective dictatorship' more likely.

Note: Topical examples should be given to illustrate all points.

Page 30

1   Sovereignty resides in that body which has supreme or ultimate decision-making power. It also implies authority, that is, consent and legitimacy. The state has sovereignty over all individuals and groups within its boundaries. In the UK, Parliament at Westminster is said to have 'legal sovereignty', i.e. it can pass, amend or repeal any law without challenge. In practice, it is subject to constraints, for example the EU, other international bodies, economic and business powers, pressure groups, media, and the electorate who have ultimate political sovereignty. Thus sovereignty is divided between the state (exercised by the executive), Parliament (which has legal sovereignty) and the voters (who have political sovereignty); it is therefore debatable where, or whether, it exists at all.

2   In UK parliamentary government, the executive (that is, government) is chosen from the majority party within the legislature (Westminster Parliament), and the government is therefore dependent on Parliament's support. Hence the government is, in theory, subordinate and accountable to Parliament (unlike the US presidential system, where the executive is separately elected and is, in theory, equal to the legislature with mutual checks and balances, and the principle of separation of powers is generally followed). In practice, in the UK, the executive tends to dominate the legislature because the electoral and party systems usually produce a strong 'majority' government which can control Parliament from within; Lord Hailsham has described this as 'elective dictatorship'.

3   In parliamentary government, the executive is chosen from within the legislature (Parliament) and is in theory subordinate and accountable – responsible – to the legislature. Parliament is therefore supposed to examine, debate, criticise and check the activities of government, to publicise executive actions, to convey public opinion to government, and to authorise the raising and spending of money by government – through, for example, debates, votes, Question Time and parliamentary committees. The ultimate form of control is a vote of no confidence in the government by the House of Commons, which would (by convention) oblige the government to resign. However, some see parliamentary control of government as inadequate: hence the concept of 'elective dictatorship' (Hailsham) – that is, the excessive power of a majority government over the legislature from within it.

4   The 'rule of law' (A.V. Dicey, 1885) is a paramount principle of any democratic constitution which seeks to equate law and justice. Its main principle is legal equality: everyone should be equally subject to the same laws – but for example in the UK, the Crown, diplomats,

MPs and often the government are not (see Chapter 8). There should also be a clear statement of people's legal rights and duties; fair and consistent trial and sentencing; and no arbitrary law or government. Justice should be an end in itself and always impartial. However, all of these principles are breached in practice in the UK: for example, by the UK's lack of a written, rigid constitution and by its often ambiguous laws; by the reintroduction since 2001 of internment (indefinite detention of some suspects without charge or trial); by inconsistent sentencing, high legal costs, and by police and judicial 'bias' (again, see Chapter 8).

Page 31

1 False

2 True

3 True

4 False

5 False

6 True

7 True

8 False

9 False

10 False

Page 31

1 Only the House of Commons is elected; not the Lords or Crown.

2 The two elements in parliamentary government are the legislature (Parliament) and the executive (government).

3 The executive is not elected; it is appointed by the Crown.

4 Ministers may be taken from the Lords as well as from the Commons.

5 The legislature is often, in practice, subordinate to the executive; but always sovereign in theory.

6 There is no necessary connection between an unwritten and a flexible constitution.

7 The UK does have constitutional laws, though they are passed in the same way as other laws.

8 A minority government has under 50 per cent of the seats in the House of Commons; its percentage vote is irrelevant.

9 A coalition government consists of two or more parties (either in a 'hung parliament' where no party has over 50 per cent of the seats, or in a crisis, such as war) – they do not merge to form a single party.

10 A manifesto is the list of policy proposals issued by any party prior to a general election. A mandate, strictly, is the assent and authority, or even duty, given to the government by the electors to govern along the policy lines indicated in the manifesto. However, voters rarely read manifestos, and cannot pick and choose between specific policies; above all, UK governments invariably win under 50 per cent of the votes cast (see Chapter 3). The authority of government to do anything is, therefore, questionable.

■ 3 Electoral systems and referenda

Page 34

● Voters know that they are not voting for a whole new government, therefore their voting behaviour often changes.

● Turnout therefore usually falls quite sharply.

● Local issues may matter more than in a general election.

● The individual candidates and their personalities may matter more.

● Media attention is focused on a single constituency, therefore many more small parties may stand candidates and the voter may have much more choice.

● Voters often use a by-election to register a protest vote against the government.

● Support for third and smaller parties often increases markedly – if only temporarily.

● In sum, by-election results are not a good basis for predicting the results of general elections.

Page 43

1 The 'bound' party list system

2 The party list system (both types)

3 STV; and the party list system may be based on multi-member, regional constituencies, or may treat the whole country as a single constituency (for example, Israel).

Advantages of multi-member constituencies:

● Voters have a choice of MPs to represent them.

● Competing MPs may work harder for their constituents.

- Different shades of thinking in one party can be represented by different MPs in one constituency.

Disadvantages:

- Constituencies would probably be larger, less homogeneous and less easy to represent.
- Blurring of accountability between different MPs.
- MPs may work less hard if others are there to do the work.

4   The alternative vote, supplementary vote and the second ballot systems.

5   AMS and AV+.

Advantages:

- Non-constituency MPs can concentrate on 'national' issues and on parliamentary versus constituency work (for example, committees).
- Maintains one-to-one relationship between constituency MPs and voters, whilst also giving a greater degree of proportionality.

Disadvantages:

- Non-constituency MPs are not personally elected by voters.
- Closed party list element gives greater power to party machines.

6   The second ballot.

Advantage:

- Produces one winner with absolute majority of votes, while also allowing sophisticated recasting of votes, or second thoughts.

Disadvantage:

- Prone to apathy and low turnout on second ballot.

7   Alternative vote, second ballot, STV, 'free' party list, AMS and AV+.

Advantages:

- More choice for voters.
- Allows electorate to vote for personalities as well as parties – may improve quality of representatives.

Disadvantages:

- Complexity.
- Undermines 'the doctrine of the mandate' – theory that the link between voters and policies is party.

8   STV, party list and AMS.

Advantages:

- Fairer and more representative.
- More 'pluralist'.

Disadvantages:

- May produce coalitions where small parties have disproportionate power.
- May produce fragmented and inefficient legislature.

9 Second and third preference votes are given the same weight as first preference votes; minority parties may have disproportionate balance of power.

10 Initiative, recall, referenda, fixed-term elections, primaries, votes for 16–18-year-olds, a presidential system, an elected second chamber, lower (or no) deposits, more devolution . . . and many others.

Page 49

1 False

2 False

3 True

4 True

5 False

6 False

7 False

8 True

9 True

10 True

Page 50

1 A referendum is a form of direct democracy where qualified voters can vote on a specific policy issue, usually with a 'yes' or 'no' answer. There are no strict rules or laws in the UK about the timing, wording or financing of referenda. An election, however, is a form of indirect democracy where qualified voters elect parties and/or candidates on a package of issues to make policy decisions on behalf of the voters. There are legal stipulations about timing, financing and procedures.

2 In 1975 a referendum was held on whether or not the UK should remain in the (then) European Economic Community – the UK's first (and, so far, only) national referendum. It was called because Harold Wilson's Labour Cabinet was very divided on the issue. Wilson wanted to stay in but the left-wingers (for example, Tony Benn) did not. Wilson wanted the outcome to be popular and legitimate, so called a referendum. The convention of collective ministerial responsibility (where ministers must demonstrate public unity) was suspended. All of the main parties and newspapers supported a 'yes' vote and it won by a two-thirds majority.

In 1997, two referenda were held on devolution – for Scotland and for Wales. Nationalist sentiment in Scotland was strong (led by the Scottish Nationalist Party) due to the discovery of North Sea oil, perceived economic benefits of EU membership and poor treatment of Scotland by long-serving Conservative governments. The Scots were offered both a devolved Parliament and tax-varying powers (+/- 3 per cent) for that Parliament. The result was strongly 'yes/yes'.

In Wales, nationalist sentiment was less strong, with the Welsh mainly wanting to preserve and promote their distinctive language. The result was 'the little yes' with just over 50 per cent voting 'yes' on a 50 per cent turnout. The weaker Welsh assembly – with no primary legislative or tax-varying powers – reflects this.

3 The UK is a representative democracy with a sovereign (ultimate law-making) Parliament. Referenda undermine the principle of parliamentary sovereignty; MPs should make decisions as we have elected them to do – especially according to traditional conservative theory. (Although in theory, referenda in the UK are merely advisory, in practice no Parliament or government could ignore the result.) Referenda also enable politicians to absolve themselves of responsibility for making difficult decisions.

Often, the issues involved are too complex to be reduced to a simple 'yes/no' answer. One example is the possible future referendum on whether the UK should join the euro. It is a complex economic, political and social issue but much media coverage has simplified it to 'losing the pound' (emotive). Another example is the EU constitution; it is over 300 pages long. Most voters will not read it and those who do may agree with some parts and disagree with others.

The result is not always decisive, as seen in the very close Welsh referendum in 1997. This undermines its legitimacy.

Too many referenda may result in voter apathy and hence low turnouts, which distort the results and undermine their legitimacy. For example, the referendum on whether London wanted a mayor and Greater London Authority only had a 34 per cent turnout. Also, in this referendum, two quite different issues were combined in a single question, which limited voter choice.

Finally, there are no rules or laws in the UK about the holding of referenda. The financing and information – or propaganda – on each side of the issue may, therefore, be very unbalanced – for example, in the 1975 European referendum where huge sums were spent on the 'yes' side. In the 1990s, the Labour government was criticised for using state funds to support the campaign for a 'yes' vote in the referenda on devolution. There are no guidelines about which issues are important or controversial enough to warrant referenda (why not moral issues such as abortion or hanging?). UK governments can hold them at whim, when they believe that public opinion is on their side – to legitimise what they want to do anyway.

■ 4 Political parties and MPs

Page 56

A party system implies political decision-making and representation on the basis of formal, organised groups of (more or less) like-minded people who stand candidates for election on a common policy programme. A one-party system means that only one party is allowed to put up candidates for election; all other parties are banned. This is a non-liberal democratic system and it operated in Nazi Germany, etc. A dominant party system, on the other hand, means that many parties exist and more than one party may have the chance of winning power, but one party is in power over long periods of time – for example, the Conservatives in the UK for two-thirds of the twentieth century.

Page 61

- Forced withdrawal from the European Exchange Rate Mechanism (ERM – the prelude to the single currency) on 'black Wednesday' in 1992, which seriously dented the Conservatives' reputation for economic competence

- Bitter Conservative party disunity over Europe, especially the smack-of-firm-compromise 'wait and see' approach to a single European currency in 1997

- Unpopular Conservative policies e.g. rail privatisation

- Air of arrogance and hubris – for example, 'sleaze', arms to Iraq, BSE, reluctance of Conservative ministers to accept responsibilities and resign

- Minority government by end of 1996. Government dependent in Commons on Northern Irish Unionists, hence abandonment of IRA ceasefire early in 1996

- Unpopularity of Major – and subsequent Conservative leaders – versus Blair

- Conservative newspapers largely turned against them

- 'Time for a change' after 18 years of Conservative power – widely held public sentiment

Labour benefited by:

- Internal reforms, for example some reduction in trade union power; one member, one vote in elections for party candidates.

- John Smith's death in 1994 allowed creation of 'new' Labour by the more modernising Blair – notably, the abandonment of Clause Four in 1995.

- Rapid centralisation of party and presentation around the leader and spin-doctors at party headquarters, and highly polished campaigns.

- Abandonment of traditional socialist – or even social democratic – principles and acceptance of market economics, low taxation, inflation and interest rates.

- Pre-election commitment to maintain existing income tax levels for a five-year term and existing spending levels for two years, 'welfare to work', tough law and order policies especially for juvenile offenders.

It was difficult for the Conservatives to criticise what were, largely, their own policies.

- Labour's desire for power, combined with growing party discipline, largely silenced the left-wing Labour dissidents.

- New, quite radical proposals for constitutional reform appealed to many voters.

Lack of 'clear blue water' between the two main parties in 1997 threatened to squeeze the Liberal Democrats but – despite getting a lower vote than in 1992 – they won over twice as many seats due to careful targeting of their limited resources and skilful tactical voting by anti-Conservative voters (this means ignoring your favourite candidate and, instead, voting for the candidate most likely to defeat your least favoured candidate). The Liberal Democrats further enhanced their success in 2001 and 2005.

Page 63

1 Representation, participation, mandate; political recruitment, campaigning and financing for candidates; policy coherence, stability and accountability for government; a basis for choice, ideological identity and information on political issues for voters; a mechanism for political change.

2 In a 'dominant party system' one party is in power over exceptionally long periods of *time* – for example, the Conservatives in the UK for two-thirds of the twentieth century – regardless of the size of their majority. An 'elective dictatorship' occurs when the governing party has such a large *majority* in the Commons that they can overwhelmingly dominate it.

3 The Liberal Democrats.

4 1900.

5 Clause Four was the most 'socialist' reference in the Labour Party's founding constitution to 'common ownership' – hence its abolition in 1995.

Page 64

Despite significant improvements since the 1997 general election, parliamentary candidates and MPs are still by no means 'representative' of the electorate in their social background; as some exam questions put it, they are still predominantly white, male, middle-aged and middle class. This is partly because of discrimination in the process of selection of candidates; and partly because working-class people, young people, women and ethnic minorities are slower to come forward as candidates (because of pressures of work, financial constraints, or lack of political background, contacts or self-confidence). In the early 1990s, the Labour Party adopted a policy of all-women short-lists in many constituencies, and a record number of female Labour MPs were elected in 2005. Since the 1997 election, minor 'family friendly' reforms have been introduced in the Commons – such as fewer late-night sittings – which make it slightly easier for women, especially, to serve as MPs.

Page 69

1   MPs are elected legislators in a national assembly with the additional task of scrutinising the executive in the UK's system of parliamentary government. Thus their essential roles – making laws, representing the people and controlling the executive – are unchanged. MPs today probably seek, increasingly, to represent their voters' views and not simply their voters' interests as the MPs themselves judge them (i.e. MPs are, increasingly, 'delegates' and not just representatives in the Burkean sense) – hence most hold regular 'surgeries' to meet their constituents and take up their grievances.

    However, in recent years, MPs have tended to see themselves more as professional politicians pursuing a long-term career, often full-time (rather than treating politics as a part-time hobby, as MPs in the nineteenth and even twentieth centuries tended to do). UK MPs average 20 years in the Commons, far longer than in most comparable countries. They also have increasing links with outside bodies such as private businesses, charities and pressure groups, through paid consultancies and sponsorship.

2   As MPs become increasingly careerist, they are more likely to heed their party leadership and toe the party line, since their jobs usually depend upon the party. Thus they may be less independent-minded, less likely to revolt and more likely to be 'lobby fodder' for the national and/or local party, which may mean that they represent voters' views or interests on controversial issues less well (for example, only one Scottish Labour MP – Dennis Canavan – rebelled in 1998 over the government's unpopular policy on Scottish university tuition fees). MPs' growing links with outside interests fuelled the 'cash for questions' scandals of the 1990s (Smith, Hamilton, Aitken, etc.) and prompted the Nolan Inquiry and subsequent curbs on paid advocacy by MPs. Heavy lobbying of MPs by outside interests may distract MPs from focusing on their own constituents' interests. However, they have become more 'representative' of the voters since the 1997 election in terms of social background – for example, record numbers of female, black and Asian MPs. In sum, the answer depends upon the interpretation of the key word 'representative'.

Page 70

1   True

2   True

3   False

4   True

5   False

■ 5 Public opinion and pressure groups

Page 74

'Power' is the ability to act, or to make others act, as you wish, regardless of their consent. It is different from 'influence', which simply means persuasive effect. Protective (or sectional) groups tend to have more sanctions available to them – i.e. more real powers, such as withholding capital or labour. Private enterprise business groups can withhold finances, and trades unions can go on strike – for example, London underground workers can withdraw their labour and force Londoners to walk to work. Promotional groups such as Shelter and the Child Poverty Action Group, on the other hand, tend to have only persuasive influence – they cannot make anyone do something against their will.

Page 78

a) **Block vote**: method of union voting, for example at 'old' Labour conferences, where a majority union vote for a particular option results in 100 per cent of that union's votes counting towards that option. This is being phased out because of its disproportionality.

b) **Closed shop**: where an individual must belong to the appropriate union or association in order to work at a particular trade or profession. Largely prohibited by legislation in the 1980s.

c) **Corporatism**: tripartite (three-way) involvement and consultation of workers' and employers' groups with the government in economic policy-making. A feature of the 1970s' era of 'consensus politics'; Thatcherism in the 1980s was anti-corporatist.

d) **Functional representation**: consultation and/or decision-making through occupational or industrial groups (rather than through parties). It was suggested as a democratic substitute for the House of Lords by Winston Churchill in the 1930s.

e) **Sequestration**: freezing and/or seizure of some or all of a union's assets by the courts, as a penalty for contempt of court (introduced in 1984 by Thatcher's government, as an alternative to imprisoning union leaders because this tended to make them into political martyrs and to boost support for the union's cause).

Page 84

In the UK, the number of political parties is relatively small (under 200), whereas the number of pressure groups runs into thousands. Political party membership in the UK is very low; under 3 per cent of UK voters are members of any political party. This percentage has declined continuously since the 1960s (when it was about 10 per cent). Over the same period, however, pressure groups' membership and participation have increased markedly. Why might this be? Tick all that may apply!

❏ Voters' disillusionment with political parties as self-serving, dishonest or simply boring

❏ The stereotype image of party politicians as 'grey men in grey suits'

❏ The lack of clear ideological and policy differences – choice – between the main parties

❏ The neglect of some key issues by the main parties

❏ The lack of scope for active and productive voter participation in party politics

❏ The scope for direct 'people power' and action in some pressure groups' methods

❏ The focus upon a single, important issue or group by pressure groups

❏ Growing public education, information and awareness of core political issues

❏ The perception that pressure groups are more honest and altruistic than are parties

❏ New pressure groups being formed to oppose existing ones

❏ The different membership of pressure groups – often younger and more diverse

❏ The greater radicalism – even extremism – of some pressure groups

On the other hand, however: parties, not pressure groups, still – and always will – form the bedrock of representative democracy in the UK. Pressure groups have no mandate from the voters (and promotional groups, especially, are often self-appointed, wholly unelected and quite unrepresentative). Pressure groups have, undoubtedly, become more important in recent years, but outright pressure group successes – in terms of aims achieved – are still not commonplace.

Page 87

1 Opinion polls may, sometimes, question an unrepresentative sample of people; they may offer limited options as answers; or they may shape the very responses they are trying to measure.

2 Promotional groups pursue a cause external to their own membership, and are often internally undemocratic; whereas protective groups seek to protect their own, select, membership, and their leaders are elected by their members.

3 Wyn Grant

4 Insider groups have close contacts with ministers and civil servants and significant influence upon policy-making.

5 Eight million UK workers currently belong to trades unions.

6 Meeting with ministers, financing political parties, sponsoring MPs, drafting and promoting private members' bills, striking, conducting

or publicising opinion polls, petitions, pickets, leaflets and letters, media adverts, demonstrations and staged public events.

7 Three per cent of UK voters are members of any political party.

8 Pressure groups do not stand candidates for election – they merely seek to influence those in political office.

9 Extra-parliamentary parties are parties with no seats in Parliament – that is, most of them.

10 The Green Party looks and acts much like the pressure group Greenpeace.

Page 87

Pressure groups vary enormously in power and influence, depending on their type, size, membership, financial resources, links with parties, methods, media coverage and current trends in government policy. Even a single event – such as a BSE crisis, a foot and mouth epidemic or an explosion at a nuclear power station – may suddenly boost the influence of an environmental pressure group. Large groups are not necessarily the most powerful. Protective groups tend to have more sanctions available to them than promotional groups, and hence more power – for example, the members of a key economic interest group may withdraw their labour or capital. Promotional groups may have considerable influence on public opinion or on government policy: for example, a large demonstration by the Countryside Alliance in 1997 persuaded the Labour government to renege for years on its manifesto promise to abolish fox-hunting; but even the largest promotional groups – such as the Stop the War Coalition (against the invasion of Iraq) – usually lack the power to change government policy.

In sum, the factors which may influence pressure group success include:

● whether they are insider or outsider pressure groups

● whether their aims or causes coincide with the ideological stance of the government of the day

● whether they are protective or promotional pressure groups

● the resources at their disposal – especially finances

● their supportive contacts and influence with the major political parties

● their supportive contacts and influence with the media

● the character of their membership – for example (for promotional groups) middle class, vocal, literate and active members; or (for protective groups) specialised, skilled and irreplaceable workers

● whether they have the support of many, or most, voters

● whether their cause coincides with a significant political occurrence such as a natural disaster or a war (reminding us of former PM

Harold Macmillan's comment that the most significant influences upon his tenure were 'Events, dear boy, events')

- their methods – whether legal or illegal, peaceful or violent, serious or fun. If they are sufficiently eye-catching, they may have influence. Disruptive tactics, such as strikes, exert power. Illegal or violent tactics may, actually, be counter-productive and create negative publicity for the pressure group and its cause. Activities which entertain as well as inform and mobilise – such as a charity concert – often have wider appeal

- the size of the pressure group.

■ 6 Parliament

Page 91

In theory, the UK Parliament – Commons and Lords together – has legal sovereignty: i.e. it can pass, amend or repeal any law and no other UK body can override its laws. The Commons and Lords share the same roles of making the law, scrutinising and controlling the executive and representing the people. These functions include debate and deliberation, and acting as a channel of communication between the government and the electorate.

'Power' is the ability to do, or make others do, something regardless of their consent, based on the capacity to coerce, i.e. to reward or punish. Parliament's power is supposed to be based on authority – for example, from elections for the House of Commons and from tradition for the House of Lords. However, since the House of Lords is wholly unelected, it has much more limited powers (laid down by the Parliament Acts of 1911 and 1949) than does the Commons. The Lords cannot touch money bills. They have the power to delay other bills for a maximum of one year, after which the Commons can 'invoke the Parliament Act' and simply override the Lords. The only kind of bill which the Lords can block entirely is any bill seeking to extend the life of Parliament beyond its five-year maximum term.

Given that the Commons is elected and the Lords is not – and given their different legal powers – the two chambers perform their roles in different ways. For example, the Commons has more legitimate authority in scrutinising the executive and especially in representing the British people.

Page 102

Externally:

- EU
- Economic power bodies – domestic and transnational
- USA
- Other international institutions – UN, NATO, IMF, etc.
- Devolved bodies such as the Scottish Parliament

- Pressure groups
- Media
- Referenda
- Ultimately: the political sovereignty of the electorate

Internally:

- Government from within Parliament

Conclusion:

In theory, there are no absolute, formal limits to the sovereignty of the Westminster Parliament. In practice, there are significant constraints.

Note: As always, credit will be given in exams for topical examples for every point.

Page 104

1 1707 – Queen Anne, the Scotch Militia Bill

2 An outline of proposed legislation, before publication of a bill

3 The Parliamentary Counsel of 30 lawyers – part of government, not Parliament

4 First reading, second reading, committee stage, report stage, third reading, amendments in the Upper House, royal assent

5 A committee of MPs and peers combined

6 The official record of proceedings in the Commons

7 No – but she/he must become impartial

8

   a) Decides allocation of time to parties and MPs

   b) Exercises casting vote on a bill where votes are tied; by convention, arranges for vote to be taken again

   c) Selects chairmen for, and allocates bills to, standing committees

9 Currently Michael Martin

10 Written rules on the conduct of Commons business

11 A time limit on debate in the Commons; the Speaker decides whether to allow a vote on it, and 100+ MPs must win a majority vote for motion to be carried

12 The Government and Opposition chief whips, who between them arrange special debates, etc.

13

   a) Circulate weekly notice of Commons business to MPs

   b) Arrange pairing, ensure that MPs vote as required, and count the votes

c) Convey backbench opinion and recommendations for promotion to the party leadership

14 Government and Opposition backbenchers arrange permanent 'pairs' at the beginning of each Parliament; they can then be mutually absent on important votes (with the permission of the whips).

15 Suspending or expelling the MP from the party (not from Parliament)

16 For more detailed information

17 To investigate citizens' complaints of maladministration by government departments

18 The government's account at the Bank of England

19 1979 – a minority Labour government

20

a) The Parliamentary Labour Party – all Labour front and backbenchers in the Commons

b) All Conservative backbenchers; not frontbenchers

■ 7 Executive

Page 106

- Contacting the relevant government department
- Contacting their local MP (who should pass on and pursue the complaint)
- Asking their MP to contact the parliamentary Ombudsman
- Going to an administrative tribunal
- Going to the UK courts for a legal hearing
- Going to the European Court of Human Rights or European Court of Justice
- Using the media
- Using the internet – even setting up a specific website
- Mobilising or setting up a relevant pressure group
- Working through a useful political party
- Taking individual direct action (legal or illegal)

Page 109

- Seniority within the party
- Popularity within the party
- Genuine policy consensus
- Policy-making experience and expertise

- Policy successes and failures
- Political and personal loyalty to the PM
- Managerial and administrative competence as head of department
- Media competence and popularity
- Ideological balance across the party
- Geographical balance across the country
- Rewarding backbench effort, loyalty and competence
- Bringing political challengers in 'under the thumb' of collective responsibility
- Size of the parliamentary pool
- (For Labour especially): political correctness – for example, women, gays and ethnic minorities
- Involuntary reshuffles due, for example, to forced ministerial resignations

Note: as always, credit will be given in exams for topical examples for every point.

Page 119

1 True

2 True

3 False

4 True

5 True

6 False

7 True

8 True

9 False

10 False

Page 122

1 Patronage, declarations of war, signing treaties

2 Collective policy-making by the team of senior ministers with the Prime Minister first among equals

3 Walter Bagehot (1867)

4 Richard Crossman (1963)

5 Formula One tobacco advertising exemption; the Dome; Amsterdam Treaty; invasion of Iraq; referendum on a new EU constitution

6 Party, Parliament, EU, media, pressure groups

7 PM's character, style of leadership and experience; degree of party unity and policy consensus; state of economy, policy successes and failures; popularity of government; proximity of election

8 To reward ministerial successes and punish failures, to reward loyalty and punish disloyalty, to introduce new blood and fresh ideas

9 A carefully cultivated and exceptionally personal, populist, 'hands on' style and image, distanced from both his Cabinet and his party

10 The UK has a system of parliamentary government: i.e. fusion, not separation, of the legislature and the executive

11 Parliament

12 Permanence, neutrality and anonymity

13 Civil servants are permanent, non-elected career bureaucrats who must serve under successive governments of any party

14 Civil servants, in theory, have no policy-making power, and therefore – unlike ministers – should not be publicly accountable for the actions of their department.

15 Job cuts; civil servants being blamed and sacked for policy errors (contrary to convention); civil servants being sacked for being politically incompatible with their political masters (contrary to convention)

■ 8 Rights and liberties

Page 130

- Judicial review means that the UK courts and judges have the power to decide whether the policies and actions of central and local governments are legal or illegal.

- When asked, UK courts and judges can decide that, for example, ministers have exceeded their powers, or have not taken an action which they should have done, or have simply done something wrongly according to the law.

- There is no general right to judicial review – it is at the discretion of the courts and judges.

- UK judges do not have the power to challenge the sheer merit, efficiency or justice of an executive decision – unless it is actually illegal.

- UK judges do not have the power to challenge a law of Parliament – unless it conflicts with EU law. They can usually only interpret and enforce statute law as it is written.

Effectiveness:

- The effectiveness of judicial review has increased in recent years, in the sense that the sheer number of cases brought against the government has increased a lot.

- This has been a growing check against elective dictatorship.

- This has also been a growing protection of individual rights and liberties.

- The UK Human Rights Act has increased the effectiveness of judicial review.

However:

- Much depends on the public's access to, the time and the cost of legal action.

- UK judges have been accused of being 'executive-minded' – that is, too sympathetic to the views and interests of the government and state, as against the rights and liberties of UK citizens.

- Above all, a majority government in effective control of a sovereign Parliament can overturn court decisions simply by passing new legislation.

Conclusion: not sufficiently effective.

Note: Examiners will, as always, credit students who can use topical examples throughout and who can suggest appropriate reforms at the end of their answers.

Page 130

Judicial independence refers to the judges' separation and autonomy from the other parts of the state. Thus, they should be structurally separate from the legislature and executive, and should not be subject to any form of pressure or influence from the politicians. UK judges, for example, are not trained by the government. Whereas judicial independence is a matter of external arrangements, judicial neutrality is an internal state of mind: judges should not let their personal or political opinions affect their professional conduct in any way. They should uphold the rule of law and protect individual rights and liberties in a fair and impartial way regardless of either external political pressures or of their own personal views.

Page 137

Case for the Human Rights Act:

UK residents can now use the UK courts for human rights issues, whereas before 2000 they usually had to go all the way to the European courts – often involving considerable time and expense (though this option is, of course, still available even though the UK now has its own Bill of Rights).

According to some observers (for example, pressure groups such as Liberty and Charter 88), basic civil liberties in the UK are always under threat with a majority government within a sovereign Parliament in effective control of a flexible, unwritten constitution. They point to the draconian 'anti-terrorism' laws passed through Parliament in a single day in 1998 which were extended to cover environmentalists and animal rights activists. The 2001 anti-terrorism law, which reintroduced internment, was particularly harsh. They also say that the growing political emphasis on law and order (for example, the introduction of child jails for 12–14-year-olds in 1998), together with growing police powers, state surveillance and a quite conservative judiciary, have all added to the threat.

The situation in Northern Ireland – where rights of political activity and legal equality, residence, movement, privacy, jury trial, freedom from arbitrary detention and from 'cruel and inhuman punishment', etc. were long curtailed – demonstrated the fragility of basic liberties in the UK.

The rule of law demands a clear statement of citizens' rights and duties, which has long been lacking in the UK.

The Human Rights Act has imposed more legal limits on governments' actions, which are often guided only by convention and are therefore effectively above or beyond the law.

Since the UK is already a signatory of the European Convention on Human Rights, it was simple and logical to incorporate it into domestic law.

Case against the Human Rights Act:

Which rights should be entrenched? How general or specific should they be? There is still not political or party consensus on these questions.

How entrenched should the UK Bill of Rights be? Some critics feared excessive rigidity, but the fact that ordinary – and sometimes very illiberal – parliamentary statute laws take precedence over the provisions of the UK Human Rights Act is now, perhaps, causing greater concern.

Many existing UK laws conflict with the Human Rights Act – for example, the Police Act, Prevention of Terrorism Acts, Criminal Justice Acts, etc. (though this is precisely why defenders of civil rights wanted more legal protection for human rights in the UK). The issues of state security versus citizens' liberties, and privacy versus freedom of information and expression, are especially fraught.

All governments are reluctant to increase constraints against themselves and against the state. The UK Human Rights Act is, therefore, conspicuously weak.

It is hard to reconcile majority and minority rights, or collective versus individual rights, or freedom versus equality.

Left-wingers are suspicious of a Bill of Rights which may entrench 'liberal' principles such as individual property rights and undermine 'socialist' principles such as collective trades union and workers' rights.

Many (such as Griffith) do not trust the judges to interpret and enforce a Bill of Rights in a liberal-minded and progressive way, because they see

British judges as unrepresentative, conservative and 'executive-minded'. The UK Bill of Rights has inevitably transferred some power from elected MPs to non-elected, unaccountable judges, and it has also made the judges more overtly 'political'.

Every Bill of Rights has some qualifying clauses allowing for the restriction of rights, for example 'in the national interest', and some are scarcely worth the paper on which they are written.

Rights in the UK were said by some (especially Conservatives) to be adequately protected already through Parliament and the Ombudsman, the 'rule of law', the courts (including the European Courts), administrative tribunals, pressure groups and the media, etc.

Note: By 2005, many students still seemed unaware that the European Convention on Human Rights has already been incorporated into UK law and that the UK now has its own, domestic, Human Rights Act. Too many answers are, therefore, still 'set in the future', with students discussing whether a referendum should be held to decide the issue. The other main confusion is the notion that this has anything to do with the European Union; to repeat, the European Convention and Court of Human Rights, and the UK Human Rights Act, have nothing at all to do with the European Union! Students should not, therefore, even mention the EU in answer to questions about the Human Rights Act. Nor were any of these legal arrangements 'imposed' upon the UK; they have all been entirely voluntary.

Page 138

In many ways, civil liberties in the UK are protected. Judges should enforce the law in an independent and neutral way, now including the UK Human Rights Act which has given judges more scope for protecting the civil liberties of citizens: for example, granting anonymity to Maxine Carr (the former girlfriend of Soham murderer Ian Huntley) upon her release from prison.

The use of judicial review also safeguards individuals against illegal government action. For example, the courts have ruled against the government's policy of internment of foreign terror suspects. There has been a significant growth in the use of judicial review in the last 20 years. There are now around 5,000 such cases each year, perhaps because citizens are becoming more aware of their civil rights, or because judges may be becoming less executive-minded (that is, pro-government).

Judges also conduct inquiries into controversial political issues, such as the Macpherson Inquiry into the death of Stephen Lawrence, which may eventually result in fairer and less racist policing.

Also, judges now speak more openly about their views on government policy and civil liberties – for example, against internment and cuts in jury trials. On balance, UK judges have become more liberal and less pro-state in their rulings over the last decade. There has been growing, and often open, conflict between the government and the judges for this reason.

The European Court of Justice enforces EU law and helps to protect the civil liberties of UK citizens: for example, it ruled against discriminatory retirement ages for men and women in the UK. The European Court of Human Rights has had an even longer history of protecting UK civil liberties: for example, it has ruled against the ban on gays in the army, torture in UK prisons and corporal punishment in state schools.

Pressure groups can also protect civil liberties. For instance, the Snowdrop campaign helped to ensure the ban on most handguns, thus protecting the right to life. Media campaigns may also highlight certain issues, especially the freedom of expression.

However, civil liberties are not fully protected.

Many (such as Griffith) argue that UK judges are not sufficiently independent – for example, they are appointed by a government minister – and that they have a narrow and largely conservative personal agenda, given their socio-economic background (overwhelmingly white, male, public school, Oxbridge). Lord Atkin argued that they are 'more executive-minded than the executive' – for example, Lord Hutton's inquiry into the death of Dr Kelly in 2004 was widely seen as a pro-government 'whitewash'.

Pressure groups such as Exit (pro-euthanasia) and Fathers4Justice (who threw purple flour bombs at the PM in the Commons in 2004) are rarely successful – and one person's civil liberty may be another's constraint. For example, Naomi Campbell's successful court battle for a privacy ruling undermined wider public freedom of information and media freedom of expression.

The police sometimes hinder civil liberties through their curbs on legitimate demonstrations (for example, police violence against an anti-arms fair protest in 2003 and against a pro-hunting demonstration outside Parliament in 2004). A BBC programme in 2003 also exposed rampant racism among some police officers.

Parliamentary sovereignty is potentially the biggest hindrance to civil liberties. A majority government in control of a sovereign Parliament with a flexible, unwritten constitution has a lot of power. For example, the government is legislating to introduce compulsory national ID cards. Parliament may even pass retrospective law, such as the backdated abolition of the double jeopardy rule.

Therefore, despite many safeguards, civil liberties are far from fully protected in the UK and, under an exceptionally authoritarian 'new' Labour government, they are under increasing threat.

Page 139

1   False

2   True

3 True

4 True

5 True

6 False

7 True

8 False

9 True

10 False

■ 9 Local government and devolution

Page 146

A councillor is a member of a local executive body, whereas an MP is a member of the national legislature. Both are elected to represent a local area; but a 'ward' is smaller than a 'constituency' and, whereas a councillor is purely local, an MP is expected to represent both constituency and national interests (according to the traditional conservative view). An MP is a sovereign law-maker, and local councils – like everyone else – should work within the law of the land (rule of law). MPs may pass laws (such as the Local Government Act 2000 which extended the system of directly elected mayors) which can alter the structures or powers of local councils, or even abolish them completely. MPs are also meant to scrutinise and control the executive, both central and local; councillors are therefore subordinate to MPs. The only kind of law which councillors may make is delegated (secondary) legislation, for example local government by-laws. Their functions are executive and administrative rather than legislative – they decide and provide local services such as education, housing, refuse collection, fire and police, roads and harbours, leisure and social services. Some of these are 'mandatory', i.e. local government is obliged by law to carry out certain functions, such as housing the homeless; others are 'permissive', i.e. optional, such as providing local libraries and nurseries.

Page 152

Advantages of local government:

- Is more responsive to the needs of the local areas (knows what the issues are, can act more quickly)

- Allows an element of local democracy and added tier of political participation and representation

- Is closer to the people and therefore more accessible

- Is more accountable and subject to public control because it is closer to the people it serves

- Imposes checks and balances on the centre

- Upholds liberal democratic principles of decentralisation and pluralism

- Some areas, for example Scotland and north England, often not well represented by Westminster and Whitehall

- Allows regional parties access to power

- Provides training and recruitment ground for the centre

- Relieves the centre of some workload and pressure

- May be more efficient and cost-effective than central bureaucracy

- Is more legitimate because it is based on more tangible local culture and reflects regional, not national, political attachments

Disadvantages of local government:

- May thwart (stronger?) mandate of central government and provoke damaging conflicts between the centre and the regions

- May mean inconsistent, uncoordinated and unjust provision of services across the country

- May be unduly costly, bureaucratic or even corrupt

- May mean local elective dictatorship of one strong and/or radical and/or irresponsible party on a minority vote

- Strong local government is contrary to the constitutional principles of a unitary state; too much decentralisation may even threaten the unity of the UK

- Alternatively, if it is too weak, it may not provide adequate checks and balances on central government and may, instead, simply generate voter apathy

Page 159

1 The structure of local government in the United Kingdom is a little bit complicated and, at the same time, local councils do not have very much real power in the UK's centralised system.

2 Labour has introduced directly elected local mayors.

3 34 per cent.

4 The passing down of limited law-making powers from central to local or regional bodies, with the centre remaining sovereign – i.e. the state remains unitary.

5 Devolution entails the passing down of limited decision-making powers and the centre remains sovereign; federalism entails much

stronger decision-making powers for local bodies and the central power is no longer sovereign.

6 The abolition of tuition fees, foundation hospitals and fox hunting in Scotland.

7 The Welsh Assembly has only limited local executive and administrative powers.

8 The Welsh Assembly has no primary legislative or tax-varying powers, unlike the Scottish Parliament. It has limited, local, executive powers over the spending of money and provision of services.

9 Because of Northern Ireland's unique history, political and religious divisions.

10 Conservative critics of devolution fear that it might be the first step towards the complete break up of the United Kingdom.

Page 159

1 True

2 True

3 False

4 True

5 False

■ 10 The European Union

Page 162

1 'Sovereignty' means the legitimate location of power of last resort over any community. It may be defined purely in legal terms as the power to make binding laws which no other body can set aside or overrule. It may also be viewed as the autonomous power of a community to govern itself – a territorial concept relating to the powers of independent nation states. The voters are said to have the 'political sovereignty' to rule themselves and elect and remove governments, i.e. the 'people power' at the root of the legitimacy of the UK Parliament and government which justifies the democratic claims of the UK political system. The location of sovereignty is not always easy to pinpoint, for example in federal systems such as the USA.

2 The most obvious legal limitations are that by signing EU treaties – Rome, SEA, Maastricht, Amsterdam, Nice – the UK has subordinated itself to the dictates of EU laws, regulations and directives. The Factortame case is an example, together with its implications for the qualitatively new role of the UK courts in being able to veto UK

statutes when they conflict with EU law. There has been a loss of control over many areas of economic policy – for example, agriculture, tariffs and trade, the beef ban, the single currency in future, etc. Other areas include fishing, the environment, conditions of work (the 48-hour working week, the minimum wage, etc.). Territorial sovereignty has been limited by the 'four freedoms' and the erosion of state boundaries. Given QMV, loss of sovereignty is a matter of degree.

Page 167

1   The European Parliament is composed of 732 MEPs. It performs similar functions to the UK House of Commons – representation, debate and scrutiny – but it has more limited powers. It can veto the EU budget – and in the 1980s it rejected the budget five times. It can dismiss the Commission with a two-thirds majority. The Parliament can also suggest amendments to draft legislation from the Commission, about 70 per cent of which are accepted by the Commission. The Maastricht Treaty gave it more powers: for example, to veto certain forms of legislation, to veto Commissioners' appointments and to investigate voters' complaints of EU maladministration. The new EU constitution will give the European Parliament a much more prominent role in the framing of new laws. It will have a right of 'co-decision' (that is, its agreement must be obtained) with the Council of Ministers across a much broader spectrum of policy including energy, the environment and transport, aspects of social security, home affairs and justice issues.

2   The Parliament is the only directly elected body of the EU but has fairly limited powers – hence, say critics, the 'democratic deficit' at the heart of the EU. Paradoxically, as it stands, the EU (through the Council of Ministers) strengthens national governments and bureaucracies at the expense of national parliaments and voters. If the European Parliament was to be given more genuine law-making power and ability to control the Commission and Council, that would further democratise the EU on the one hand, and reduce the potential for 'elective dictatorship' within the UK, on the other. The EU Parliament should also remain in Brussels; and the much-abused system of travel expenses and other perks for MEPs should be scrapped, to save millions of pounds for the taxpayers – who might, then, have more respect for the European Parliament.

Page 171

1   True

2   False

3   False

4   True

5   False

Page 173

1   Advantages:

- Lasting peace and security after two great European wars
- A common free market and free trade
- The advantages of large-scale markets
- Enhanced economic competitiveness and consumer rights
- Greater world influence in the global economy through 'pooled' sovereignty
- An added tier of democratic representation
- Curbs on national elective dictatorship and more power for UK regions
- Protection of the environment, health and safety and UK workers' rights
- Further civil rights through the ECJ
- Enhanced collective security against international crime and terrorism
- 'An ever closer union among the peoples of Europe'
- Cultural diversity and choice from food to fashion

2   Disadvantages:

- Loss of sovereignty in its various forms
- (Perception of) loss or dilution of national and cultural identity
- Loss of emotive national symbols such as the pound or imperial measurements
- Economic imbalances and drains between richer and poorer member states
- Widespread consequences of any future euro instability or weakness
- Difficulties of EU management and coordination, especially with enlargement
- Over-centralisation and ignorance of diverse needs of local regions
- EU inadequacies in foreign policy, conflict and crisis management – for example, Kosovo
- Risks and costs of waste, inefficiency and corruption
- Disadvantages to non-EU states and their trading partners (for example, the Commonwealth and the UK) of protective EU trade agreements (GATT)
- The 'democratic deficit' created by the non-elected institutions of the EU

Page 174

1   1957

2   Rome

3   Norway and Switzerland

4

    a)   Ultimate authority and power

    b)   The principle established by the Maastricht Treaty that, within the EU, 'decisions should be taken at the lowest possible level compatible with efficiency and democracy'

    c)   The creation of a sovereign authority over and above member states

5   Desire for peace and security after two wars; awareness of growing economic and social interdependence and desire for greater international co-operation; advantages of large-scale markets; greater world influence; challenge to US and other major economies

6   A sense of superiority and national pride after victory in war; hankering after imperial status; international status and links with USA and Commonwealth; sense of political and geographical difference; left-wing dislike of capitalist aspects of EU; right-wing xenophobia

7   1973

8   1975

9   1979

10

    a)   Qualified Majority Voting, in the Council of Ministers

    b)   The Single European Act 1986

    c)   Member states have lost further power to the Council

11   They see it as a bastion of free market capitalism

12   They fear loss of sovereignty and 'national' identity

13   *For:* European economic integration requires a single currency; it would enhance Europe's competitiveness against USA and Japan; currency transaction costs would be eliminated; the currency speculators would be weakened; business stability and certainty would be enhanced

    Against: Loss of national sovereignty; loss of government's ability to adjust currency value against external shocks; loss of wealth, employment and power from weaker to stronger member countries

14   Agreement on minimum employment rights, sexual equality, freedom of information and other social improvements throughout the EU

15   It is a number that represents perfection and completeness.

Page 175

The EU (then the Common Market) was formed in 1957 by six states. It now has 25 member states.

The UK joined in 1973. This meant that the UK Parliament lost 'legal' or legislative sovereignty both *de jure* and *de facto* (i.e. both in theory and in practice) in areas where European law took precedence. This loss of sovereignty has since increased, with the growing scope of European intervention and with reforms of European voting procedures. The most important reform was the change from unanimous voting in the Council of Ministers – i.e. any one country could veto any policy – to qualified majority voting, under the Single European Act 1986. For example, in 1993 the UK was overruled on the principle of a 48-hour working week.

In 1975 a national referendum was held on the UK's continuing membership of the then EC. Technically, this was merely 'advisory', and so, in theory, Parliament's legal sovereignty was not affected. In practice, however, Parliament could not have ignored the referendum result, which was a two-thirds 'yes'. Similarly, in theory, Westminster could legislate to leave the EU at any time, but in political practice that seems difficult and unlikely. There are promises of future referenda in the UK on a new European constitution and on the euro. The EU has, therefore, provided the impetus for more 'direct democracy' within the UK.

From another perspective, the primacy of EU law has curbed the dangers of 'elective dictatorship' of a single party majority UK government within a sovereign Parliament – for example, the EU has obliged the UK government to extend national holiday laws and rights for part-time workers.

Since UK and European courts are required to enforce European law rather than domestic law where there is conflict between the two, Parliament has also lost some legal sovereignty to both the UK courts and the ECJ.

Elections to the European Parliament were first held in 1979, adding a new layer of representative democracy to the UK political system. However, the European Parliament – the only elected institution of the EU – is still relatively weak. Since the main decision-making bodies of the EU – the Council of Ministers and the European Commission – are not elected, membership of the EU has also meant some loss of the 'political' sovereignty of the UK electorate – the so-called 'democratic deficit'.

The sheer quantity and impact of EU law upon the UK has given the UK constitution an increasingly codified and rigid character, as well as modifying its unitary nature.

Membership of the EU has increased the powers of UK Prime Ministers: for example, in membership of the European Council with its twice-yearly summits; in signing EU agreements such as Maastricht and Amsterdam; and in appointing European Commissioners and civil servants.

Membership of the EU has also increased the policy-making powers of UK Foreign Secretaries in the Council of Ministers; and it is widely held to have increased the power of civil servants.

Most obviously, membership of the EU has profoundly divided the two main UK political parties, Labour especially in the 1970s and the Conservatives especially in the 1980s and 1990s. Also, the rise of small parties which are more or less hostile to the EU, such as the UKIP and the Greens, has dented the main parties' votes in secondary elections (i.e. local, London and EU elections). However, this has had a lot to do with PR electoral systems; the small (and sometimes single-issue) parties have much less impact at general elections.

The EU court has protected many civil liberties against UK law, for example in relation to retirement ages, food and water standards and employment rights of part-time workers.

The emphasis on 'subsidiarity' in the Maastricht Treaty has encouraged devolution and decentralisation within the UK.

Finally, many UK pressure groups are increasingly focusing their attention on EU rather than on domestic decision-making institutions – a reliable indicator of the shifting balance of power and influence. For example, the Committee of Professional Agricultural Organisations (COPA), comprising most of the national farmers' organisations including the UK's National Farmers' Union, is based in Brussels where it can effectively lobby the relevant EU institutions, especially the Commission. Similarly, most UK local authorities – especially those who receive EU financial aid – now have a European office to maintain effective contacts, again, especially with the Commission; and local authority by-laws (for example, on weights and measures) are often based on EU regulations.

Whether the impact of the EU upon UK political processes has been, on balance, positive or negative is a matter of highly subjective and sometimes very emotive assessment. It has certainly done more to divide the main parties than any other issue for the last half century; but it has probably also done more to enhance the rights and freedoms of UK citizens than has any of those parties.

References and useful websites

■ References

Bagehot, W. (1867) *The English Constitution*, Fontana, London

Burke, E. (1774) 'Letter to Constituents in Bristol', in *Edmund Burke: Selections from his Political Writings and Speeches*, Thomas Nelson & Sons, London

Crossman, R. (1963) *Introduction to Bagehot's 'The English Constitution'*, Fontana, London

Dicey, A.V. (1885) *Law of the Constitution*, Macmillan, London

Foley, M. (1993) *The Rise of the British Presidency*, MUP, Manchester

Gerth, H.H. and Mills, C.W. (eds) (1948) *From Max Weber: Essays in Sociology*, Routledge and Kegan Paul, London

Grant, W. (1989) *Pressure Groups, Politics and Democracy in Britain*, Philip Allan, London

Griffith, J. (1991) *The Politics of the Judiciary*, Fontana, London

Hailsham, Q. (1976) 'Elective dictatorship: The Dimbleby Lecture', *The Listener*, 21 October

Hennessy, P. (1990) *Whitehall*, Fontana, London

Kellner, P. (1980) *The Civil Servants*, MacDonald and Jane's, London

Madgwick, P. (1986) 'Prime ministerial power revisited', *Social Studies Review*, May

Miliband, R. (1983) *The State in Capitalist Society*, Verso, London

Montesquieu, C-L. (1748) *The Spirit of the Laws*, Free Press, Illinois

■ Useful websites

http://news.bbc.co.uk

http://news.bbc.co.uk/2/hi/uk_news/politics/81344.stm

http://news.bbc.co.uk/1/hi/in_depth/europe/2003/inside_europe/default.stm

http://www.direct.gov.uk/Homepage/fs/en

http://www.faxyourmp.com/index.php3

http://www.number-10.gov.uk/output/Page1.asp

http://www.politicos.co.uk

http://www.theyworkforyou.com/

http://en.wikipedia.org/wiki/Main_Page

http://www.YouGov.com

Glossary

absolute majority Over 50 per cent of votes or seats

absolute monarchy A hereditary head of state with total political power

administrative law The law as applied to executive and administrative bodies, especially government

adversary politics A period when the two main parties are polarised, advocating very different policies

authority Rightful, legitimate power based on consent

backbenchers MPs in the House of Commons who are not, in addition, members of the government, the shadow government or major spokespersons for their party

bicameral legislature A legislature with two houses or 'chambers'

bill Draft law going through Parliament

by-election Election in a single constituency when an MP dies, loses the seat through disqualification or quits for other reasons

Cabinet Combined heads of executive policy departments and team of senior policy-makers

Cabinet committees Small sub-groups of ministers, chosen by the Prime Minister, to aid policy-making

Cabinet government Collective policy-making by a united team of senior ministers with the Prime Minister *primus inter pares* (first among equals)

case law Judicial interpretation of the law in test cases which sets a precedent for future, similar cases

civil disobedience Non-violent but unlawful action as a form of political protest

civil law Concerns disputes between individuals or groups in society and the aim of proceedings is compensation

civil rights Those rights granted to citizens in law by a particular state

civil servants Permanent, impartial, non-elected career administrators and officials of the government

civil service anonymity Civil servants should not be publicly accountable for the work of the department; the minister in charge is answerable to Parliament and public for government policy and administration, according to the convention of individual ministerial responsibility

civil service neutrality As permanent, non-elected, career officials who serve under successive governments of any party, civil servants should not let political or personal bias influence their work (though they are allowed to vote)

class or partisan dealignment The breakdown, since the 1970s, of long-term patterns of consistent voting for a political party which were based mainly on social class

coalition government Two or more parties in executive office

collective Cabinet responsibility The convention that ministers make policy decisions collectively and, if ministers disagree so strongly with a policy that they cannot defend it in public, they should resign

citizenship An individual's legal membership of, and recognition by, a state which grants mutual rights and obligations between state and citizen

consensus politics A period when the two main parties share very similar policies

constituency a geographical area represented by an elected MP

constituents Residents of a local area represented by an MP

constitution The set of rules and principles by which a state is governed

constitutional monarchy An impartial (non-party political), largely symbolic, hereditary head of state whose powers are exercised by, and on the advice of, ministers, in theory subordinate to the will of Parliament, the people and the rules of the constitution

conventions Unwritten customs which are traditionally regarded as binding, but which have no legal force

corporatism Tripartite (three-way) involvement and consultation of workers' and employers' groups with the government in economic policy-making

criminal law Concerns offences against society or state, and the aim of proceedings is punishment

cross-benchers Independent peers without any party affiliation

Crown The permanent, abstract institution which embodies the supreme power of the state in the UK, culminating in the monarchy

delegated legislation Laws made by bodies other than Parliament – for example, ministers or local authorities – by powers passed to them by Parliament

democratic socialists Radical left-wing 'old' Labour advocates of extensive collective ownership, workers' democracy, welfare and equality of outcome

departmental select committees Commons' committees of backbench MPs from all of the parties, which scrutinise each government department's policies, activities and spending

devolution The delegating of some legislative or executive powers from central to regional bodies

direct democracy 'people power', or self-government of the people, by the people, for the people

elective dictatorship Lord Hailsham's thesis of excessive executive (government) power, between elections, over Parliament and the public

electoral deposit The sums of money required from each candidate who stands in an election

Eurosceptics People doubtful about, or quite hostile to, the UK's involvement in the EU and further European integration

executive The branch of state responsible for running the country through the execution and administration of laws and policies; often also called the 'government'

executive agencies Organisations of civil servants, structurally separate from the departments and headed by a chief executive but still, in theory, subject to ministerial responsibility

federal constitution A constitution where the central and local powers are equal and autonomous, with mutual checks and balances against each other

federalism A system of greater decentralisation, where the central and local powers are equal and autonomous, with mutual checks and balances against each other – thus, there is no sovereign centre

flexible constitution A constitution which requires no special procedures for amendment, but can be changed by an ordinary Act of Parliament

franchise The right to vote

general election The election of all Westminster MPs to the House of Commons at intervals of no more than five years

government The executive, policy-making branch of the state

Green Paper A consultation paper preceding a bill

hereditary peers Lords whose right to sit and vote in the chamber derives purely from a title inherited within the family

Her Majesty's Opposition The second largest party in the legislature and an official part of the constitution

hung parliament A parliament where no one party has over 50 per cent of the seats

independent candidate A candidate who is not a member of any political party

indirect/representative democracy The election by qualified citizens of candidates to political office to make decisions on behalf of the electorate

individual ministerial responsibility The convention that ministers should be publicly accountable for all of the actions of their departments, and should resign in the event of serious departmental or personal error

influence Persuasive effect on others' ideas or actions

insider groups Pressure groups which are regularly consulted by the ministers and civil servants who make policy decisions in the groups' special areas of interest and influence

internment Indefinite detention of suspects without charge or trial (introduced in the UK in 2001)

judicial independence The freedom of judges from the influence of the executive or legislative branches of the state

judicial neutrality The absence of political or personal bias amongst judges

judicial review Court rulings on government policies and actions

judiciary The branch of state responsible for the interpretation and enforcement of the laws – that is, the judges

Law Lords The most senior judges in the UK

laws Rules of state which are enforceable by the courts and judges

legislative devolution The passing down of limited law-making powers from central to local or regional bodies, with the centre remaining sovereign – i.e. the state remains unitary

legislature The branch of state responsible for the making of laws or 'legislation'

liberal democracy A system of individual representation and protection of individual rights based on free, regular and competitive elections, constitutionalism and the rule of law

life peers Members of the Lords appointed by the Prime Minister of the day, for their lifetime only, whose titles are not hereditary

lobbying Influencing politicians and policy-makers

local government A system of executive and administrative devolution – decentralisation – where local people are elected to run local services

mandate The authority of the government, granted by the voters, to govern according to the promises in their manifesto

manifesto Booklet of policy proposals issued by every party before each general election

minority government An executive with under 50 per cent of the seats in the House of Commons

monarch The individual person upon whom the Crown is conferred

monarchy The institution of hereditary rule by a royal family

money bills Government bills concerned mainly with the raising or spending of public money

nation A group of people who share a sense of common culture, based on common ties of, for example, language, religion, race, territory and/or history

natural rights Those rights to which, according to some philosophers, everyone is entitled simply by being human

'new' Labour A term used by Tony Blair for the first time at the 1994 Labour Party conference to describe the modernised, more right-wing Labour Party, repositioned to attract more middle-class voters

New Right conservatives Economic Conservatives – Thatcherites – who emphasise private property, the free market, individual enterprise and self-help, reducing inflation, public spending and taxation

oligarchy Political elitism, or rule by the few

Ombudsman A parliamentary bureaucrat whose job is to investigate public complaints about government maladministration

outsider groups Pressure groups which are not consulted by the policy-makers because they have aims and/or methods which conflict with those of the government of the day

parliamentary government Overlap or 'fusion' between Parliament and government: that is, the executive (government, i.e. PM and ministers) is chosen from within the legislature (Parliament, i.e. MPs and peers); and the executive is, in theory, subordinate to the legislature.

parliamentary privilege The exemption of MPs from some ordinary laws under the special laws and customs of Parliament

parliamentary sovereignty Parliament has supreme law-making power, and can make, amend or repeal any law without challenge from any other UK body or institution

party A formal, organised group of (more or less) like-minded people who stand candidates for election on a common policy programme

party whips Senior MPs in the Commons, or peers in the Lords, who have been selected by the leadership of their party to act as a channel of communication and party discipline between the leadership and the party members in each House

pluralism Diverse and competing centres of power – especially many parties and pressure groups

political culture The predominant set of political values held by the citizens of a particular state

political socialisation The instilling of political attitudes and values through agencies such as family, media, education, peer group, church, etc.

political sovereignty The ultimate electoral power and authority of the voters

power The ability to do, or make others do, something based on the capacity to reward or punish

presidentialism A style of government leadership (often attributed to Prime Minister Tony Blair) that is populist and personalised, aloof from Cabinet and dismissive of Parliament

presidential system A system where the executive is separately elected from the legislature and the two bodies are in theory equal, possessing checks and balances against each other

pressure groups Organisations which do not stand candidates for election but seek to promote a cause or to protect a particular section of society by influencing government, Parliament or the public

prime ministerial government Policy-making dominated by the Prime Minister rather than by Cabinet

private bills Laws which concern individual or group interests

private members' bills Bills introduced by backbench MPs of any party rather than by the government

promotional/cause groups Pressure groups which seek to promote a specific cause external to their own membership

proportional representation Umbrella label for systems of election which produce seats in proportion to the parties' share of votes cast

protective/sectional/interest groups Pressure groups which seek to protect the interests of their own members as a particular section of society

public bills Laws which concern the general public interest

public opinion A general sense of the views of the population as expressed in elections and opinion polls – or the majority view on a given issue at a given time

public opinion poll A survey of the views of a sample of the voting public to assess wider public opinion

qualified majority voting (QMV) A weighted system of voting (according to countries, population sizes) used in the EU Council of Ministers where several member states must vote together to block a decision, across a growing range of policy areas

referendum A direct public vote on a political issue or policy (plural: referenda)

representation A form of indirect democracy reflecting the views, interests and/or typical social background of the electorate

representative government A form of political decision-making by elected representatives who should reflect the views, interests and/or typical social background of the electorate

responsible (party) government Executive accountable to Parliament and public (through party system, manifesto and mandate); or wise and sensible government in the best interests of the people

retrospective law Backdated law. The sovereign UK Parliament can decree that a law takes effect before it was written

rights Entitlements – for example, to some kind of freedom or equality or security

rigid constitution A constitution which requires a special legal process for change

royal prerogative The formal powers of the Crown

rule of law A principle which seeks to ensure 'just' law which is applicable to all; thus there should be legal equality, clear, consistent and impartial laws and an independent judiciary

safe seat A constituency which one particular party is virtually certain to win every time

separation of powers Non-overlapping personnel and powers of the legislature, executive and judiciary

separatism Complete political independence of a territory

simple majority More votes or seats than any other single candidate or party; not necessarily 50 per cent

social democrats Moderate 'old' Labour advocates of a mixed economy and moderate welfare

society The body of people within and under the power of the state

sovereignty Ultimate legal and political power and authority

sponsored MPs MPs (usually Labour) whose campaign costs are aided by trades unions or other pressure groups

standing committees Commons' committees of backbench MPs from all parties in the Commons, which scrutinise proposed legislation

state The formal, abstract, sovereign political power over a given territory, usually comprising legislature, executive and judiciary and usually possessing a legal monopoly of coercive power

statute Act of Parliament – a law passed by Commons, Lords and Crown

subsidiarity The principle (enshrined in the Maastricht Treaty) whereby decisions should be taken 'at the lowest possible level' compatible with efficiency and democracy – i..e. encouraging decentralisation down to member states

supranational institution A sovereign body over member states with laws that take precedence over national law

tactical voting Ignoring your favourite candidate or party and, instead, voting for the candidate or party most likely to defeat your least favoured candidate or party

trades unions Organisations which represent groups of workers in negotiations with their employers and their wider policy interests

traditional political conservatives Older school of Conservatives who emphasise social stability and consensus, traditional institutions (for example, monarchy, Church and Lords), the nuclear family and public duty

unconstitutional action An action which breaks any part – that is, any rule – of the constitution

unitary constitution A constitution with one sovereign legislature which has ultimate law-making power and authority over all other bodies within the state

unwritten/uncodified constitution A set of rules not contained in a single, legal document but deriving from many different sources (some written and some not, some with the force of law and some not)

White Paper The draft document of a bill

written constitution A set of state rules outlined in a single, legal document

Index

Page numbers in **bold** indicate where the term has been defined in the text